Invent To Learn:
Making, Tinkering, and Engineering
in the Classroom

Invent To Learn:
Making, Tinkering, and Engineering in the Classroom

Sylvia Libow Martinez & Gary Stager, Ph.D.

Constructing Modern Knowledge Press

Constructing Modern Knowledge Press
21825 Barbara St.
Torrance, CA 90503
www.InventToLearn.com

EDU039000   EDUCATION / Computers & Technology
EDU034000   EDUCATION / Educational Policy & Reform

ISBN: 978-0-9891511-0-8

Copy editor: Carla Sinclair
Illustrator and cover design: Yvonne Martinez

Reviews

"Learning is often confused with education. Martinez and Stager clearly describe "learning learning" through engagement, design and building. The best way to understand circles is to reinvent the wheel."
— Nicholas Negroponte, Founder MIT Media Lab and One Laptop per Child

"*Invent to Learn: Making, Tinkering, and Engineering in the Classroom* is the most important book of the 21st century for anyone interested in children and learning. The title says it all. Children learn best by making things whether physical or virtual. The authors highlight antecedents to this burgeoning new movement. Martinez and Stager describe making and tinkering as part of a long intellectual tradition and mention contributions of diverse luminaries such as Leonardo, Piaget, and Papert. This guidebook offers insights and suggestions as to how to bring making, tinkering, and engineering into learners' lives through classroom and out-of-school settings. Ideas and resources for implementing the ideas are clearly articulated. This beautifully written book opens up an exciting and stimulating educational adventure."
— Cynthia Solomon, Ed.D. Co-inventor of the Logo programming language and author of *Computer Environments for Children: A Reflection on Theories of Learning and Education*

"Sylvia and Gary have created a dynamic masterwork that engages readers from the opening sentence to the last. The craft of making things becomes a philosophical cornerstone to a true education, as this book makes abundantly clear. Rather than rant against the status quo, this book shows both why the transformation of education is essential, and presents specific strategies to make these changes. In many parts of the world, education has lost its way, and this book provides a map back to the educational experiences that are both tremendously effective and a great deal of fun as well."
— David Thornburg, Ph.D., Director, Thornburg Center

"Rarely does an education book come along that provides a cogent philosophical basis and an understanding of learning, thinking and teaching, as well as providing practical guidance for setting up effective digital-age learning and "making" environments. Sylvia Martinez and Gary Stager's *Invent To Learn: Making, Tinkering, and Engineering in the Classroom* provides both the background and a path for educators to create engaging learning opportunities to help students not only develop skills and strategies that will prepare them for a complex world, but empower them to use their creativity to solve problems, ask questions, and continually learn. This book articulates what we know in our hearts is best for our students – to allow them to play, experiment and invent as they learn. I encourage you to immerse yourself in this book, share it with your colleagues, and together start experimenting with creating "maker" learning environments and watch the magic happen!"
— Holly Jobe, President, International Society for Technology in Education

"Educators will be hard pressed to find a more essential, important book for making sense of not just the exciting, game-changing "maker" technologies that are currently exploding around us, but of the absolutely powerful learning opportunities they present for our students as well. Sylvia Martinez and Gary Stager are a teacher's perfect guides into this fast growing, innovative world of creative problem solving and construction using an array of new, innovative computing devices, many of which fit in our pockets. Even more, *Invent to Learn* creates a required new context for modern learning, and it offers an accessible roadmap for re-imagining schools, classrooms, and personal practice. It's a must read for those wanting to remain relevant in their students' learning lives."

— Will Richardson, Author of *Why School? How Education Must Change When Learning and Information Are Everywhere*

"Sylvia Martinez and Gary Stager have been passionate advocates for the need for children to learn by doing, making and building for over twenty-five years. With the explosion of the "Maker Movement," there is finally a movement built around their ideas. *Invent to Learn* is a must-read for any teacher, parent or student who wants to define their learning as more than just answers on a test. The ideas and resources in this book will inspire anyone to start making powerful artifacts of their learning."

— Chris Lehmann, Principal, Science Leadership Academy

"*Invent to Learn* is filled with inspiration and practical ideas that I cannot wait to share with colleagues. Gary and Sylvia have provided not only the rationale and history, but also practical how-tos in a thoughtful book perfect for teachers, parents and administrators. I expect the number of maker spaces to grow as this book makes them feel much more accessible to all teachers and schools. You will finish the book inspired to make programming, invention and making a reality."

— Shelly Luke-Willie, Elementary School Principal, Chadwick International School – Songdo, South Korea

"Thank you Gary and Sylvia. Your fresh, lively and fascinating book can help us to re-invent schooling by making it relevant. Too many educators are closing student minds, chasing scores, following prescriptive curriculum. There is another way and this book will help all who want to see engaged students, support for creativity and 'making' and even a historical and philosophical context for thinking differently."

— David Loader OAM, Author of *The Inner Principal*, Associate Professor and Principal Fellow – Melbourne Graduate School of Education, Melbourne University.

"Transforming education is a long overdue promise that we have not been able to fulfill. This may be because our intentions went one way, our beliefs another, and tools and resources the opposite. *With Invent To Learn: Making, Tinkering and Engineering in the Classroom*, Sylvia Martínez and Gary Stager offer a profound and very engaging book about bringing innovation to the classroom and show us a path towards reinventing education. They have aligned theory, practice, and tools to place in our hands, minds, and hearts an integrated vision and a powerful vehicle to finally refresh our educational systems. I have renewed hopes that this time, along with Sylvia and Gary, we can make it happen."

— Eleonora Badilla-Saxe, Ed.D. University of Costa Rica

"Here is a book that encourages everyone to be a learner, doer and maker of things that intrigue them. A challenge is now put to everyone, but especially teachers, to make learning a personal journey for each of their students. The challenge is to trust in children, and allow them to create, fail, share, succeed and understand in a manner that will endure."
— Stephen Costa, Deputy Head of Junior School,
Methodist Ladies' College – Melbourne, Australia

"I'm so excited to share *Invent to Learn* with my colleagues. Sylvia and Gary have written a very important book about how and why the maker movement can save our kids and their education system. Schools need more learning by doing, making, and inventing. This book serves as an incredibly informative, entertaining, and practical guide to the exciting world of making, tinkering, and engineering in the classroom."
— Jaymes Dec, Teacher and Innovation Specialist at the Marymount School
– New York City

"A lucid guide to create and shape new and exciting learning environments for all, where digital devices are the learners' technology, the constructing tools to make, to invent, to understand… The maker movement flows gracefully to the classroom."
— Leda Milena Muñoz García, Ph.D., Director of Fundación Omar Dengo
(Costa Rica's Computers in Schools NGO)

"The scope of the book is broad, but even better it is a great read for those interested in a chance to really think about education. Provocative, stirring, enlightening and opens the fun of education, where relationships between people who want to learn get together get to play in creative activity. The book has at its educational heart what some will see as educational anarchy, but that it simply because they want to control learning rather than allow it to grow though the discovery of solutions to things that we think about. An essential book for conservatives who have the answers yet still seem to be reluctant to learn through thinking about how we learn."
— Peter Crawley, Head of School, St Hilda's School – Gold Coast, Australia

"We desperately need to ignite an invention revolution in our schools to engage learners in solving the complex problems facing our world. *Invent to Learn* takes you through an enlightening journey to understand the history behind the ideas that support this approach, and will get you ready to bring 3D printing and Arduino programming into your classroom! Are you ready to turn your students into Makers? They'll remember you forever for the wonder you're about to bring into their lives... read this book!"
— Michael Furdyk and Jennifer Corriero Co-founders, TakingITGlobal.org

"Sylvia Martinez and Gary Stager bring more than a half century of experience to this must read for educators wanting to break free from the grip of today's education "reform." Sylvia and Gary don't just study and summarize others' work. The thoughts in this book come from working with hundreds of teachers, students, and schools throughout the world. I have had the pleasure of working with both authors and have seen first hand how the principles in this book have helped teachers and students learn to invent their lives."
— Dennis Harper, Ph.D., Founder and CEO of Generation YES

"Having grown up inspired by the spirit of invention and DIY by Thomas Edison and the Wright brothers, and more recently by Elon Musk and Limor Fried, I am thrilled to see this excellent, comprehensive and in-depth resource. An enormous amount of research and explanation is evident in this book. It's a must-have for the many young people and their mentors who want to be part of the new generation of makers who are inventing the future!"

— Roger Wagner, Creator of HyperStudio, Author of 1st Book on Assembly Programming for the Apple II, Educational Technology Innovator

"To learn is to reinvent ourselves. In *Invent to Learn*, Gary and Sylvia have crafted a pragmatic title that describes what it looks like for learners and educators to think, know and do in the modern world. At a time when endless testing and test preparation are the norm, *Invent to Learn* is a necessary support for educators to develop compelling arguments for more powerful ways of learning."

— Brian C. Smith, ICT Facilitator at Hong Kong International School

"Ready or not, the maker movement is coming your way. In this timely book, authors Sylvia Martinez and Gary Stager help us understand why making-to-learn makes such good sense for today's students. They build their case on a strong foundation of learning theory (with some Renaissance history included for good measure). Then it's off on a guided tour of the maker landscape. There's no talking down to the non-technical as we learn about everything from 3D printers to Raspberry Pi. Best of all, the authors offer a wealth of ideas and prompts for incorporating the maker movement into projects that will yield meaningful, memorable, beautiful work. Let the messiness begin."

— Suzie Boss, author of *Bringing Innovation to School: Empowering Students to Thrive in a Changing World*

"*Invent To Learn* is essential reading for those of us who are bringing the making and tinkering philosophies into our classrooms. This book gives context to the Maker Movement that is so popular today by including a history that the path of education, learning, and making has taken. It stresses the importance and relevance of allowing for the time and space for children to explore and tinker with physical and electronic objects. It is packed with ideas and resources for all models of learning environments."

— Tracy Rudzitis – Digital Media Teacher @ The Computer School NYC

"I have often been asked what the 21st century classroom should look like, and my response remains the same, like the classrooms of the Renaissance, or if that is too far back, how about your kindergarten class? This book evokes the critical relationship of equating the notion of education to creating an environment where persistent revelations and discoveries are made everyday in the classroom. Both Gary and Sylvia understand that for teachers to teach in the way they aspire to teach, it will take the insights of this book, and plenty of courage. Gary and Sylvia give the readers the chance to realize this potential. I love books that are full of the pragmatics of effective teaching and learning! Well done!"

— Ron Canuel, President and Chief Executive Officer, Canadian Education Association

Contents

To Seymour Papert – Thank you for your vision, friendship, and for having the audacity to believe we can all do better by children.

Acknowledgments

Kristy Acero
Ed Baafi
Paulo Blikstein
Karen Blumberg
Josh Burker
Joshua Callman
Andrew Carle
Chris Champion
Amy Dugre
Jaymes Dec
Erin Mumford Glenn
Gary Greenberg
Ted Hamory
Brian Harvey
Charisse Hewitt-Webster
Michelle Hlubinka
Paul Jones
Guy Kawasaki
Leon Martinez
Vivian Martinez
Yvonne Martinez
Henry Mielarczyk
Rob Mielarczyk
Maryann Molishius
Caine Monroy

Nicholas Negroponte
Henry Petersen
Juan Pena
Mitchel Resnick
Peter Reynolds
Bob Rhodes
Will Richardson
Eric Rosenbaum
Tracy Rudzitis
Brian C. Smith
Super-Awesome Sylvia
Sparkfun
Stacked Del Amo Mall
Arlene & Brian Stager
Kate Tabor
The Oaks
David Thornburg
James Todd
Cynthia Solomon
Andrew B. Watt
Rick Weinberg
Mirabel Wolf

Introduction

Playrooms and games, animals and plants, wood and nails must take their place side-by-side with books and words. — Angelo Patri

The words written nearly a century ago by the great American educator, Angelo Patri, could not be truer today. (Patri, 1917) For generations, children enjoyed classrooms rich in the objects of childhood as well as opportunities to use such materials in formal and informal ways. Play and experimentation were prized as the work of childhood.

Until recently, teachers studied how to create interdisciplinary projects in which the playful inclinations of children were leveraged in the construction of meaning. Elementary classrooms had centers where children could explore with deliberate materials and get lost in the flow of learning something in depth. Primary teachers were polymaths who not only taught the 3 Rs, but also brought the academic subjects to life through the arts.

Through the mid-1980s, learning to play the piano, make puppets out of Pop-Tarts boxes, create handmade math manipulatives, and teach physical education were requirements of those qualifying to become elementary school teachers. The Piagetian idea that "to understand is to invent" (Piaget, 1976) shaped how teachers taught and how children learned.

The past few decades have been a dark time in many schools. Emphasis on high-stakes standardized testing, teaching to the test, de-professionalizing teachers, and depending on data rather than teacher expertise has created classrooms that are increasingly devoid of play, rich materials, and the time to do projects.

Fortunately, there's a technological and creative revolution underway that may change everything.

No one would argue that computers have changed every aspect of life over the past few decades. As computers become smaller, more powerful, and cheaper at the same time, they become embedded into objects and tools, changing the way that people interact with tools. For the first time, "smart" tools allow people to design their own objects and quickly fabricate them in the real world.

Online communities serve as the hub of a digital learning commons, allowing people to share not just ideas, but the actual programs and designs that they have made. This ease of sharing lowers the barriers to entry as newcomers can easily use someone else's code and design as building blocks for their own creations.

Amazing new tools, materials, and skills turn us all into makers. Using technology to make, repair, or customize the things we need brings engineering, design, and computer science to the masses. Hundreds of thousands of adults and children alike are frequenting Maker Faires, hackerspaces, and DIY (Do-It-Yourself) websites. A growing library of print literature in magazine and book form, and even reality television, inspire learners of all experiences to seize control of their world. Fortunately for educators, this "maker movement" overlaps with the natural inclinations of children and the power of learning by doing. The active learner is at the center of the learning process, amplifying the best traditions of progressive education. This book helps educators bring the exciting opportunities of the maker movement to every classroom.

Dale Dougherty, the founder of *Make* magazine, says:

> Yet the origin of the Maker Movement is found in something quite personal: what I might call "experimental play." When I started *Make* magazine, I recognized that makers were enthusiasts who played with technology to learn about it. A new technology presented an invitation to play, and makers regard this kind of play as highly satisfying. Makers give it a try; they take things apart; and they try to do things that even the manufacturer did not think of doing. (Dougherty, 2013)

Children's seminal learning experiences come through direct experience with materials. Digital fabrication devices such as 3D printers and physical computing, including Arduino, MaKey MaKey, and Raspberry Pi, expand a child's toy chest and toolbox with new ways to make things and new things to make. For the first time ever, childhood inventions may be printed, programmed, or imbued with interactivity. Recycled materials can be brought back to life.

While school traditionally separates art and science, theory, and practice, such divisions are artificial. The real world just doesn't work that way! Architects are artists. Craftsmen deal in aesthetics, tradition, and mathematical precision. Video game designers rely on computer science. Engineering and industrial design are inseparable. The finest scientists are often accomplished musicians. The maker community brings children, hobbyists, and professionals together in a glorious celebration of personal expression with a modern flare.

One might try to marginalize robotics or 3D fabrication as having nothing to do with school or as just a super-charged hobby. The maker community could be dismissed as the scouting of the 21st century. However, today's new low-cost, flexible, creative, and powerful materials should be viewed as building blocks for today's children. The sorts of projects made possible by these materials may make readers nostalgic for what primary education used to be and reinvigorate project-based learning. Classrooms could once again become places of great joy, creativity, and invention. That would be a very positive outcome, but the maker revolution offers even more profound implications for education.

Making is a way of bringing engineering to young learners. Such concrete experiences provide a meaningful context for understanding abstract science and math concepts. For older students, making combines disciplines in ways that enhance the learning process for diverse student populations and opens the doors to unforeseen career paths.

Google's Chairman Eric Schmidt is not only "flabbergasted" that computer science is rarely taught in schools, and then only to a handful of students, but reminds us that in the Victorian era, the same people who wrote poetry also built bridges. (Robinson, 2011) Lewis Carroll wrote fairytales and was a mathematician. Even today, engineers have revolutionized the film and music industries. Schools would be well served by nurturing polymaths.

Tinkering is a powerful form of learning by doing, an ethos shared by the rapidly expanding maker community and many educators. It celebrates the best of what it means to be human. One of the most endearing things about the maker movement is how many children are celebrated as heroes, leaders, and innovators.

When 3D printing, precision cutting, microcomputer control, robotics, and computer programming become integral to the art studio, auto shop, or physics lab, every student needs access to tools, knowledge, and problem-solving skills. Most importantly, it obliterates the distinction between a vocational and academic education. When the same hardware and process skills are required in the physics lab as the art studio as the auto shop, schools need to no longer sort students into imaginary tracks for jobs that no longer follow those arbitrary rules.

Today, we have the capability to give every child the tools, materials, and context to achieve their potential, unencumbered by the limited imaginations of today's education policy makers. There are multiple pathways to learning what we have always taught, and things to do that were unimaginable just a few years ago.

Even if you don't have access to expensive (but increasingly affordable) hardware, every classroom can become a makerspace where kids and teachers learn together through direct experience with an assortment of high- and low-tech materials. The potential range, breadth, power, complexity, and beauty of projects have never been greater thanks to the amazing new tools, materials, ingenuity, and playfulness you will encounter in this book.

This book doesn't just advocate for tinkering or making because it's fun, although that would be sufficient. The central thesis is that **children should engage in tinkering and making because they are powerful ways to learn.**

Throughout this book, we assume that the reader is familiar with traditional classrooms in Western primary and secondary (K–12) schools. We use the term "teacher" to refer to any adult working with young people in an educational capacity. "Classroom" refers to wherever teaching takes place, including a club, summer camp, neighborhood hangout, or community center. You may teach in a traditional school, non-traditional school, vocational school, or homeschooling setting. Your school may have rigid schedules and segregated subjects or more flexibility. One setting is not more privileged than another. We hope that you can read between the lines when we say "classroom," "school," or "teacher," and that you can translate to your individual setting without prejudice.

We will also use the term "makerspace" as a generic term throughout the book. We are not advocating a certain kind of space that is separate from where your students meet right now. There is no list of required equipment that defines a makerspace. We share examples of teachers who create effective makerspaces regardless of physical constraints. The growing maker movement includes laboratories, hackerspaces, fab labs, shop classrooms, studios, museums, community tech shops, and DIY clubs. These spaces share the ideals of making, tinkering, collaborative learning, and invention.

Warning! Danger!

We have made every attempt at accuracy while writing this book. Prices are bound to change, technology will advance, products will be updated or even disappear, and URLs are likely to break. If this book is your best friend, "The Google," should be your second best friend.

To save space and knowing that you cannot click on a book, we have shortened some very long URLs using Bitly.com which will redirect you to the actual URL. We hope this website remains active! For your convenience, all URLs, books, and resources mentioned in this book can be found on the resource page of the InventToLearn.com website.

CHAPTER OVERVIEW

The chapters in this book attempt a progression from the big ideas of the giants of education on whose shoulders we stand towards the specific things teachers can do to encourage these ideals today.

CHAPTER 1 AN INSANELY BRIEF AND INCOMPLETE HISTORY OF MAKING
The modern maker movement is placed in a historic educational context.

CHAPTER 2 LEARNING
Constructionism is a learning theory strongly resonant with the maker movement. We look at learning through the lenses of making, tinkering, and engineering.

CHAPTER 3 THINKING ABOUT THINKING
We explore ways to think about design, the process of invention.

CHAPTER 4 WHAT MAKES A GOOD PROJECT?
That's a good question! We have some answers.

CHAPTER 5 TEACHING
What do making and constructionism look like in the classroom?

CHAPTER 6 MAKING TODAY
Making in the classroom is not new; we connect new materials to time-honored learning opportunities.

CHAPTER 7 THE GAME CHANGERS
Three activities of the modern maker movement can revolutionize learning: fabrication, physical computing (robotics, Arduino, etc.), and programming.

CHAPTER 8 STUFF
You were wondering where the shopping list was!

CHAPTER 9 SHAPING THE LEARNING ENVIRONMENT
How to create a learning environment (physical, emotional, and intellectual) that is most conducive to making.

CHAPTER 10 STUDENT LEADERSHIP
The maker movement is an opportunity for students to become leaders and advocates in their school and community.

CHAPTER 11 MAKE YOUR OWN MAKER DAY
Share the fun of making with everyone.

CHAPTER 12 MAKING THE CASE
How to convince others that invention, making, and makerspaces belong in your school.

CHAPTER 13 DO UNTO OURSELVES
How can teachers learn to do and teach things that didn't exist when they went to school?

CHAPTER 14 RESOURCES TO EXPLORE
Websites, books, kits, parts, software, online stores, and more to build your maker classroom.

ABOUT THE AUTHORS

Sylvia Libow Martinez

Sylvia Libow Martinez is president of Generation YES, a non-profit organization that works with schools around the world to empower young people with leadership roles in the effort to improve education with modern technology.

Prior to joining Generation YES, Sylvia oversaw product development, design, and programming as Vice President of Development for Encore Software, a publisher of game and educational software on PC, Internet, and video game platforms. Sylvia also developed Math.com, the award-winning website that provides math help to millions of people worldwide.

Sylvia spent seven years as executive producer at Davidson & Associates/Knowledge Adventure, a leading educational software developer. She designed, developed, and launched dozens of software titles including *Math Blaster: Algebra*, *Math Blaster: Geometry*, and *Maurice Ashley Teaches Chess*. In addition, she was responsible for Educast – the first Internet service for teachers that provided teachers with free news, information, and classroom resources.

Prior to joining Davidson & Associates, Martinez spent six years at Magnavox Research Labs, where she developed high-frequency receiver systems and navigation software for GPS receivers.

Sylvia has been a keynote and featured speaker at national and international education technology conferences in areas ranging from the use of the Internet in schools, Web 2.0 technologies, student leadership, digital citizenship, project-based and inquiry-based learning with technology, and gender issues in science, math, engineering, and technology (STEM) education. In 2010 she served on the National Assessment of Educational Progress (NAEP) 2014 Technology and Engineering Literacy assessment planning committee.

She holds a Master of Educational Technology from Pepperdine University, and a Bachelor of Science degree in electrical engineering from the University of California, Los Angeles.

Gary S. Stager, Ph.D.

Since 1982, Gary Stager has helped educators on six continents make sense of the digital age. He is considered one of the world's leading experts and advocates for computer programming, robotics, and learning-by-doing in classrooms. In 1990, Gary led professional development in the world's first laptop schools and played a major role in the early days of online education. In addition to being a keynote popular speaker at some of the world's most prestigious education conferences, Gary is a journalist, teacher educator, consultant, software developer and director of STEM at The Oaks School in Hollywood, California.

When Jean Piaget wanted to better understand how children learned mathematics, he hired Seymour Papert. When Papert wanted to create a high-tech alternative learning environment for incarcerated at-risk teens, he hired Gary. This work was the basis for Gary's doctoral dissertation and it documented Papert's most recent institutional research project.

In 1999, *Converge* magazine named Gary a "shaper of our future and inventor of our destiny." The National School Boards Association recognized Gary with the distinction of "20 Leaders to Watch" in 2007. The June 2010 issue of *Tech & Learning* magazine named Gary as "one of today's leaders who are changing the landscape of edtech through innovation and leadership." CUE presented him with its 2012 Technology in Learning Leadership Award, a recognition shared with the likes of George Lucas and Marc Andreesen.

Gary was the new media producer for *The Brian Lynch/Eddie Palmieri Project – Simpatico*, which won the 2007 Grammy Award Winner for Best Latin Jazz Album of the Year. He is also a contributor to *The Huffington Post* and a Senior STEM and Education Consultant to leading school architecture firm, Fielding Nair International. His advocacy on behalf of creativity, computing, and children led to the creation of the Constructivist Consortium and the Constructing Modern Knowledge summer institute.

Sylvia and Gary in a jet engine

The Hundred Languages

No way. The hundred is there.

The child
is made of one hundred.
The child has a hundred languages
a hundred hands
a hundred thoughts
a hundred ways of thinking
of playing, of speaking.

A hundred always a hundred
ways of listening
of marveling, of loving
a hundred joys
for singing and understanding
a hundred worlds
to discover
a hundred worlds
to invent
a hundred worlds
to dream.

The child has
a hundred languages
(and a hundred hundred hundred
*   more)*
but they steal ninety-nine.
The school and the culture
separate the head from the body.

They tell the child:
to think without hands
to do without head
to listen and not to speak
to understand without joy
to love and to marvel
only at Easter and at Christmas.

They tell the child:
to discover the world already
*   there*
and of the hundred
they steal ninety-nine.

They tell the child:
that work and play
reality and fantasy
science and imagination
sky and earth
reason and dream
are things
that do not belong together.

And thus they tell the child
that the hundred is not there.

The child says:
No way. The hundred is there.

Loris Malaguzzi (Founder of the Reggio Emilia Approach)
Translated by Lella Gandini (Edwards, Gandini, & Forman, 2012)

Chapter 1 – An Insanely Brief and Incomplete History of Making

I do not think there is any thrill that can go through the human heart like that felt by the inventor as he sees some creation of the brain unfolding to success. Such emotions make a man forget food, sleep, friends, love, everything.
— Nikola Tesla

Making things and then making those things better is at the core of humanity. Ever since early man started his first fire or clubbed his first seal, humans have been tinkerers. Farming, designing weapons for hunting, and building shelter were early forms of engineering. Tinkering was a way of controlling the environment and a vehicle for intellectual development. Throughout history, art and science, craft and engineering, analytic thinking, and personal expression have coexisted in communities, industry, culture, commerce, academia, and in the heads of creative people. Throughout history there has been an acceptance of the intuitive sense that peak learning results from direct experience.

If you are an educator who creates opportunities for making and inventing in your school or classroom, know that you are in good company. These are indeed exciting times to learn by doing. There have never been more fascinating or powerful materials available for personal expression and knowledge construction. Who knows? The maker movement may represent our best hope for reigniting progressive education. As you embark on a personal adventure to bring making, tinkering, and engineering into your classroom, know that you are not alone. You stand on the shoulders of giants and there is a rapidly growing community of makers available to help.

A KINDA SORTA HISTORY LESSON

Leonardo da Vinci (1452–1519) was the quintessential Renaissance man. He was a creative inventor, artist, sculptor, architect, engineer, musician, mathematician, and anatomist who dabbled brilliantly in a dozen other fields. Ushering in the Scientific Renaissance, da Vinci used his powers of observation, rather than the prevailing medieval practice of using the Bible and classical Greek writings, as the basis for science. Many of his inventions were ahead of their time and some of his important scientific discoveries were lost to history, but one can confidently say that Leonardo da Vinci was a maker – perhaps the greatest maker of all time.

Unsung Heroes

Philosopher Jean-Jacques Rousseau (1712–1778) made waves when he published *Emîle, or On Education*, a book that celebrated the natural abilities of the child and the importance of allowing children to develop freely in nature. He believed that individuals were blessed with innate goodness and competence and has been called "the inventor of childhood." At a time when education for children was characterized by memorization and beatings, Rousseau's philosophy was extraordinary.

Johann Pestalozzi (1746–1827) was inspired by Rousseau and believed that learning was natural and resulted from a balance between heart, head, and hand. Pestalozzi believed in nurturing children, and put this theory into action by rescuing orphans abandoned in the aftermath of Napoleon's armies. Like Piaget more than a century later, Pestalozzi thought that learning resulted from the learner's first-hand experiences and self-activity. Pestalozzi's theories also portend Piagetian stage development by recognizing that learning occurs from the concrete to abstract, known to unknown, and simple to the complex. He favored things and deeds over words. He believed that there was much to learn from nature, play, and observing the world.

Pestalozzi was a huge influence on one of his students, Friedrich Froebel (1782–1852), who built upon Pestalozzi's ideas in the design of kindergarten, the first formalized educational institution for young children. In naming his system of schooling "a children's garden," Froebel gave great consideration to what children could learn by interacting with the natural world. Planting seeds, observing their growth, caring for the resulting plants, and harvesting the resulting crops provided a rich laboratory for a young child. Froebel also created provocative objects that could be used in multiple ways through play and experimentation called "gifts," followed by more guided material-based activities called "occupations." You might think of the Froebel gifts as the first educational toys. In fact, the Milton Bradley Company was one of the largest manufacturers of Froebel's gifts as kindergartens spread across the globe and parents wanted their children to learn from the Froebel gifts at home. Froebel's aesthetic sense also inspired generations of architects and artists, including Frank Lloyd Wright, whose own son attended an early kindergarten, and perhaps not too coincidentally, invented "Lincoln Logs" as an adult.

Italian medical doctor, Maria Montessori (1870–1952), embraced many of Froebel's ideas, notably the deliberate use of materials for learning specific concepts in creating her approach to educating poor preschoolers.

PIAGET

Swiss psychologist and epistemologist Jean Piaget (1896–1980) formalized and confirmed many of the ideas of John Dewey, Montessori, Froebel, and Pestalozzi with his theories of constructivism and stage development. Piaget advanced the idea of genetic epistemology in *To Understand is to Invent*, which advocated the "…use of active methods which give broad scope to the spontaneous research of the child or adolescent and requires that every new truth to be learned, be rediscovered, or at least reconstructed by the student and not simply imported to him." (Piaget, 1976) This theory of learning came to be known as *constructivism*. The learner constructs knowledge inside their head based on experience. Knowledge does not result from receipt of information transmitted by someone else without the learner undergoing an internal process of sense making.

Piaget also called for interdisciplinary learning and made a plea for schools to create polymaths. Such educational experiences by teachers would aid students in the construction of meaning.

> What is needed at both the university and secondary level are teachers who indeed know their subject but who approach it from a constantly interdisciplinary point of view – i.e., knowing how to give general significance to the structures they use and to reintegrate them into overall systems embracing the other disciplines with the spirit of epistemology to be able to make their students constantly aware of the relations between their special province and the sciences as a whole. Such men are rare today. (Piaget, 1976)

Learning by making, tinkering, and engineering is consistent with Piagetian theories. "Students who are thus reputedly poor in mathematics show an entirely different attitude when the problem comes from a concrete situation and is related to other interests." (Piaget, 1976) In the following passage, he rejects the popular notion that some or most students are no good at math, but the larger point refers to learning in any discipline.

> Every normal student is capable of good mathematical reasoning if attention is directed to activities of his interest, and if by this method the emotional inhibitions that too often give him a feeling of inferiority in lessons in this area are removed. In most mathematical lessons the whole difference lies in the fact that the student is asked to accept from

> outside an already entirely organized intellectual discipline which he may or may not understand. (Piaget, 1976)

Piaget reminds teachers not to present students with pre-organized vocabulary and concepts, but rather provide students with a learning environment grounded in action.

> Abstraction is only a sort of trickery and deflection of the mind if it doesn't constitute the crowning stage of a series of previously concrete actions. The real cause of failure in formal education is therefore essentially the fact that one begins with language instead of beginning with real and material action. (Piaget, 1976)

Piaget's colleague, Seymour Papert, would later frame the educational establishment's favoring of the former approach over the latter as a battle between instructionism and constructionism.

John Dewey and the Progressive Era

John Dewey (1859–1952) rejected the mechanistic ideals and highly regimented factory schooling that resulted from the industrial revolution. He viewed the process of education as continuous growth across a lifetime, resulting from personal motivation and resistant to external forces or what would later become known as behaviorism. Dewey wrote extensively about the critical role community, democracy, and experience play in shaping the educational process. He advocated for students to be actively engaged in authentic interdisciplinary projects connected to the real world. In Dewey's view, education should prepare children to solve problems in a methodical fashion resulting from careful observation and previous experience. Dewey said that schools should be concerned with the intellectual, social, physical, and emotional needs of each person while subordinating the standards of adults to the needs of children. The iterative design methodology that characterizes modern making may be found in the words of John Dewey.

> It is part of the educator's responsibility to see equally to two things: First, that the problem grows out of the conditions of the experience being had in the present, and that it is within the range of the capacity of students; and, secondly, that it is such that it arouses in the learner an active quest for information and for production of new ideas. The new facts and new ideas thus obtained become the ground for further experiences in which new problems are presented. The process is a continuous spiral. (Dewey, 1938)

Amateur crafts, like sewing, weaving, carpentry, woodworking – even farming, hunting, and fishing – have been necessities and avocations for millennia. Hobbyists have always embraced art, music, and dance. Since the 17th century, "gentleman amateurs" dabbled in science and made important contributions to knowledge of the natural world. Amateur science among the general populace is more recent, but no less robust. *Popular Science* began publishing in 1872, *Popular Mechanics* in 1902, and *Boy's Life* in 1911. Authors like Jules Verne and H.G. Wells published popular books of science fiction around this time. These publications, among others, brought the innovations of the industrial revolution to amateurs. Progressive era exploration of the world, oceans, heavens, and machinery generated great interest in home-based tinkering, experimentation, and invention. Dewey not only wrote articles for *Popular Science* magazine, but was also heavily influenced by the relatively new evolutionary theories of Charles Darwin. As in today's maker movement, connections between ideas, people, and disciplines are complex and abundant.

Today, computers, microcontrollers, sophisticated software, and the Internet are allowing amateurs to collaborate with each other and professional scientists in significant ways. Norm Stanley began a speech to the First Annual Citizen Science Conference in June 2002 by saying:

> Science, as we know it today, would not be what it is without the contributions of amateurs. In fact I think it not too brash a statement to assert that basic science and what we know as the scientific method was largely developed by amateurs. From alchemists in search of the philosophers' stone to monks investigating nature in pea gardens to the gentlemen amateurs of the 17th century on, they were developing the experimental/observational/hypothetical approach of modern science. True, with the passage of time the role of the amateur, working independently, has diminished as experimental techniques became highly sophisticated and string and sealing wax no longer sufficed for doing cutting-edge science. Despite vicissitudes, amateur or recreational science remains healthy today, as witness the present gathering. (Stanley, 2002)

Amateur astronomy has been popular since the invention of the telescope. Chemistry sets captured the imagination of children for 200 years from the late 18th century until the late 20th century when ninnies suddenly determined that fire, chemistry, and fun were just too dangerous for young people.

One of the most popular purveyors of chemistry sets during the 20th century was A.C. Gilbert (1891–1984), a medical doctor, Olympic medalist, inventor, and master salesman. Gilbert pioneered the modern construction kit when he invented Erector Sets in 1911. The Erector Set was set apart from other kits by the inclusion of a motor that allowed the construction of moving models. Aggressive marketing to boys and a sales pitch to adults promised that playing with Erector Sets would reduce the "problems with boys" plaguing society. This claim proved so convincing that Gilbert convinced the United States government to withdraw their plans to ban toy production during World War I. This earned Gilbert the nickname, "the man who saved Christmas." (Watson, 2002)

In addition to Erector Sets, Gilbert published his own magazines touting the virtues of his products, which included other building materials, chemistry sets, microscopes, magic tricks and model trains. Gilbert was even a hundred years ahead of the current badge craze being hyped as today's educational revolution.

> Gilbert touted the Erector as a "real engineering" toy and created the "Gilbert Institute of Erector Engineering." A boy could "win degrees, honors, a handsome diploma, valuable prizes and a salary through free membership" in the Institute. Diplomas for First Degree, Second Degree and Third Degree Engineers were awarded with a gold "E.M.E" fraternity pin for the third degree Master Engineer. Gilbert even offered to write a reference for the winner to any business house stating this accomplishment. (Hill, n.d.)

Tinker Toys, Meccano, Lincoln Logs, LEGO, and other construction kits would follow Erector. All of these toys could be used to construct fanciful models of things, but not the things themselves. The game-changing "toys" available to today's girls and boys are capable of making real things.

All Aboard!

In the late 1950s, The Tech Modern Railroad Club (TMRC) at the Massachusetts Institute of Technology was filled with makers who, according to journalist Steven Levy, became self-proclaimed "hackers." These hackers not only spurred generations of remarkable innovation in computer hardware and software development, but were an early maker community.

Members of the TMRC fell into two groups based on interest and aptitude. The "knife-and-paintbrush" contingent loved trains. They read railroading magazines, arranged club rail trips, and worked on improving the TMRC's large train layout. The Signals and Power (S&P) subcommittee was largely concerned with what went on underneath the train layout, in other words, how the trains operated. Each group reflected a particular style and shared a meticulous attention to detail. Yet they represented two synchronistic systems – the art and science of model railroading. These distinct groups reflect common preferences and learning styles found in classrooms today.

The increasing complexity of track switching and the simultaneous control of several trains required the S&P committee to find novel ways to repurpose telephone equipment. The late-night obsessions of the TMRC also coincided with a chance to use MIT's gigantic computer systems during the hours they were idle. Learning to control the computer and get it to do things it was not intended to do enhanced the model railroading and vice versa. The "Midnight Requisitioning Committee" would scrounge for electronics parts that could be used to "hack" the large computer or their toy trains. Quickly the boundaries between the two pursuits blurred.

Hack had long been a term of art at MIT used to describe the elaborate pranks for which the institute's students had gained infamy. Now those who achieved feats of control over a system, "…imbued with innovation, style, and technical virtuosity," were prestigiously referred to as hacks and their perpetrators, hackers. (Levy, 2010)

In 1959, MIT borrowed a TX-0 computer that no longer required programming by handing over punch cards to the computer room operator. Terminals with a keyboard, called Flexowriters, could be typed on and generate a paper tape that could be fed directly into the TX-0. Instead of waiting hours for the results of your computer program to be handed to you, the result could be experienced immediately. This immediacy made it possible for the first time to modify a program while sitting at the computer. (Levy, 2010) This new level of interactivity raised the roof on "personal" computing and sent the passion of the TMRC members skyrocketing through the stratosphere. The hackers would do anything necessary to learn more and increase access to "the machine." It would not be long before their programs made music, played games, and performed computational tricks never before imagined on what were enormous multimillion dollar accounting machines.

> Hackers believe that essential lessons can be learned about the systems – about the world – from taking things apart, seeing how they work, and using this knowledge to create new and even more interesting things. (Levy, 2010)

Outsiders in their own institution, the hackers formed a computer culture unique to its surroundings, complete with its own values, heroes, legends, and goals. Quickly a "Hacker Ethic" emerged that challenged seemingly arbitrary rules and artificially scarce computing resources. It included the following principles:

- "Access to computers – and anything that might teach you something about the way the world works – should be unlimited and total. Always yield to the Hands-On Imperative!
- Mistrust Authority – Promote Decentralization.
- Hackers should be judged by their hacking, not bogus criteria such as degrees, age, race, or position.
- You can create art and beauty on a computer.
- Computers can change your life for the better." (Levy, 2010)

Such values are noble, creative and egalitarian – nothing like the way in which the media portrays hackers. Fifty years later, the motto of the maker movement, "If you can't open it, you don't own it," and the emphasis on learning by doing resonates with the Hacker Ethic dating back to MIT a half century ago.

SEYMOUR PAPERT: FATHER OF THE MAKER MOVEMENT

Mathematician, computer scientist, artificial intelligence pioneer, psychologist, educator, inventor, epistemologist, activist, and author Seymour Papert was born in 1928 in South Africa. His father was an entomologist who frequently moved the family around South Africa. Papert tells the story of playing with automobile gears beginning at the age of two and attributes much of his thinking about think-ing to those experiences. His tale is one of learning through tinkering.

> I became adept at turning wheels in my head and at making chains of cause and effect: "This one turns this way so that must turn that way so..." I found particular pleasure in such systems as the differential gear, which does not follow a simple linear chain of causality since the motion in the transmission shaft can be distributed in many different ways to the two wheels depending on what resistance they encounter. I remember quite vividly my excitement at discovering that a system could be lawful and completely comprehensible without being rigidly deterministic... Anything is easy if you can assimilate it to your collection of models. If you can't, anything can be painfully difficult. What an individual can learn, and how he learns it, depends on what models he has available. (Papert, 1980)

Papert takes great pains to declare that one particular experience, no matter how rich, might not have the same effect on other learners. To Papert, "the most powerful idea of all is the idea of powerful ideas." (Papert, 1980) His life's work has been creating tools, theories, and coercion-free learning environments that inspire children to construct powerful ideas through firsthand experience.

> A modern-day Montessori might propose, if convinced by my story, to create a gear set for children. Thus every child might have the experience I had. But to hope for this would be to miss the essence of the story. I fell in love with the gears. This is something that cannot be reduced to purely "cognitive" terms. Something very personal happened, and one cannot assume that it would be repeated for other children in exactly the same form. My thesis could be summarized as: What the gears cannot do the computer might. (Papert, 1980)

When Piaget sought a greater understanding of how children construct mathematical knowledge in the late 1950s, he hired a mathematician, Papert. Years earlier, Papert had to sneak out of South Africa, where he was labeled as a dissident prohibited from international travel due to his anti-Apartheid activi-ties. From his days as a child, the insanity of Apartheid caused Papert to become fascinated by the nature of thinking, an interest that suited his collaboration with Piaget, whose life's work was as an epistemologist

Following several years of work with Jean Piaget, Papert was invited by Mar-vin Minsky to join the MIT faculty. It was during his first day at MIT that Papert began tinkering with computers, and over the next few years he and Minsky col-laborated on pioneering work in the field of artificial intelligence. In 1968, Papert's interest in learning, mathematics, and computing led to the invention of the Logo programming language along with Cynthia Solomon, Wally Feurzig, and others. At a time when few adults had ever seen a computer, Papert sought to make them for children. He not only advocated that children should use computers, but that they should make things with them via programming. Logo was developed as a language for making things and for learning powerful ideas while making things. To this day, versions of Logo, including Scratch, remain the most popular programming environments for children.

> The computer is the Proteus of machines. Its essence is its universality, its power to simulate. Because it can take on a thousand forms and can serve a thousand functions, it can appeal to a thousand tastes. (Papert, 1980)

It did not take long for Papert to turn his sights on the troublesome nature of schooling. In *Teaching Children Thinking*, a paper originally written in 1968, Seymour Papert makes an audacious claim:

> The phrase, "technology and education" usually means inventing new gadgets to teach the same old stuff in a thinly disguised version of the same old way. Moreover, if the gadgets are computers, the same old teaching becomes incredibly more expensive and biased towards its dumbest parts, namely the kind of rote learning in which measurable results can be obtained by treating the children like pigeons in a Skinner box. (Papert, 1972a)

His words seem revolutionary for 1968, but sadly remain as a perceptive critique of schooling today. The maker movement represents a bright spot in a world that too often uses computers biased towards the least empowering aspects of formal education.

Four decades ago, Papert questioned why computers were being used by schools in such unimaginative ways. His words might be used today to question why the institutionalized "educational technology" community appears so ignorant of the affordances created by the maker movement.

> Why then should computers in schools be confined to computing the sum of the squares of the first twenty-odd numbers and similar so-called 'problem-solving' uses? Why not use them to produce some action? There is no better reason than the intellectual timidity of the computers-in-education community, which seems remarkably reluctant to use the computers for any purpose that fails to look very much like something that has been taught in schools for the past centuries. (Papert & Solomon, 1971)

In a stunning 1971 paper, *Twenty Things to Do with a Computer*, Seymour Papert and Logo co-creator Cynthia Solomon proposed educative computer-based projects for kids. They included composing music, controlling puppets, programming, movie making, mathematical modeling, and a host of other projects that schools should aspire to more than 40 years later. Papert and Solomon also made the case for 1:1 computing and stressed the three game changers discussed later in this book.

> The school computer should have a large number of output ports to allow the computer to switch lights on and off, start tape recorders, actuate

slide projectors and start and stop all manner of little machines. There should also be input ports to allow signals to be sent to the computer.

In our image of a school computation laboratory, an important role is played by numerous "controller ports" which allow any student to plug any device into the computer... The laboratory will have a supply of motors, solenoids, relays, sense devices of various kids, etc. Using them, the students will be able to invent and build an endless variety of cybernetic systems. (Papert & Solomon, 1971)

Computer game design was viewed as a way of learning powerful mathematical concepts, even in 1970. Papert's 1972 paper, *Teaching Children to be Mathematicians vs. Teaching About Mathematics,* (Papert, 1972b) continued the progressive tradition of advocating for children to have real experiences rather than be taught subjects. Throughout his career, Papert viewed the activities and values now embraced by the maker movement as consistent with progressive ideals of education.

It is 100 years since John Dewey began arguing for the kind of change that would move schools away from authoritarian classrooms with abstract notions to environments in which learning is achieved through experimentation, practice and exposure to the real world. I, for one, believe the computer makes Dewey's vision far more accessible epistemologically. It also makes it politically more likely to happen, for where Dewey had nothing but philosophical arguments, the present day movement for change has an army of agents. The ultimate pressure for the change will be child power. (Papert, 1996)

In conversation over the years, Papert frequently argued that the technology of a previous era allowed the ideas of Dewey to take root in humanities subjects, but had little impact on allowing children to experience powerful ideas of mathematics and science. As a result, the teaching of science and math remained just as impersonal and didactic as it had for centuries, ultimately reintroducing coercion into otherwise progressive schools. Papert attributed much of that failure to what he called "idea aversion," (Papert, 2000) and to a lesser extent, the absence of computational technology that would afford opportunities for learners to have direct firsthand experience with what are now commonly referred to as the STEM subjects.

I think that the great thinkers about education – the Deweys and the Piagets and the Montessoris and the Vygotskys – they all see the same fault in our education system. I think the differences between them are absolutely minor compared with the situation of sticking with the system as it is. But although they had the right idea, like Leonardo da Vinci and his airplane, they didn't have the infrastructure to be able to implement it. So, are we going to continue using the new technology to implement what was only there because there wasn't the technology? (Papert, 2006)

Despite school's resistance to change, Papert had great confidence in teachers' ability to increase their personal fluency so that "...powerful advanced ideas can become elementary without losing their power." (Papert, 1998)

Papert developed the theory of constructionism and wrote three profound books about learning with computers, *Mindstorms, The Children's Machine,* and *The Connected Family.* Each book was intended for a different audience: academics, educators, and parents respectively. The message of learning by actively constructing knowledge through the act of making something shareable is consistent across all three books, whether he was talking about programming, robotics, or media making.

Seymour Papert delights in a kid's computer programming

In addition to his work as an educator and evangelist for educational computing, school reform, and constructionism, Papert spent nearly 40 years creating new "objects to think with" and computationally rich materials. He and his colleagues developed countless dialects of Logo, the first programmable robotics construction kits with LEGO. Papert was a major force behind 1:1 computing in Maine and the creation of the One Laptop Per Child initiative creating a low-cost laptop for children in the developing world.

During Papert's last institutional research project he created an alternative learning environment entirely designed to support constructionism inside a prison for teens. It was during this project that constructionism was expanded to include a wider variety of non-computational materials, often in concert with computers to create hand-crafted classical guitars, ultra-light airplanes, films, telescopes, photography, animal habitats, publications, and more. The continuum of low- and high-tech materials allowed for learning through the construction of shareable artifacts not normally associated with school.

PROGRESSIVE EDUCATION STAGES A COMEBACK

For a brief period during the 1960s and '70s, progressive education reemerged in the United States and other industrialized economies. The Sputnik crisis spurred investment in hands-on science programs, mathematics manipulatives were in vogue, and school arts programs bloomed. Society's attention to matters of civil rights, democracy, war, and peace led to attempts at less coercive schooling and a greater emphasis on individuality within a democratic context. Summerhill and The British Infant School movement inspired open education, classroom centers, and project-based learning across the globe. Herbert Kohl, Jonathan Kozol, John Holt, Ivan Illich, Jerome Bruner, Lillian Weber, and Vito Perrone enjoyed the greatest influence on classroom practice since John Dewey.

As in the previous period of progressivism, efforts were made to change curricular content, combine subjects, reconfigure class organization and age segregation, create authentic learning experiences connected to the world outside of the school, reject behaviorism, and resist external assessment.

Howard Gardner's 1983 introduction of the theory of multiple intelligences recognized what good teachers had known for ages: intelligence comes in many forms and humans learn differently. Hands-on learning through the sort of rich projects advocated by makers offers flexible opportunities for students to learn in their personal style or styles. Classroom projects that welcome various problem-solving strategies provide fertile ground for the expression of multiple intelligences. (Gardner, 1983) (Shearer, 2009)

The Reggio Emilia Approach

In the early 1960s, the Italian city of Reggio Emilia decided to rebuild its community still ravaged by World War II by investing heavily in the education of its very youngest citizens. The system of municipal infant and toddler centers and preschools created by Loris Malaguzzi and his colleagues were built upon the philosophies of Dewey, Piaget, Vygotsky and others who placed the child at the center of the learning process. The Reggio Emilia Approach is highly sensitive to local culture and community, and respects the rights, needs, talent, and questions of children. Educational activities emerge from the interests of children, and the environment is "the third teacher," after the parent and teacher. A wide variety of materials are used for knowledge construction and to express understanding through the "hundred languages of children." In the classrooms, atelier (studio), and community of Reggio Emilia you will find the tiniest toddlers using real tools in pursuit of authentic problem solving. The primary role of the teacher in a Reggio-inspired setting is as a researcher charged with understanding the thinking of each child and preparing the environment for that child's natural intellectual growth. There may be no more consistent model of learning through making, tinkering, and engineering than found in the work of our Italian colleagues. Carlina

Rinaldi, the president of Reggio Children, offers a glimpse into the Reggio Approach's thoughtful reinvention of school:

> The word, 'project' evokes the idea of a dynamic process, an itinerary. It is sensitive to the rhythms of communication and incorporates the significance and time of children's investigation and research. The duration of a project can be short, medium or long, continuous or discontinuous, with pauses, suspensions and restarts.
>
> The term, 'curriculum' (along with the corresponding terms 'curriculum planning' or 'lesson planning') is unsuitable for representing the complex and multiple strategies that are necessary for sustaining children's knowledge-building processes. (Rinaldi, 2006)

We are blessed with 50 years' worth of wisdom, research, and documentation from the Reggio Emilia Approach. This may represent the world's most mature model of sustained constructionism and progressive education. The lessons of Reggio Emilia have profound implications for every level of education, not just preschool. While the subtlety, beauty, and wisdom of the approach could and should be studied for a lifetime, we suggest that readers of this book pursue the Reggio Emilia resources listed later in this text.

MAKING MAKES A COMEBACK

Computer Hobbyists

The invention of the microcomputer led to an explosion of interest in hobbyist computing from the mid-1970s through the mid-1980s. It was these hobbyists and their social clubs, such as Silicon Valley's Homebrew Computer Club, that led to the invention and popularity of personal computing. Steve Jobs and Steve Wozniak, founders of Apple Computer, were members of the Homebrew Computer Club. Other clubs existed around the world for the purpose of sharing knowledge, parts, and circuits with other enthusiasts. Periodicals from that period, including: *Byte, Creative Computing, Compute, Dr. Dobb's Journal* (still in print), and *Logo Exchange* spread the joy of computer programming to hundreds of thousands of hobbyists around the world. The hobbyists planted the seeds for the explosive growth of Silicon Valley.

The Capital of Making

In 1985, Nicholas Negroponte, along with Jerome Wiesner, Seymour Papert, and Marvin Minsky, created the MIT Media Lab. Negroponte imagined a convergence of technology, multimedia communication, and design. In the original proposal for the Lab, Negroponte drew a sketch of how the computer, broadcast and motion picture, and publishing industries had an area of intersection in a Venn diagram representing their narrow common interests. A second sketch showed how those three industries would soon be indistinguishable from one another, a prediction that quickly became reality. Negroponte said that at the Media Lab, "…new theories of signals, symbols and systems will emerge from the merger of engineering, social science and the arts." (Brand, 1988) The Media Lab embraced polymaths and became a grand center for tinkering across the lines of traditional disciplines. The Media Lab reinvented university research and development while inspiring competitors around the world to create their own media labs.

The Media Lab's playful spirit of learning by doing made it the birthplace of many of the ideas and materials embraced by the modern maker movement. The MIT Media Lab has a special knack for taking complex, expensive, and foreboding technology and making it accessible to laypeople, even children. Programmable LEGO robotics sets, Scratch, and MaKey MaKey are but three of the Lab's inventions popular in classrooms and kids' bedrooms around the world. One Media Lab invention is the invention of other labs for invention – the FabLab. Graduates of the Media Lab are inventing new products and companies that are fueling the maker movement. The maker family tree has a deep set of roots at MIT and another in Silicon Valley.

Fab

In his 2005 book, *Fab: The Coming Revolution on Your Desktop – from Personal Computers to Personal Fabrication*, MIT Professor Neil Gershenfeld described the next technological revolution as one in which users would make the tools they need to solve their own problems. Gershenfeld predicted that for the cost of your school's first computer, you would soon have a Fabrication Lab or fab lab – a mini high-tech factory – capable of making things designed on a computer. In the near future, such factories may fit on your desktop. Gershenfeld tells readers that Seymour Papert was the first to blur "…the distinction between toys and tools for invention, culminating in the integration of play and work in the technology for personal fabrication." Gershenfeld also mentions how Papert always believed that children should invent, as well as use, technology. The longstanding obstacles to children constructing their own computers was a "thorn in our flesh," said Papert. (Gershenfeld, 2007)

Gershenfeld's MIT course, "How to Make Almost Anything," became enormously popular among students across a wide spectrum of academic disciplines. When art, science, engineering, computer science, and crafting meet whimsy, a new era of personal empowerment emerges. You could design a bicycle in the shape of Matisse's *Blue Nude Number Two* and then email it to your sister in Australia. ("Scientific American Frontiers: You Can Make it On Your Own," 2003) Gershenfeld was surprised to learn that students with "skills best suited for arts and crafts" were able to create complete functioning systems. He was also surprised to see that these inventions were not only highly personal, but executed by students working alone, when in a corporate context such products would be the work of teams. Personal ownership of an idea can lead learners to exceed all expectations. (See "Stager's Hypothesis" later in this book.)

In *Fab,* Gershenfeld describes a collaborative culture that emerged during classes in his own "FabLab." His depiction is not dissimilar from what we find in K–12 maker classrooms. In just a few sentences, Gershenfeld addresses collaboration, design, teaching, learning, and curriculum in makerspaces.

> The final surprise was how these students learned to do what they did: the class turned out to be something of an intellectual pyramid scheme. Just as a typical working engineer would not have the design and manufacturing skills to personally produce one of these projects, no single curriculum or teacher could cover the needs of such a heterogeneous group of people and machines. Instead, the learning process was driven by the demand for, rather than supply of, knowledge. Once students mastered a new capability, such as waterjet cutting or microcontroller programming, they had a near-evangelical interest in showing others how to use it. As students needed new skills for their projects they would learn them from their peers and then in turn pass them on. Along the way, they would leave behind extensive tutorial material that they assembled as they worked. This phase might last a month or so, after which they were so busy using the tools that they couldn't be bothered to document anything, but by then others had taken their place. This process can be thought of as a "just-in-time" educational model, teaching on demand, rather than the more traditional "just-in-case" model that covers a curriculum fixed in advance in the hopes that it will include something that will later be useful.

Students will learn, they will invent, they will teach, they will collaborate, and they will share knowledge when it best suits their needs, interests, and style. The maker culture gets smarter when it buzzes with activity. Paradoxically, it may be an absence of the external pressures of schooling – assessment, curriculum, lecture, and demands for note-taking that leads to the greatest achievement.

Gershenfeld's work teaches us that everyday objects can have intelligent features built in and fab labs may be created in developing communities. Such fab labs allow locals to meet specific needs by shaping low-cost digital technology. Different communities have unique requirements that now could be satisfied by technology they invent and fabricate for themselves.

Moi?

You may be asking, "All that tinkering and high-tech wizardry may be fine for MIT professors and students, but what does it have to do with my school?"

The most obvious implication is for the ways computers are used in school. Making and personal fabrication are a clear departure from the status quo. Instead of training another generation to perfect secretarial skills via word processor instruction or drilling basic skills, computers can and will be used to shape the world of the student. Policy shifts are already afoot in the U.K. where in 2012, the government announced that they were scrapping the national ICT curriculum because, in the words of the British Secretary of State, "It is harmful and dull." (Barnett, 2012) The government proposes to replace the emphasis on information literacy and productivity applications – things quickly learned naturally – with computer science.

Although much work needs to be done to define what K–12 computer science means and how teacher preparation needs to change, such curricular shifts will likely spread worldwide.

Many educators, beginning in the 1960s with Seymour Papert, Alan Kay, and Cynthia Solomon, recognized that computers could be powerful knowledge incubators where formal ideas could be concretized through computer programming and debugging. Educators who were focused on outcomes or who were unfamiliar with the sorts of sophisticated thinking their students were experiencing were quick to question the value of programming in school. Others dismissed it as "only for some children." Today, the personal fabrication and physical computing revolution allows the very same intellectual experiences to result in tangible products more likely to be admired by adults. Just as Logo programming gained respect when it teamed with LEGO bricks to propel robotics into the classroom 25 years ago, new construction toolkits breathe life into exciting project-based learning.

Schools should seize any opportunity for students to learn and express their knowledge in new and exciting ways. Classrooms need to reflect the world their kids live in and leverage new tools to amplify human capacity.

Fab Labs Go to School

As early as 2003, Mike Eisenberg of the University of Colorado Boulder began to publish articles and papers about the potential for new computationally enhanced materials and personal fabrication to support constructivist learning in K–12 schools.

> Why should educational technologists be interested in these devices? Briefly, the answer is that these new technologies can vastly extend and reinvigorate the best traditions of student-driven design and construction. (Eisenberg & Buechley, 2008)

In 2008, Paulo Blikstein of Stanford University started working with K–12 schools to create digital fabrication labs called the FabLab@Schools project. As part of FabLab@School, he built the first fabrication lab in a School of Education in the U.S. and began teaching the first course (outside of the MIT Media Lab) for graduate students and teachers to design new projects for K–12 education using a fab lab or makerspace. Blikstein says,

> I realized that digital fabrication had the potential to be the ultimate construction kit, a disruptive place in schools where students could safely make, build, and share their creations. I designed those spaces to be inviting and gender-neutral, in order to attract both the high-end engineering types, but also students who just wanted to try a project

with technology, or enhance something that they were already doing with digital fabrication. (Blikstein, 2013)

In 2011, Blikstein hosted the first FabLab@School conference at Stanford, drawing K–12 educators from around the world who then became the leaders of many "first ever" makerspaces in their own schools.

TODAY

June 2012 saw two national magazines, *Wired* and *Make*, feature cover stories on summer technology projects for kids and parents. Newsstands across the U.S. alerted laypeople to the tinkering revolution and new opportunities for intergenerational learning. Articles about personal fabrication could be found in specialized magazines and newspapers for the past few years, but now children are being placed in the center of the revolution.

Since Gershenfeld published *Fab*, the availability and mainstream popularity of personal fabrication has skyrocketed. Three forces have made his predictions accessible and affordable: physical computing with Arduino and other micro-controllers, low-cost 3D printers and cutters, and programming. Each of these innovations has profound implications for classroom practice and school reform. A growing library of accessible print materials, countless websites, social networks where makers share ideas, and Maker Faires around the world support these game changers.

The quarterly magazine *Make* is the Gutenberg Bible of the burgeoning "maker" community. Dale Dougherty (*Make's* founder and publisher) and Mark Frauenfelder (editor-in-chief) first noticed the growing energy and participation at the intersection of craft, engineering, computer science, and whimsy. Think of *Make* as a combination of *Popular Mechanics* meets computer science and fabrication. Its pages delight readers with projects featuring programming, robotics, amateur space exploration, backyard ballistics, cigar box guitars, and old VCRs turned into automatic cat feeders. The magazine celebrates and inspires ingenuity, innovation, and creativity, as should your school. No school library is complete without a subscription.

When soldering, prototyping, programming, and inventing return to the lives of children, remarkable projects result. Arduino is a low-cost (approx. $25–$30) open source programmable micro-controller that allows you to build robots and "intelligent" machines of varying sophistication out of broken toys, electronic parts, and increasingly sophisticated sensors. Arduino continuously adds functionality, as its price remains constant or even goes down. Arduino is the standard robotics controller used by hobbyists and industry alike. It belongs in the toolbox of school children.

Arduino variants like the "Lilypad" expand the student toolbox to e-textiles – computers you can wear. The Lilypad Arduino includes buttons, sensors, lights, and sound elements that become part of garments and "soft sculptures" when circuits are sewn with conductive thread. Now your school T-shirt can feature a dancing light pattern, or directional signals may illuminate the back of a kid's sweatshirt while they ride their bike. Code libraries for Arduino are freely shared online, allowing learners to download a program similar to their needs and then modifying it to their personal specifications. Reading and "remixing" another person's computer program is a sophisticated form of literacy students need today.

3D printers and precision cutters are breaking the $1,000 barrier. These desktop machines allow a user to design an object on a computer with increasingly simple software and then print or cut the actual object. Kids view the ability to print their own toys, tools, and models with a sort of blasé attitude described by Alan Kay's adage that, "Technology is anything that wasn't there when you were born."

The Spring 2012 Bay Area Maker Faire, organized by *Make* magazine, attracted over 100,000 children and adults who came together for a weekend of tinkering, crafting, inventing, showing-off, learning, and making together. In addition to the fall New York City and spring San Mateo fairs, local communities around the world are encouraged to make their own Mini-Maker Faires. Maker Faires, like the hackerspaces, fab labs, and tech shops popping up all over the world, are remarkably rich learning environments where novices learn alongside experts. These communal learning spaces have access to equipment that an individual or school may not yet be able to own. Schools would be wise to create similar learning environments. Already, a growing number of schools have their own fab labs or are hosting their own Maker Days.

There is a growing body of literature to inspire a teacher or parent interested in making with children. In addition to *Make* magazine, there is *Howtoons, Fifty Dangerous Things (You Should Let Your Children Do), Made by Hand: Searching for Meaning in a Throwaway World, Unbored,* and the *Geek Dad/Geek Mom* series' of books. Books such as *62 Projects to Make with a Dead Computer (and Other Discarded Electronics)* combine this generation's passion for environmentalism with electronics, science, engineering, and arts and crafts. Websites like *Makezine* and *Instructables* feature countless project ideas and tutorials. "Sylvia's Super Awesome Maker Show" is a series of Web videos by an elementary school student who shares her love and knowledge of making and fabrication with learners of all ages. There are millions of Scratch projects designed and programmed by children and shared online. Online communities are the new guilds, where access to expertise, mentors, and affinity groups are a mouse click away.

One might even consider the popularity of reality television as a manifestation of our desire to make things and have authentic learning experiences with experts. If you want to learn to build a shed, dance the Paso Doblé, bake a soufflé, or be a drunken loser, there is an expert you can apprentice with, if only through a screen. The primal human need to be creative is bursting out in thousands of ways across the culture. At the same time, too many schools are stifling individuality and personal expression.

The maker community is bringing time-honored forms of craft and handiwork back into the lives of children. You may knit an intelligent scarf, recycle a pile of junk into an underwater robot, or build a remarkable cardboard arcade, like Caine, a 9-year-old kid in Los Angeles, did. In 1988, Seymour Papert wrote about the computer as material with which you can make things and other powerful ideas. Nearly a decade earlier, Papert described the computer as mud pie. At last, this vision of computing being as handy as a pencil or paper mâché is becoming a reality.

The maker ethos values learning through direct experience and the intellectual and social benefits that accrue from creating something shareable. Not only are there a plethora of exciting high-tech materials available for childhood knowledge construction, but the growing popularity of making things has led to many "low-tech" innovations to spice up hands-on learning. Makedo is a series of reusable connectors and hinges for turning cardboard packaging materials into elaborate structures and play objects. Sugru is a space-age material that allows you to make a shape or stick two objects together as you might do with clay, but within 24 hours it air sets as rubber. Best of all, the plethora of new materials lets children build actual things, not just models of things.

Kids have always made things – tree houses, skateboards, soapbox cars, doll houses, forts, and igloos. They have learned socially through collaborative play and construction by putting on shows, experimenting with roles, and performing magic tricks. The major difference today is computation. As Brian Silverman says, "A little bit of programming goes a long way. It is like a jet assist" in solving problems or building exciting things. (Silverman & Kay, 2013)

Empowerment

In the late 1960s, Seymour Papert began asking, "Does the computer program the child or the child program the computer?" The growing list of creative technology accessible to children represents the closest realization of the goal of empowering the human in this cybernetic relationship. Beyond fluency, personal fabrication, programming, and physical computing shift the emphasis from passive consumption to active creation and invention.

Personal fabrication is more than inventing alarm clocks that run away and hide when you press the snooze button; it is revolutionizing every field dependent on design. Gone are the days of tedious calculation, speculation, sketches, or cardboard models. Now you can make the actual thing you are trying to test. Best of all, gone are the days of helplessness, dependency, and consumption. Making lets you take control of your life, be more active, and be responsible for your own learning.

A Rainbow in the Clouds

Kid makers possess a skill set and self-efficacy that will serve them well in school, as long as they are engaged in interesting activities worthy of their capacity for intensity. Despite the swirling politics and external pressures on schools, the maker movement may offer teachers cause for optimism. The stuff of making is super cool and gives those teachers so inclined another chance to reanimate progressive education. If your administrator likes to buy shiny new things, then there are plenty of things to buy that actually amplify the potential of children. Silicon Valley billionaires are endorsing the non-profit, Code.org, which advocates for kids to learn computer programming. The Association for Computing Machinery is advocating for computer science to be a curriculum staple from kindergarten to twelfth grade and the brand new Next Generation Science Standards by the National Academies of Science makes explicit calls for meaningful assessment, interdisciplinary knowledge, inquiry, and engineering.

> In the future, science assessments will not assess students' understanding of core ideas separately from their abilities to use the practices of science and engineering. They will be assessed together, showing that students not only "know" science concepts; but also that they can use their understanding to investigate the natural world through the practices of science inquiry, or solve meaningful problems through the practices of engineering design. ("Next Generation Science Standards," 2013)

None of the experiences advocated in this book or the materials that enable them are inconsistent with the imaginations of children or with the types of learning experiences society has long valued. Making is a stance that puts the learner at the center of the educational process and creates opportunities that students may never have encountered themselves. Makers are confident, competent, curious citizens in a new world of possibility.

This book is intended to be aspirational. Like Papert, we believe in kid power and know that teachers hold the key to liberating the learner. The values, tools, and activities of the maker movement enrich and acclerate that process.

Chapter 2 - Learning

Some of the most crucial steps in mental growth are based not simply on acquiring new skills, but on acquiring new administrative ways to use what one already knows. — "Papert's principle" described in Marvin Minsky's Society of the Mind

CONSTRUCTIVISM AND CONSTRUCTIONISM

Constructivism is a well-established theory of learning indicating that people actively construct new knowledge by combining their experiences with what they already know. Constructivism suggests that knowledge is not delivered to the learner, but constructed inside the learner's head. New knowledge results from the process of making sense of new situations by reconciling new experiences or information with what the learner already knows or has experienced. This profoundly personal process underlies all learning. In this sense, the new buzzword of "personalized learning" is redundant. All learning is personal. Always.

Constructivism is often misunderstood as meaning that learning only occurs alone. This is not the case. Learning is often socially constructed. Talking and working with others is one of the best ways to cement new knowledge.

We believe that "constructionism," a similar-sounding term coined by Seymour Papert, is the learning theory that most strongly resonates within the maker movement and should be taken seriously by anyone investigating classroom making.

Papert defined constructionism as:

From constructivist theories of psychology we take a view of learning as a reconstruction rather than as a transmission of knowledge. Then we extend the idea of manipulative materials to the idea that learning is most effective when part of an activity the learner experiences as constructing a meaningful product. (Papert, 1986)

Papert's constructionism takes constructivist theory a step further towards action. Although the learning happens inside the learner's head, this happens most reliably when the learner is engaged in a ***personally meaningful activity outside of their head*** that makes the learning real and shareable. This shareable construction may take the form of a robot, musical composition, paper mâché volcano, poem, conversation, or new hypothesis.

This is much more than "hands-on" learning. The "meaningful" part of constructionism is not just touchy-feely new age language. It acknowledges that the power of making something comes from a question or impulse that the learner has, and is not imposed from the outside. Questions like "How can my car go faster?" or "I like the way this looks, can I make it prettier?" are treated as valid, and in fact, potentially more valid than criteria imposed by anyone else, including a teacher. Learners are empowered to connect with everything they know, feel, and wonder to stretch themselves into learning new things. We seek to liberate learners from their dependency on being taught.

The maker movement is terribly exciting in the ways it celebrates the virtues of constructionism, even if the advocates of learning by making have no formal knowledge of the theory underlying their passions.

Constructionism is a learning theory – a stance about how you believe learning occurs. It is not a curriculum or set of rules. This book explores the strategies for teaching and classroom organization with modern materials and processes to support constructionism.

MAKING, TINKERING, AND ENGINEERING

Making, tinkering, and engineering are ways of knowing that should be visible in every classroom, regardless of the subject or age of the students. In a makerspace these processes may be defined loosely:

- **Making** is about the active role construction plays in learning. The maker has a product in mind when working with tools and materials.
- **Tinkering** is a mindset – a playful way to approach and solve problems through direct experience, experimentation, and discovery.
- **Engineering** extracts principles from direct experience. It builds a bridge between intuition and the formal aspects of science by being able to better explain, measure, and predict the world around us.

Making – Messing About With Transformative Materials

Making is about the act of creation with new and familiar materials. Children have always made things, but their tool palette and canvas have expanded remarkably in recent years.

Making something is a powerful, personal expression of intellect. It creates ownership even when what you make isn't perfect. Researchers have identified "The IKEA Effect" in which people who make things value their creations, even flawed creations, more than the same things created perfectly by experts. (Norton, Mochon, & Ariely, 2011)

The modern maker movement also embraces the ability to share not only the products, but the joyful process of making with videos, blogs, and pictures. Mark Frauenfelder, editor-in-chief of *Make* magazine, wrote about this "virtuous circle" of DIY enthusiasts who enjoy documenting their projects online and inspiring others:

> I've joined this virtuous circle myself. Whenever I build a new guitar or a new gadget for my chicken coop, I post a description or a video about it on my blog. Many people have emailed me to let me know that my projects have spurred them to do their own projects. They've told me that making things has changed the way they look at the world around them, opening new doors and presenting new opportunities to get deeply involved in processes that require knowledge, skill building, creativity, critical thinking, decision making, risk taking, social interaction, and resourcefulness. They understand that when you do something yourself, the thing that changes most profoundly is you. (Frauenfelder, 2011)

Maria Montessori said, "The hands are the instruments of man's intelligence." But intelligence is not only in the act of making, it's in extending ones own intelligence with interesting materials and tools. When used enough, the materials and tools of the maker become part of the intellectual laboratory that can be used to solve problems.

In the 1960s, computers were massive machines used only by the military and large corporations. Papert's genius was in seeing the computer as a rich, playful material that could be used by children as they learned about the world.

In their paper *Computer as Material: Messing About with Time*, Papert and Franz write:

> We mention one other closely related point of interest. The phrase "messing about" in our title is, of course, taken from a well-known paper by David Hawkins. (Hawkins, 1965) Marvelously entitled "Messing About in Science," it describes how he and Eleanor Duckworth introduced children to the study of pendulums by encouraging the students to "mess about" with them. This would have horrified teachers or administrators who measure the efficiency of education by how quickly students get to "know" the "right" answers. Hawkins, however, was interested in more than right answers. He had realized that the pendulum is a brilliant choice

of an "object to think with," to use the language of Papert's *Mindstorms*, one that can build a sense of science as inquiry, exploration, and investigation rather than as answers.

Just as pendulums, paints, clay, and so forth, can be "messed around with," so can computers. Many people associate computers with a rigid style of work, but this need not be the case. Just as a pencil drawing reflects each artist's individual intellectual style, so too does work on the computer. (Papert & Franz, 1987)

The idea of computers as "material" stands in contrast to the typical uses of computers in schools, then and now. Three categories of usage were outlined in Robert Taylor's seminal book on the subject, *The Computer in School: Tutor, Tool, Tutee* (Taylor, 1980). Taylor framed potential uses of the computer as either:

1. **A tutor.** The computer displays instruction and conducts assessment.
2. **A tool.** The computer allows the student to perform academic tasks easier or more efficiently.
3. **A tutee.** The student learns by programming (tutoring) the computer.

Despite being published in 1980, Taylor's classification of computer use in schools remains accurate today. The computer as tool and tutor remain dominant.

To Papert, the strength of the computer lies in none of these categories. It is a material to be "messed about with." The act of messing about, which we might call tinkering, is where the learning happens. The computer provides a flexible material that the child can weave into their own ideas and master for their own purposes.

It might seem that what we are talking about here is the "tutee" use, or children learning to program computers. However, there is a subtle difference. In the *Computers as Material: Messing about with Time* article, Papert and Franz describe students investigating the concept of time. The teacher showed her students how a candle would gradually extinguish when covered with a bell jar. How, she asked, can we measure how long it will take for the candle to go out?

This simple prompt created a wealth of challenges and learning opportunities for these students on their journey to solve this problem. They invented multiple ways to measure time, from counting heartbeats to constructing sand-filled homemade hourglasses. The quest to build these timers and clocks was driven by the need for accurate measurement of time, not the teacher's directions. In fact, there were very few teacher directions aside from the challenge to answer the question.

The classroom was "well stocked with materials," even "junk," which gave the children a rich source of material when they brainstormed about measuring time in new ways. Eventually the students used computers to help measure time. They programmed timers and counters on the computer, alongside the ones they built from the other materials on hand. In building these devices, they naturally came across problems that needed to be solved – engineering obstacles, inconsistencies, and mathematical concepts like precision. They built, tested, and re-built their clocks and timers to solve these problems and get better results.

The object of the lesson was not to build a timer or to program a computer. The object was to empower children to use their brains and anything they could put their hands on to solve a problem.

Could the lesson have been learned without the computer? Perhaps, but including the computer as part of the materials used to solve the problem gave the students a richer and more relevant experience. In the modern technological age we live in, there is simply no way to mess around with mathematical and scientific ideas without the computer.

The conclusion of the article recommends how best to use computers in schools. Remember, this is from 1987!

> Seek out open-ended projects that foster students' involvement with a variety of materials, treating computers as just one more material, alongside rulers, wire, paper, sand, and so forth.

> Encourage activities in which students use computers to solve real problems.

> Connect the work done on the computer with what goes on during the rest of the school day, and also with the students' interests outside of school.

> Recognize the unique qualities of computers, taking advantage of their precision, adaptability, extensibility, and ability to mirror individual students' ideas and constructions of reality.

> Take advantage of such new, low-cost technological advances as temperature and light sensors, which promote integration of the computer with aspects of the students' physical environment.

> While the theme of this article has been the role of the computer in the educational process, let us clearly state that the ideas underlying our teaching strategies were formulated by educators and philosophers whose lives long predated the invention of the computer, and whose ideas can be applied to any learning situation and to any material. Our emphasis, as was that of Piaget, Dewey, Susan and Nathan Isaacs, and others, is clearly on the inquiry and the learner, not on the specific curriculum or facts to be learned. In this undertaking, all materials are created equal, although admittedly the computer did add unique and powerful aspects to the learning process. (Papert & Franz, 1987)

"Computer as material" may be the most powerful idea we will explore in this book as we further develop the concepts of making, tinkering, and engineering in the classroom. In future chapters we will support these ideas with more practical suggestions for teachers, such as how to develop good prompts and select the best kinds of materials, both digital and physical, to promote intellectually empowering experiences.

Tinkering – A Mindset For Learning

Tinkering is a uniquely human activity, combining social and creative forces that encompass play and learning.

In most school activities, structure is valued over serendipity. Understanding is often "designed" by an adult committee prior to even meeting the students. Play is something you do at recess, not in class where students need to "settle down" and "be serious." Schedules and bells tell students where to be and what they are to learn. Textbooks set the pace of learning, and teachers tend to follow the pattern of chapter assignments and tests. Too often, kids are hooked on teachers and teachers have a faith-based relationship with the textbook.

This is evident when you ask students what they are doing in math and they answer, "Chapter 12." The reason for all this structure is not that it benefits the learner. In reality, it benefits the teacher-as-manager and the administrators in the system. The structure makes it easier for one teacher to teach a one-size-fits-all curriculum to large numbers of same age students. None of the constraints of school are for the benefit of learning – they create a more manageable, homogeneous, efficient platform for teaching a predetermined bit of content.

Creating a learning environment that deliberately breaks this teacher-as-manager focus is difficult, yet necessary. It requires a new teacher mindset and also requires giving students explicit permission to do things differently.

When we allow children to experiment, take risks, and play with their own ideas, we give them permission to trust themselves. They begin to see themselves as learners who have good ideas and can transform their own ideas into reality. When we acknowledge that there may be many right answers to a question, it gives children permission to feel safe while thinking and problem solving, not just when they answer correctly. When we honor different kinds of learning styles it becomes acceptable to solve problems without fear.

In *Epistemological Pluralism and the Revaluation of the Concrete,* Sherry Turkle and Seymour Papert argue that equal access to mathematics and science (including computer science) for women is not just a matter of historical gender inequity, but a basic imbalance in valuing only "abstract, formal, and logical" ways to think about science.

> The concerns that fuel the discussion of women and computers are best served by talking about more than women and more than computers. Women's access to science and engineering has historically been blocked by prejudice and discrimination. Here we address sources of exclusion determined not by rules that keep women out, but by ways of thinking that make them reluctant to join in. Our central thesis is that equal access to even the most basic elements of computation requires

an epistemological pluralism, accepting the validity of multiple ways of knowing and thinking. (Turkle & Papert, 1991)

They go on to describe other ways of knowing and learning, contrasting the planner with checklist in hand to the *bricoleur* (tinkerer in French) who, "... resembles the painter who stands back between brushstrokes, looks at the canvas, and only after this contemplation, decides what to do next." (Turkle & Papert, 1991)

The message is clear in many classrooms that there is only one way to approach learning. It's taken on face value that science is analytical, math is logical, art is creative, and so on. Contemplation is time wasted and there is only one way to solve problems. Children hear these messages loud and clear – "This subject isn't for me," or worse, "School isn't for me."

In her book *The Second Self*, Sherry Turkle describes tinkering as an alternate, but equally valuable approach to science, calling it "soft mastery" in contrast to the "hard mastery" of linear, step-by-step problem solving, flowcharting, and analytical approaches. (Turkle, 1984)

School, especially in science and math classes, typically only honors one type of learning and problem-solving approach, the traditional analytical step-by-step model. Other more non-linear, more collaborative, or more artistic problem-solving styles are often dismissed as "messy" or "intuitive" with the implication that they are not reliable.

There is also a clear implication of gender roles in these adjectives – soft mastery skills are most often attributed to women, while hard mastery skills are more often attributed to men. When school favors hard mastery over soft mastery, we implicitly ask some children to ignore their own best instincts. We figuratively tie one hand behind their backs.

The point is not that tinkering is good for one type of student and not others. Tinkering is not what you do with the students who "can't do regular work" or just something to make girls feel comfortable. Adopting a tinkering mindset in your classroom allows all students to learn in their own style.

A lot of the best experiences come when you are making use of the materials in the world around you, tinkering with the things around you, and coming up with a prototype, getting feedback, and iteratively changing it, and making new ideas, over and over, and adapting to the current situation and the new situations that arise.

I think there are lessons for schools from the ways that kids learn outside of schools, and we want to be able to support that type of learning both inside and outside of schools. Over time, I do think we need to rethink educational institutions as a place that embraces playful experimentation." — Mitchel Resnick (Rheingold, 2011)

Tinkering, when presented as a way to approach problems in an iterative, contemplative fashion, can take its rightful place in schools next to analytical approaches to problem solving.

Tinkering as Play

Tinkering is what happens when you try something you don't quite know how to do, guided by whim, imagination, and curiosity. When you tinker, there are no instructions – but there are also no failures, no right or wrong ways of doing things. It's about figuring out how things work and reworking them. Contraptions, machines, wildly mismatched objects working in harmony – this is the stuff of tinkering. Tinkering is, at its most basic, a process that marries play and inquiry. (Banzi, 2008)

"Play is the work of the child" is an oft quoted maxim from Maria Montessori, echoed by Jean Piaget, "Play is a child's work," and even Fred Rogers, "Play gives children a chance to practice what they are learning." But play is not a chore, nor is it the opposite of work; Stuart Brown in the book *Play: How it Shapes the Brain, Opens the Imagination, and Invigorates the Soul*, says the opposite of play is depression.

Play is called recreation because it makes us new again, it re-creates us and our world. (Brown & Vaughan, 2010)

Both Abraham Maslow, "Almost all creativity involves purposeful play," and Dr. Benjamin Spock, "A child loves his play, not because it's easy, but because it's hard," understood that play can be fun, creative, purposeful, and mindful at the same time. Play is not a frivolous waste of time. When children are deeply involved in play, they are learning. Their passion, flow, and sense of timelessness mirror the actions of the tinkerer. (Csikszentmihalyi, 1991) It is through these activities that children stretch to become the people they are meant to be.

Play creates a zone of proximal development of the child. In play a child always behaves beyond his average age, above his daily behavior; in play it is as though he were a head taller than himself. As in the focus of a magnifying glass, play contains all the developmental tendencies in a condensed form and is itself a major source of development. (Vygotsky, 1978)

Edith Ackermann, a colleague of both Jean Piaget and Seymour Papert, has spent her career investigating the intersections of learning, teaching, design, and digital technologies. She says that play and design are similar:

Both design and play involve breaking loose from habitual ways of thinking, and making dreams come true! This, in turn, requires 1. an ability to imagine how things could be beyond merely describing or representing how things are (ask what if, do as if, inventing alternative ways); and 2. a desire to give form or expression to things imagined, by projecting them outward (thus making otherwise hidden ideas tangible and shareable). Both are about building and iterating. Messing around with materials, or giving the head a hand often sparks a maker's imagination and sustains her interest and engagement: you get started and the ideas will come. You persevere and the ideas will fly. (Ackermann, 2010)

Engineering as Inventing

We tried all the systems that had been tried before, then we tried our own systems and we tried some combinations that no one had ever thought of. Eventually, we flew. — Orville Wright

The origin of the word "engineer" is a maker of an "engine," which is from the Latin word *ingenium*, meaning a clever invention. Engineering is the application of scientific principles to design, build, and invent.

In the K–12 context, "science" is generally taken to mean the traditional natural sciences: physics, chemistry, biology, and (more recently) earth, space, and environmental sciences. . . . We use the term "engineering" in a very broad sense to mean any engagement in a systematic practice of design to achieve solutions to particular human problems. Likewise, we broadly use the term "technology" to include all types of human-made systems and processes – not in the limited sense often used in schools that equates technology with modern computational and communications devices. Technologies result when engineers apply their understanding of the natural world and of human behavior to design ways to satisfy human needs and wants. (National Research Council, 2012)

We teach children science and math so they can make the world a better place, not so they can pass tests. Edith Ackermann says:

In the practice of design, the purpose is not to represent what is out there (or model how things are) but to imagine what is not (or envision how things could be) and to bring into existence what is imagined. Creators are fabricators of possibilities embodied: They both make and make-up things! (Ackermann, 2007)

Unfortunately, we think of engineering as being something very serious that one studies in college. In fact, engineering is something that is perfectly compatible with young children. When we encourage children to build with sand, blocks, paint, and glue, we are simply asking them to take what they know about science and apply it to the real world. In the truest sense, children are natural engineers and we can create classrooms that celebrate this fact.

Engineering is concrete. Engineers make things that work in the real world, within constraints of time, budget, and materials. Constraints make life interesting, and dealing with constraints creates opportunities for ingenuity and creativity. Engineers plan, but they also experiment and tinker. Yet, most kids are deprived of engineering experiences until they endure 12 years of abstractions. Knowledge construction follows a progression from concrete to the abstract, but the abstract is not "better." It's just a different way of knowing. If the playful, creative inclinations of young children were nurtured in an engineering context, their understanding of the increasingly elusive math and science facts would be developed in a meaningful natural context.

The just-released Next Generation Science Standards state that each citizen should learn engineering practices that include "defining problems in terms of criteria and constraints, generating and evaluating multiple solutions, building and testing prototypes, and optimizing – which have not been explicitly included in science standards until now." ("Next Generation Science Standards," 2013) Let's hope that these standards are interpreted to mean real engineering that is playful and creative.

In his paper *How Kids Learn Engineering: The Cognitive Science Perspective*, researcher Christian Schunn explores how to support early engineering learners (Schunn, 2009). His research points to several contradictions in the way students are taught science and math. In many classrooms, students are presented with endless "basic skill" lessons on scientific vocabulary, lab safety, theory, or even history lessons about famous scientists before actually engaging in hands-on activities. Sometimes, there are no activities at all – just the facts.

Such front-loading techniques do not work. They bore students and by the time the activity is presented, many will have lost interest. Engaging children as quickly as possible in real projects creates an authentic context for learning a specific science formula or math equation since students realize they need that skill or information to continue *their* projects. Good projects create the need for learning more. This is much more powerful than a checklist or threat of a bad grade.

In this book, we will use making, tinkering, and engineering as lenses through which to explore ways to enhance children's learning.

Tinkering, Engineering, and "Real Work" — Sylvia

It seems that to many people, tinkering connotes a messiness and unprofessionalism that doesn't apply to "real" jobs in scientific fields.

I believe just the opposite is true — tinkering is exactly how real science and engineering are done.

I like to think I have a unique perspective on this. After graduating from UCLA with an electrical engineering degree I went to work at an aerospace company on a research project to create the world's first GPS satellite navigation system. It was fun, exciting work because we were building something that we knew would change the world. The task was literally theoretically impossible, which made it even better. The hardware was too slow, the software didn't exist, the math was only a theory, and existing navigation systems weren't built to handle what we needed. I was thrown together with an assortment of mathematicians, scientists, hardware gurus, engineers, and programmers who weren't used to working together. The military pilots we collaborated with didn't trust any of us or our new-fangled ideas, which created even more interesting team dynamics. There were many days when we just sat around and talked through the problems, went to try to them out in the lab, and watched our great ideas go up in smoke. Then we did it again...and again...and again... until it worked.

It was the essence of tinkering. We tinkered with ideas, methods, with hardware and software, always collaborating, always trying new things. There was no "right answer," no "scientific method," and sometimes the answers came from the unlikeliest sources or even mistakes. There were flashes of insight, fighting, battle lines drawn, crazy midnight revelations, and the occasional six-hour lunch at the local pool hall.

My flash of insight, 20 years later, is that perhaps we should avoid squeezing all serendipity out of STEM subjects in a quest to teach students about a "real world" that exists only in the feeble imagination of textbook publishers. Tinkering is the way that real science happens in all its messy glory.

Chapter 3 – Thinking About Thinking

*You can't think about thinking without thinking
about thinking about something.*
— Seymour Papert

Now that we have laid some groundwork about learning and the historical roots of tinkering and making, we turn to thinking. Why thinking? Because it's something that teachers need to think about.

Educators talk a lot about school, classrooms, learning, and children, and not a lot about thinking. Thinking is more than a mechanical act performed by the brain. Brain science is still far from being able to tell what someone is thinking. The outward clues about what's going on inside a child's head can be confusing, contradictory, and vary from child to child and even from day to day. But it's the job of every teacher to learn how to watch children for signs of thinking, and to point that child in the direction of deeper learning. The early childhood educators of Reggio Emilia, Italy, teach us that the primary role of the teacher is as "researcher" whose job is to understand the thinking of each child.

How do we know what a child is thinking? We don't. That's the fun part. The first step is to mindfully watch and listen to children as they work. What kinds of strategies are they employing to solve problems? What do they do when frustrated? What do they say to you, to themselves, and to their peers when they are in learning situations? A teacher who is paying close attention to a child should strive to answer these and similar questions. Teachers should be concerned with making thinking visible, or making private thinking public. Making is a way of documenting the thinking of a learner in a shareable artifact. Stages of a project "under construction" offer important evidence of productive thinking or scaffolding opportunities.

This chapter is not about brain science, epistemology, or theories of thinking. It's about how teachers can watch, listen, and learn about children's thinking in ways that help create a more productive context for learning.

Thinking is never done in the abstract. As Seymour Papert says, "You can't think about thinking without thinking about thinking about something." (Papert, 2005) That is why the process of tinkering is very helpful to learn about thinking. Tinkering gives deep clues to a patient observer about thinking.

There are many who believe that their own success in learning can be transferred to others by sharing the thinking patterns and steps they successfully use to solve problems. As the theory goes, if others simply memorize these successful thinking patterns, then they too will be successful.

However, learning as a transfer of thinking patterns does not work. When people learn, they construct knowledge based on what they already know and have experienced. This is context specific and different for each person.

SCHOOL THINKING

Nowhere in school is this attempt to transfer thinking patterns more evident than in science and math classes, the S and M of STEM (Science, Technology, Engineering, and Math). STEM is a popular acronym for the subjects that government and business leaders value and want schools to teach. In recent years, the acronym STEM has become popular when describing subjects deemed necessary for United States economic progress and global competitiveness. There are many pronouncements about improving STEM education, why STEM is important for global economic completion, and why students should study STEM subjects.

But the "jobs of the future" do not need scientists who have memorized the periodic table. In fact, business leaders say they are looking for creative, independent problem solvers in every field, not just math and science.

Yet in most schools, STEM subjects are taught as a series of memorized procedures and vocabulary words, when they are taught at all. In 2009, only 3% of high school graduates had any credits in an engineering course. (National Science Board, 2012) Technology is increasingly being relegated to using computers for Internet research and test taking.

In school, this explicit teaching of facts and procedures is rampant in almost every subject area. In science, it's called "the scientific method" and often includes steps such as:

- Observe something and/or do research.
- Construct a hypothesis.
- Make a prediction based on your hypothesis.
- Test your hypothesis by doing an experiment.
- Analyze the results of your experiment.
- Determine if your hypothesis was correct.

The steps vary slightly between models. However, no matter the actual words on the checklist, or how many steps are included, we teach them to children as if they descended on stone tablets. Teachers devise songs or mnemonic devices to help students memorize the rigid steps. Then students memorize the vocabulary words that go along with the scientific method: hypothesis, fair test, variables, control groups, reliability, validity, etc. Finally, students fill out worksheets to match the vocabulary words with the correct definitions and put the steps in order.

This is not science. Science is about wonder and risk and imagination, not checklists or vocabulary memorization. Alan Kay laments that much of what schools teach isn't science at all, it's science appreciation. (Kay, 2007)

Bruno Latour, an influential anthropologist, studied the way that scientists really do their work in his book, *Science in Action: How to Follow Scientists and Engineers Through Society.* (Latour, 1987) What he discovered was that tinkering is closer to the way real scientists, mathematicians, and engineers solve problems. Tinkering is not just an uninformed or immature way that science happens. Sure, scientists make plans. They also follow hunches, iterate, make mistakes, re-think, start over, argue, sleep on it, collaborate, and have a cup of tea. Tinkering encourages making connections, whereas school tends to favor "clean" disconnected problems with clear, unambiguous step-by-step solutions.

> For planners, mistakes are steps in the wrong direction; *bricoleurs* [French for tinkerers] navigate through midcourse corrections. *Bricoleurs* approach problem-solving by entering into a conversation with their work materials that has more the flavor of a conversation than a monologue. (Turkle & Papert, 1991)

In many cases, science is taught by telling students the end of the story first. The history of math and science is full of interesting problems that people have tackled over centuries. Often, people solved these problems with brute force methods – building buildings that collapse or launching voyages into unknown lands with little information. After a lot of hard-won experience, a theory is born to explain it. Now we teach children the theory as if that came first and is all that matters.

The world is full of crazy, weird, seemingly unexplainable things that push the boundaries of imagination, yet some child living today will figure out the answer. Too often, we teach as if all scientific problems are solved and the steps are fixed. It's like teaching music theory without allowing children to hear or play actual music.

The scientific method is often misapplied in school to design and invention problems. The scientific method may work for testing a guess about how the world works, but it is not applicable to things that don't yet exist.

"Design thinking" and "computational thinking" are hot topics in education today. While the objectives of students developing the thinking skills required by design or computation are laudable, teaching them outside of a meaningful context is likely to fall short of those goals. The best way to ensure the development of design thinking is for students to be engaged in authentic design activities. The surest path to computational thinking is a student engaged in computer programming. Taking the computer out of computational thinking or production out of design leaves the students with an impoverished view of 21st century skills. It would be a shame if students came to view such powerful ideas with the ennui normally reserved for algebra.

Design in the real world is often a process of deliberate tinkering. Edith Ackermann says:

> Designing (*projettare* in Italian) can be seen as the flipside of reflective abstraction: an iterative process of mindful concretization, or materialization of ideas (*concrétisation réfléchie* in French). To design is to give form, or expression, to inner feelings and ideas, thus projecting them outwards, making them tangible. (Ackermann, 2007)

Of course in the real world there are goals to be met like delivery dates, budgets, and other constraints. Sometimes the goals may be less clear, as you struggle to come up with something "better" even though no one quite knows what that means. Sometimes you work for days or weeks, making small incremental steps; sometimes things come in a flash of brilliance. But rarely in the real world do difficult projects start out with a perfect road map.

Yet in school, there is often a rigid "design process" with stages that imply a linear progression from start to finish. Whether teaching writing, video production, or brainstorming a useful invention, it seems most efficient to provide students with step-by-step assistance, tools, and tricks to organize their thoughts and get to a finished product as quickly as possible.

This well-intentioned support may in fact have the effect of stifling creativity and forcing students to create products that simply mirror the checklist they have been given. Students, especially the "good" students who have been well-trained to follow directions, will march through the steps with little thought at all. The intermediate products, mindmap, or lab notebook becomes the goal, with students trying to guess the secret objectives inside the mind of their teacher.

By looking at how real-world designers, engineers, and scientists engage in deliberate tinkering, we may discover a way for teachers to guide students to think more critically without coercion.

DESIGN MODELS FROM THE REAL WORLD

The computer has transformed engineering and design. Pre-computer, design was a meticulous process of calculating by hand, building models when possible, and relying on all known data about the problem to be solved. For large engineering projects, the most reliable design methodology was the waterfall method. This method relied on sequential steps of gathering requirements and data, planning, building, testing, and deployment. It was called the waterfall method because like water in a waterfall, it's easy to go one way, and very hard to go the opposite way.

In the waterfall method of design, you complete each stage before progressing to the next stage. You hope that your planning is so good that anything actually built from that plan is perfect. Because, for example, if you build the 22nd floor of a skyscraper and realize that your plan didn't include proper fire escapes, you can't afford to tear down the building, re-plan, and start over again.

When the risk of making a mistake is costly, it makes sense to use the waterfall method. However, if the risks of making a mistake are *not* expensive or dangerous, then it makes sense to explore different design methodologies.

As computers became more and more ubiquitous, designers found that they could greatly decrease the risk of mistakes by creating simulations of engineering designs on the computer. The computer has allowed designers to tinker with the design in ways never before possible. It has changed what used to be risky and expensive to risk free and inexpensive.

Weisman Art Museum designed by Frank Gehry, Minneapolis

Buildings by Frank Gehry and I.M. Pei with impossible angles and custom computer-manufactured parts are the outcome of this revolution in computer-enhanced design. Companies like the Amsterdam-based Freedom of Creation use high-end computer-controlled fabrication devices to print designer furniture, jewelry, and household fixtures on demand – something impossible just a few years ago.

Advances in manufacturing based on computation not only makes one-of-a-kind production possible, but it also allows for mass customization. You can buy an iPod in a choice of colors, not just because an artist visualized the options, but because a computer scientist, industrial designer, and engineer made it possible to make such changes easily at a low cost. The maker movement reminds us regularly that art and science are inseparable.

When designing physical products, there is a time when planning must end and you must commit to building something. You can tinker with a bridge design while it's on the computer, but once you start building it in the real world, the design tinkering has to stop.

In electronics, you can place components on a "breadboard" and try out various circuits. If you make a mistake or don't like a result, you pull out the wires and try again. Fabrication allows you to quickly build prototypes on an inexpensive 3D printer until you are satisfied enough to commit to a finished design.

In the world of digital products, like software, apps, and websites, this design philosophy can go a step further. You can tinker even as you build, spiraling through a series of stages as you make progress. These modern, tinkering-friendly design models are known by various names including "rapid prototyping," "spiral design," "iterative design," and "agile development."

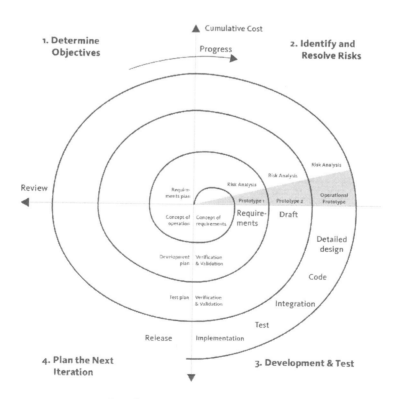

Spiral Design Model (Boehm, 1988)

Tinkering-Friendly Design Models

All design starts with an idea. But spiraling, iterative design does not require that the entire product be completely planned at the beginning. The goal is to build something as quickly as possible in order to check your assumptions and move forward. The planning, doing, checking, adjusting, re-planning, fixing, improving, sharing, etc. move in a spiral fashion through these phases again and again.

The goal is to make constant forward progress through a series of gradually improving prototypes (products that can be tested in the real world, but aren't final), thus the alternate name, "rapid prototyping."

This is why all Google apps and sites are perpetually in "beta," meaning an unfinished state. Google puts apps in front of the public as part of their design process so that they can get feedback from users, watch usage patterns, and decide which features (if any) should be changed or added. Some projects may take a surprise turn when an obscure feature becomes a user favorite. Some projects die a quick death, saving time and money in the long run.

Rapid prototyping takes advantage of the fact that changing a digital product like an app is relatively inexpensive and risk free.

Even when building products for the physical world, the rapid prototyping model can be very useful. The quicker you can get a prototype complete, the better the feedback you can get from people who use your product. Electronic products can be protoyped on a breadboard where wires and parts are easily connected, disconnected, and reconnected until the designer is satisfied with the result. A product designer can quickly build product concepts using inexpensive fabrication technology before committing to final manufacturing.

Another design model used by programmers and engineers is called the "iterative development model." Similar to spiral design, it "iterates" through steps of design and development so that lessons are quickly learned and incorporated into the next cycle.

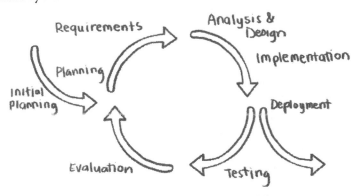

Iterative Development Model

The distinctions between these various professional design and development models are not that important for the purposes of this book. What is important to understand is that the iterative, cyclical nature of these modern, real-world models looks nothing like the linear, step-by-step design models or scientific method found in most textbooks.

DESIGN MODELS FOR LEARNING

In the classroom, iteration through multiple design cycles is useful and relevant. Not only is it more "real world" than linear methods, it matches the inclination of children to do something quickly rather than spend a lot of time planning.

As students go through multiple design cycles, they develop a better understanding of the requirements, tools, and materials as they make tradeoffs and try to improve their prototype. These cyclical phases allow the teacher to see progress and make sure that students are moving forward towards a goal, not procrastinating until the last minute.

> Multiple design cycles enable children to develop a more complex, more complete understanding of relevant engineering concepts. Early in a design task, students tend to focus on superficial aspects of models, often misunderstanding the functional aspects of the design and making poor conceptual connections between models and engineering design. (Schunn, 2009)

The number and length of phases can be adjusted to match students' age and the nature of the project. For young children, the time it takes to get to the first creation phase should be measured in minutes!

In 2007, Mitchel Resnick, LEGO Papert Professor of Learning Research and head of the Lifelong Kindergarten group at the MIT Media Lab where Scratch was developed, wrote a paper called *All I Really Need to Know (About Creative Thinking) I Learned (By Studying How Children Learn) in Kindergarten*. This paper introduces a cycle that reflects the natural way that young children learn and play.

> The materials vary (finger paint, crayons, bells) and the creations vary (pictures, stories, songs), but the core process is the same. I think of it as a spiraling process in which children **imagine** what they want to do, **create** a project based on their ideas, **play** with their creations, **share** their ideas and creations with others, **reflect** on their experiences – all of which leads them to imagine new ideas and new projects.
>
> In going through this process, kindergarten students develop and refine their abilities as creative thinkers. They learn to develop their own

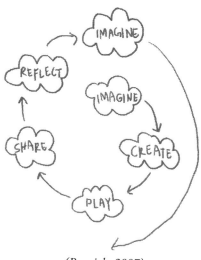

(Resnick, 2007)

ideas, try them out, test the boundaries, experiment with alternatives, get input from others – and, perhaps most significantly, generate new ideas based on their experiences. In reality, the steps in the process are not as distinct or sequential as indicated in the diagram. Imagining, creating, playing, sharing, and reflecting are mixed together in many different ways. But the key elements are always there, in one form or another. (Resnick, 2007)

The paper goes on to make the case that new technologies, such as robots, programmable devices, and Scratch are much like the best toys for children, encouraging imaginative, creative play in a way that does not, "…over-constrain or over-determine. Children with different interests and different learning styles can all use the same materials, but each in his or her own personal way."

In MIT workshops, children were deliberately shown this cycle while engaged in the process of design. It was considered an indicator of success when after each workshop, children could articulate the ideas of this approach.

We completely agree that children should be explicitly included in making the learning process understandable. It empowers children to see the whole picture and not feel like they are just following steps handed to them. Having a reflective activity at the very end of a maker class to see what tips they would give to the next class is a great idea. However, we wouldn't actually give those tips to the next class; the powerful part of that lesson is not the tips, it's the reflection.

What we fear with imposed design cycle diagrams and checklists is that children will see any set of steps as prescriptive, and as much as we tell them that it doesn't have to be done exactly like this, they will worry that they aren't "doing it right." In actuality, and as Resnick discusses, these are not distinct, sequential steps, but steps that exist in many different forms. Children, however, aren't going to read books or research papers and understand this.

The second problem with any design cycle diagram is that none of them will be perfect. Sometimes a project will require a lot of iteration during the creative process, sometimes a lot of fixing, and those iterations may happen without any sharing or testing. Design cycle diagrams are meant merely to suggest the iterative, forward-progress nature of the work to be done, and the tinkering mindset that goes along with it.

WHAT THE WORLD REALLY NEEDS IS ANOTHER DESIGN MODEL

Humans love lists, particularly teachers. Lists help us remember. Lists help us plan. Lists help us measure progress. Yet, an obsession with lists and their inherent linearity may detour the learning process by replacing making with compliance. This book has already explored the scientific method, spiral design/ rapid-prototyping, and Mitchel Resnick's Creative Kindergarten Learning Spiral. George Polya's *How to Solve It* problem-solving steps (Polya, 1945) and the writing process have long been popular in schools.

Despite an abundance of options for describing what industry might call workflow, making, tinkering, and engineering in a classroom setting is different. Classroom making is less concerned with producing a perfect product or finding one solution to a problem. We recognize that the deepest learning experiences may occur while en route to producing a product. Students engaged in direct experience with materials, unforeseen obstacles, and serendipitous discoveries may result in understanding never anticipated by the teacher. That is why curricular planning schemes like "backward design" are problematic. They assume that maximum educational value is achieved when every student gets to a goal preordained by the teacher, even if multiple paths are paved.

Design models for school also tend to use stages that offer the teacher ready-made objects to be assessed, rather than give students agency.

Existing design models may be too wordy or abstract for young learners. Time is the most precious of classroom resources. Teachers need to protect actual making from time spent on teaching the particulars of a model of making. Not all products or projects are created equally, and therefore flexibility is paramount. Making, tinkering, and engineering may require schools to undergo structural changes that support inquiry and project development over much longer periods of time than they are accustomed.

TMI

While thinking about the existing design models and our dissatisfaction with them, a popular acronym popped into our heads: TMI. In our context, TMI has its original meaning, "Too much information," but several others as well:

- Too much instruction
- Too many interruptions
- Too much intervention

Polya may have been most elegant in reducing the problem-solving process to four steps. TMI has only three – **Think, Make, Improve**. Reducing the process to three steps minimizes talking and maximizes doing. Best of all, kids of the texting generation are unlikely to forget TMI.

Think

The "think" stage incorporates many of the problem-setting, brainstorming, and planning processes found in other approaches. Thinking may include:

- Brainstorming
- Talking it out
- Predicting
- Gathering materials
- Identifying expertise
- Deciding who to work with (or to work alone)
- Setting goals

- Sketching
- Outlining
- Flowcharting
- Researching
- Planning

Make

This is the part of the process where the most action occurs. During the making process, students may:

- Play
- Build
- Tinker
- Create
- Program
- Experiment
- Construct
- Deconstruct
- Test strategies/materials
- Observe others
- Borrow code
- Share code
- Document their process
- Look for vulnerabilities in their invention
- Ask questions
- Repair their creation

Improve

At some period in the process, the maker (or team of makers) faces one of two conditions:

1. Their machine, program, story, film, or folk dance doesn't work or they are stuck.
2. They are satisfied with what they created.

The first eventuality may occur more often than the second, but in either case, there is always room for improvement. For kids, these two choices may be expressed as "Fix or Make Better."

When you get stuck, you may need to improve your thinking about the problem or find another strategy for getting unstuck. This process might include:

- Conduct research
- Talk it out
- Discuss with peers
- Look at the problem from a different perspective

- Use different materials
- Change one variable at a time
- Think about ways in which you solved similar problems in the past
- Play with it
- Find a similar project you might analyze or deconstruct
- Ask an expert
- Be cool
- Get some fresh air
- Sleep on it

"I'm done" are two words you should never hear in the maker classroom! When a student (or team of students) thinks they are finished, they should seek opportunities to improve or refine their work. Students who find themselves on a successful project development plateau might ask questions, such as: *How can I make my/our _____ faster, slower, better, more accurate, prettier, greener, cooler, stronger, smarter, more flexible, taller, shorter, more efficient, less expensive, more reliable, lighter, more elegant, easier to use?*

Invariably, attempts at improvement will lead to new making and further improvement.

Under the rarest of circumstances, a student who has solved a problem to their satisfaction or "completed" a project should be motivated to start another or share their expertise with peers.

After formulating our TMI paradigm, we discovered that Seymour Papert also viewed tinkering as "…a source of ideas and models for improving the skill of making – and fixing and improving – mental constructions." (Papert, 1993) Again, Papert reinforces the constructionist theory that making, complete with the process of making things better, leads to understanding.

There is a poster of the TMI Robot on the InventToLearn.com website for you to print out. Feel free to adapt this model for your classroom. Moving forward, we will use the term "iterative design cycle" as we discuss how to use this methodology for student projects.

INTEGRATING THE ARTS

There have been recent efforts to produce STEAM by adding the Arts to STEM. Adding more letters to an acronym is no substitute for action. To date, much of the energy behind STEM and STEAM is rhetorical. Some schools are shopping for a handful of magic STEM/STEAM beans and merely slapping a new label on old curriculum.

The desire to add the A to STEM may be rooted in a fear of math and science, a devaluing of the visual and performing arts, or both. Why is it assumed that STEM subjects are devoid of the creative disposition of artists? Will combining already underrepresented subjects reverse the trend of a narrowing curriculum? It would be a tragedy if the arts were to become even further marginalized by schools that can now point to STEAM as the reason why art and music teachers vanished.

Children deserve rich experiences across the widest range of disciplines available. The good news is that in the maker community, artistic projects and craftsmanship are highly valued. Music composition is often required in programming a computer game or making your robot dance. Oral presentation skills are necessary for pitching your invention or in narrating your film. Artistic skills, creativity, and curiosity are in high-demand by any project, no matter how technical.

Tinkering is a way of thinking that allows children to naturally integrate the arts into their learning. As a project comes together, some of the decisions made by the learner will naturally be artistic ones. *Should I paint my robot? My space game looks boring. Can I draw a cool alien planet background?* The arts and sciences are a natural marriage when students have sufficient time for project development, reflection, and revision.

Some may find it hard to believe, but for many people who love math or science, making things work is a poetic experience. Combining the arts with STEM means that children can express themselves in even more variations. Making produces experiences in which children realize such truths.

Color us cynical, but there is little historical evidence that school practice changes as the result of a re-branding exercise, like changing STEM to STEAM. Such rhetorical slight of hand is unlikely to produce more music teachers or band instruments or theatrical productions or kilns. Our focus needs to be on dismantling the artificial boundaries between subject areas erected in the late 19th century. Anything educators can do to make learning more natural accrues to the benefit of students. When you allow children to make personally meaningful projects, they develop the habits of mind required to solve their own problems.

THE ROLE OF POWERFUL IDEAS IN CHANGING EDUCATION

In his paper *Technology in Schools: To Support the System or to Render it Obsolete* (Papert, 1998), Seymour Papert says that the profound ideas of John Dewey didn't fail, but were simply ahead of their time. Experiential learning is not just another school reform destined to failure, because three reversals have taken place since the time of Dewey.

The first reversal is that children can be part of the change. Schools used to demand that students meet standards. But the time is coming when students will demand that schools live up to the standards of learning they have come to expect via their home computers. More and more young people learn independently and follow their own passions via online sites and communities, most of them not run by traditional educational institutions. We are living in a time of tremendous change when traditional institutions are trying new things, some in order to keep their grip tight on old ways, while others experiment outside those boundaries. But the voice of the learner is being heard and will continue to be heard in a way never before possible.

The second reversal Papert identifies is that the computer offers "learner technology" instead of "teacher technology." Many previous attempts at integrating technology into classrooms simply reinforced the role of teacher (videos of lectures) or replacing the teacher (drill and practice, computerized testing, etc.). However, affordable computers, sensors, and simple programming tools have become materials for the learner. This transition, if we choose to take it, "…offers a fundamental reversal in relationships between participants in learning."

The third reversal is that powerful ideas previously only available in college courses can be made understandable for young children. We believe that this is the hope of the classroom maker movement. Ideas that are the cornerstone of learning in the 21st century – from electronics and computers to mathematical and scientific concepts like feedback, population statistics, and recursion – can be learned and understood by very young children as they work with computational technology.

But this third reversal may be the most difficult – these ideas were not taught to parents and teachers when they were children. Convincing parents and teachers that today's children need to understand these new, fundamentally different concepts may be the hardest work of all.

The strategy for overcoming the last obstacle brings us full circle in thinking about thinking. For those of us who want to change education, the hard work is in our own minds, bringing ourselves to enter intellectual domains we never thought existed. The deepest problem for us is not technology, nor teaching, nor school bureaucracies – it's the limits of our own thinking.

Chapter 4 – What Makes a Good Project?

Before they invented drawing boards, what did they go back to? — *George Carlin*

To some people, *tinkering* sounds messy, *making* implies summer camp craft projects, and *engineering* is for rocket scientists. Others may say that these topics are not worthy of study in school. Luckily, there is a good deal of research and practical resources supporting the concept of "project-based learning" (see the Making the Case chapter for some of these). Educators can tap into these resources to justify creating a maker classroom to a skeptical community or administration. Best of all, these time-honored pedagogical practices will enrich your making as well.

There are several names for this kind of classroom experience. Project-based learning may be the most common, but there are variants known as problem-based learning, inquiry learning, and others. There are many websites and studies that argue the differences between these terms. They all have value and ardent supporters. We believe that they all describe similar processes for the teacher and result in similar habits of mind and successful learning for students. Suffice it to say that students with a tinkering mindset and a space full of creative opportunities will create products, tackle problems, and devise intricate inquiry strategies as they tinker, make, and build. We do not believe it is critical to superficially separate problem solving, inquiry, and creating artifacts into different types of learning.

When we talk about a "project," what we mean is work that is substantial, shareable, and personally meaningful. Some projects may take a class period or two to complete, while others may require an entire term.

When a teacher creates a well-designed prompt that capitalizes on student curiosity, kids can embark on complex, long-term learning adventures.

Inquiry begins with what students want to know and the things they wonder about. Allowing students to explore these questions drives their desire to learn.

When we build off this natural phenomenon, we support learners along the path to knowledge and understanding without expecting a right answer. Successful learning expeditions use the curriculum as the buoy, not the boat.

> Making things is better than being passive, but making good things is better still! — Gary Stager

Teachers instinctively know that projects are worthwhile, even if they do not have much experience with project-based learning. Too often the term "project" means any activity that is not worksheet-based or that takes longer than a 42-minute class period. Too many instances of unimaginative assignments turn into projects just by giving students weeks for completion. That five paragraph essay about caribou is transformed into a project when students are given two months to obsess over it. The inevitable procrastination leads to increased stress and an imperceptible improvement in quality.

In Papert's theory of constructionism, the best way to construct knowledge or understanding is through the construction of something shareable, outside of a student's head. Those artifacts are commonly thought of as projects, even though the project development process is where the learning occurs. Such artifacts are evidence of learning.

THE EIGHT ELEMENTS OF A GOOD PROJECT

1. **Purpose and Relevance.** Is the project personally meaningful? Does the project prompt intrigue in the learner enough to have him or her invest time, effort, and creativity in the development of the project?
2. **Time.** Sufficient time must be provided for learners to think about, plan, execute, debug, change course, expand, and edit their projects. Class time affords students equal access to expertise and materials; projects may also need sufficient out-of-school time.
3. **Complexity.** The best projects combine multiple subject areas and call upon the prior knowledge and expertise of each student. Best of all, serendipitous insights and connections to big ideas lead to the greatest payoff for learners.
4. **Intensity.** Children have a remarkable capacity for intensity that is rarely tapped by the sliced-and-diced curriculum. Projects provide an outlet for the exercise of that intensity. Think about how long kids can spend mastering a video game, reading a favorite book series, memorizing the attributes of Pokemon, or building a tree house, and you have a good template for successful project-based learning.
5. **Connection.** During great projects students are connected to each other, experts, multiple subject areas, powerful ideas, and the world via the Web. The lessons learned during interpersonal connections that are required by collaborative projects last a lifetime. While there is some merit in organizing student groups to "teach" collaboration, a teacher can hope to create a more natural environment in which students collaborate (or

do not) based on their own needs. Collaboration may consist of observing a peer, asking a quick question, or by working with the same teammates for the duration of a project.

6. **Access**. Students need access to a wide variety of concrete and digital materials anytime, anyplace. Personal student laptops make this possible, but we also need to think about the quality and quantity of craft materials, books, tools, hardware, software, and Internet access that allows learners to follow paths we may never have anticipated. When non-consumable materials are used, such as LEGO bricks, a sufficient quantity is necessary to ensure that students have everything they need for their projects and can leave the finished products together long enough for others to learn from them. The last thing you want is one student cannibalizing a classmate's work during project creation.

7. **Shareability**. This is the big idea of project-based learning! Students need to make something that is shareable with others. This provides a great deal of motivation, relevance, perspective making, reciprocal learning, and an authentic audience for the project. "A project is something you want to share" is a sufficient definition for learners of all ages.

8. **Novelty**. Few project ideas are so profound that every child needs to engage in its development in every class, or year after year. Yes, that means that it may be time to rethink the annual marshmallow adobe project. If one student makes a fantastic discovery during a project, others can learn from it without slavishly repeating the steps of the pioneering student. In a healthy community of practice, learning continues and knowledge is shared naturally without coerced repetition.

QUESTIONS WORTH ASKING

Is the problem solvable? The brilliant educators of Reggio Emilia, Italy, teach us that a well-designed, open-ended, learner-definable prompt is the best starting place for project-based learning. Rather than ask, "How would you make the world a better place?" Reggio educators might ask 3-year-olds, "Can you make a park for the birds who come to visit our school?" Kids immediately have a starting point they can wrap their heads around. They know about birds and parks and can build all sorts of representations. In the process they learn about birds, measurement, engineering, and collaboration and develop a plethora of powerful ideas no teacher is smart enough to anticipate.

Projects often begin with a problem statement. Yet too many school projects are based on problems unsolvable by students. That is not always a bad thing, since a student might learn a lot before appreciating the enormity and complexity of a problem. That is a worthy outcome in itself. Completely solving a problem about fixing a levee may be too advanced for kindergartners, but they could learn the complexity of the problem and gain an appreciation for the other things they need to learn.

While overly ambitious engineering problems may lead to new insights or recognition of complexity, solving social or political dilemmas are harder to debug and provide fewer opportunities for model building. Asking kids to solve world peace is a dopey project idea because they cannot get their heads or arms around such ill-defined, infinitely complex problems.

Requiring students to assume the role of people with whom they share no life experience causes other problems. This is why conference panel discussions asking school students to invent the future of education leads to a stream of banalities and audience boredom.

Is the project monumental or substantial? Schools require kids to produce all sorts of *monumental* work, like that work sheet featuring 200 similar arithmetic problems. The goal is *substantial* work, where a student wakes up in the middle of the night thinking about getting back to school to continue working on a project. When a project burns inside of them, students often exceed our expectations.

Who does the project satisfy? Is the learner as enthusiastic a beneficiary of the project as the person giving her a grade? Great projects benefit the learner more than the teacher.

What can they do with that? Anything you ask of a student should lead to the construction of a more complex question or a larger theory. Otherwise, we should rethink the assignment. Great projects, like hobbies, have a self-regulating feedback loop. Incremental success motivates a student to try something more ambitious or to enhance the project. Bugs or mistakes lead students to rethink problems and test new strategies. Powerful learning occurs in both instances.

Why Computers and Digital Technology?

The protean nature of computers as constructive material makes a wider range and depth of projects possible like never before. Computers allow students to explore powerful ideas and express themselves in a myriad of ways never before possible. Using computers in creative ways invites students to create interdisciplinary projects that demonstrate student competence and connect knowledge domains. Open-ended software supports learning diversity and allows multiple entry points into a sea of ideas.

As Seymour Papert said, "If you can make things with computers, then you can make a lot more interesting things." (Stager, 2006)

Stager's Hypothesis:
A Good Prompt is Worth A Thousand Words

For years, I have watched kids and adults in my classes do remarkable work without being taught to do so. I marveled at how participants in the Constructing Modern Knowledge institute could write a crazy project idea on the wall and then accomplish it within a matter of hours or days. I watched as graduate students told tenth grade English students to use their computers to compose a piece of instrumental music telling the story of Lady Macbeth; regardless of the students' range of expertise, they nailed it.

During my doctoral research I formed a pedagogical hypothesis which I believe answers the question of how a learner is able to accomplish more, often in a short period of time, than they could have ever achieved following a traditional curricular scope and sequence. I call this hypothesis **A Good Prompt is Worth 1,000 Words!**

A learner can exceed expectations with the following four variables in place:

1. **A good prompt**, motivating challenge, or thoughtful question
2. **Appropriate materials**
3. **Sufficient time**
4. **Supportive culture**, including a range of expertise

The genius of this approach is that it is self-evident. If you lack one of the four elements, it is obvious what needs to be done.

WHAT'S A GOOD PROMPT?

The best prompts emerge from a learner's curiosity, experience, discovery, wonder, challenge, or dilemma. When a student asks a question, that question deserves serious consideration. However, far too often teachers rob students of powerful learning opportunities by setting the prompt or being too prescriptive.

Of course there are times when you need to cover some bit of curriculum and a project would be a great way to do so. When you absolutely must design a prompt for students, here are three tips you should follow:

1. **Brevity**. The best prompts fit on a Post-It! note. They are clear, concise, and self-evident.
2. **Ambiguity**. The learner should be free to satisfy the prompt in their own voice, perhaps even employing strategies you never imagined.
3. **Immunity to assessment.** The best projects push up against the persistence of reality. What is a B+ poem or musical composition? How does an engineering project earn an 87? Most mindful work succeeds or fails. Students will want to do the best job possible when they care about their work and know that you put them ahead of a grade. If students are collaborating and regularly engaged in peer review or editing, then the judgment of an adult is really unnecessary. Worst of all, it is coercive and often punitive.

Here is an example of a bad prompt and a better one for students to explore motion, rate, and distance:

Bad prompt – Build a four-wheeled car that uses two motors, one switch and rolls from a starting line on this table and stops as close to the finish line as possible in exactly one minute.

Better prompt – Make something that will start here and end there in one minute.

The first prompt makes it highly unlikely that kids will surprise you with their ingenuity. If a student or team of students had an idea for building a supersonic flying machine that would circumnavigate the globe and land on the finish line in one minute, they will lower their sights when faced with a particularly prescriptive prompt or rubric.

Long, complicated, or overly descriptive prompts tend to reduce chances for serendipity. The richest learning often results from getting in over one's head or when encountering unforeseen obstacles. Teachers do children no favor when they spell out one way to solve a problem.

Good prompts do not burden a learner, but set them free. Add thematic units, interdisciplinary projects, and a comfortable classroom well equipped with whimsy and "objects to think with" and you set the stage for authentic student achievement.

Skew Your View

Point of view is worth 80 IQ points. – Alan Kay

Keep things fresh by mixing up the prompts or challenges you give kids. Turn a prompt upside down or look at it from a new perspective. Instead of seeing whose vehicle is fastest, host a race for the slowest machines. Rather than climbing ramps, build machines that will descend them. Pull instead of push.

Scarcity of time or resources may necessitate a fresh perspective. For example, amateur space exploration has become popular. You hang a camera and perhaps a GPS receiver to a weather balloon and launch it to the stratosphere. The results can be really cool if your parachute deploys properly and a good Samaritan finds your payload and returns it to you by mail. The best-case scenario is that your students will need to wait for any pictures. In the worst case, you launched a few hundred dollars into the ocean. Besides, photos of the earth from thousands of feet in the air are fairly predictable. Once your balloon reaches a certain altitude every photo begins to look alike (clouds) and there is still a great risk of never seeing your hardware or photos again.

Try thinking like a fourth grader! Flying a camera 100 or 1,000 feet above your school may be even better than 10,000 feet. You might see your friends at recess or your mom coming to pick you up. The experience may be more personal and less abstract than exploring high above the clouds. Not only will your gear be safe, but also there are new engineering challenges associated with tethering a balloon and stabilizing the camera for still, video, or time-lapse photography. When you skew your view, it is possible to achieve the same educational objectives in a fashion that keeps things interesting for your students. Sharing this strategy with kids may enhance their making, tinkering, and engineering experiences as well. Shifting perspective is a valuable part of the learning process.

PLANNING PROJECTS

Two pioneers of project-based learning are Sylvia Chard and Lilian Katz, educators, professors, and authors who have devoted their careers to helping teachers understand what they call "The Project Approach" to teaching. The project approach uses a framework and process that encourages both teachers and students to plan projects around their own experiences and questions. (Katz & Chard, 2000)

This framework builds on student experience to generate authentic student interest in a topic, shared knowledge, and practice in exploring the known parts of a topic before tackling the unknowns.

During the planning process, the teacher's role is an ethnographer and guide – not the rulemaker. As an ethnographer, the teacher is a researcher exploring and teasing out what students already know. The guide and support role finds opportunities for students to construct deeper understanding, sometimes by providing the right resources or perhaps asking a question just at the right time that pushes a student to dig deeper. The teacher also needs to "seize the teachable moment" and listen carefully for what students need when they need it.

You may be thinking, "Well, that's not the real world – I have standards and curriculum and lesson plans to get through…" Yes, that is a reality that many teachers face. But these are teacher concerns, not student concerns. One of the responsibilities of being a teacher is to translate the mandates of the educational system to something that helps children understand their world. The project should be the basic unit of learning.

Maryann Molishus, a teacher in Pennsylvania who has taught both second and fifth grade, shares this:

> "What do you want to learn and how do you want to share it with the class?" This is how I began second grade for many years. The ideas would start off ordinary. "I want to learn about tigers, and I will write a book about them." Then, there would continue to be requests to make a variety of animal books. Eventually there would be a child who seemed to want to challenge me – did I really mean ANYTHING? "I want to be a book critic and make my own television show," or "I want to be a scientist, mix things up, and see what happens," or "I want to make a video game." There would be a collective gasp. Surely that's not what I meant. But, I'd casually write down the requests, give a nod, and continue on with more requests until the animal book authors would begin asking to change their ideas to less traditional projects. It happened every year. And

knowing that students, both in second and in fifth grade, are surprised by what they can do means that each year my goal is always to make what seems to them to be the extraordinary the norm for my classroom.

It takes four things to be able to teach based on the interests and aspirations of young learners:

1. A strong knowledge of your curriculum and standards
2. Flexibility
3. Organization
4. Resourcefulness

You have to have a thorough understanding of the content materials and skills to figure out how to integrate the curriculum and how to include individual interests in your program. A child who wants to be a book critic, for example, has to read and write and think critically – skills that are required at all grade levels. Our television show required hours of reading, writing, rewriting, learning about the camera and filming, and video editing. In the end, the entire class was involved in the project. We even had a security guard outside the door during filming, complete with a clipboard with a list of those who were allowed entrance (his own creation).

A child who wants to "be a scientist and mix things up" could certainly be introduced to a more technical style of writing and expected to present his findings to the class, both skills required by the curriculum. While we didn't have a chemistry component in second grade science, we did study solids and liquids, and I found a way to link this unit to the student's interests. I set up a corner of the classroom with materials and created lab sheets to record data. The student (which then became a team) began to study the properties of certain solids in water and recorded their work in a lab experiment format. They were fascinated and eager to share their findings with the class.

Lesson plans are not easily recycled if students direct their own learning each year. It takes a great deal of flexibility and organization to manage several different projects to completion and to assure that your class of students is able to learn from one another and, in the end, have completed their requirements for their given grade.

If your students want to create a television show, be a chemist, or animate their stories, you either have to have the know-how (and equipment), find out how, or get someone to help you. It is unacceptable and unnecessary to deny children the opportunity to work on something they are passionate about because the teacher is not an expert in that particular field. It does help, however, to know how to ask others for help and to be able to keep current with the tools and resources that are available to educators and students. Do you have to ask other adults? No. Sometimes the other students will have great ideas about how to get the projects completed. They will willingly join in and support one another – not because they have to, but because they want to. Most of the really great projects started as an idea of one student and ended as small group or even whole class projects.

FOUR APPROACHES TO USING MATERIALS

When you wish to introduce a new technology, construction material, tool, or art supply, you may do so in one of four ways. The example below assumes the use of robotics elements, but with a little imagination, these four approaches apply to other materials as well.

1. **Specific concept.** Use the materials to teach a specific concept, such as gears, friction, or multiplication of fractions.
2. **Thematic project.** Visit a local factory, amusement park, airport, construction site, etc. and construct a model of it. Design a set for our medieval carnival.
3. **Curricular theme.** Identify a problem in Sub-Saharan Africa and build a machine to solve that problem.
4. **Freestyle.** The materials just become part of your toolbox and may be used when you see fit. This choice of media or medium requires students to develop technological fluency.

RAISING OUR STANDARDS – STUDENT WORK THAT ENDURES

Projects create memories for students. Those memories contain the skills and content learned during that project's development. The best teachers are those who inspire memories in their students, and engaging students in great projects is a powerful way to do so.

In this age of higher, tougher, meaner academic standards, any classroom practice associated with creativity is susceptible to caricature. Constructivist educators struggle with the perception that our kids can't possibly compete with their peers in India or China when engaged in project-based learning. It is imperative for constructivist educators, therefore, to raise the bar, challenging their students to achieve a high standard of quality. The value of student projects at all levels needs to be demonstrably obvious even to the most casual observer.

All too often, we are enchanted by the technical merit of a project and forget the importance of relevance, meaning, and sufficient evidence of understanding. Adults are often quick to celebrate students' success with technology and neglect to consider the overall impact of student project work.

Rather than concentrating on purpose, relevance, sufficient time, complexity, connections, access, shareability, or novelty, we are distracted by the technology, and the project suffers for it. A powerful project inspires student memories because of the learning that takes place during its creation, not because a student successfully navigates the technical vagaries of the software or hardware used during its creation.

Artists, musicians, filmmakers, authors, poets, and crafts people do not set out to produce or consume content. They work tirelessly to draw, write, paint, film, compose, play, build, knit, sew, act, or direct to create personally meaningful objects, sights, sounds, or memories. In the rare instance, others will value such personal expression.

We suggest that educators plan and evaluate student projects based on a loftier set of goals. Teachers should embrace the aesthetic of an artist or critic and create opportunities for project development that strive to satisfy the following criteria. Ask if the project is:

- Beautiful
- Thoughtful
- Personally meaningful
- Sophisticated
- Shareable with a respect for the audience
- Moving
- Enduring

That last variable is the highest standard of all. Does the student project have a chance of enduring? Will it make a contribution to knowledge or be a source of student pride? Will a parent frame the work or preserve it in a scrapbook? Artists have no idea if their creation will endure, but that is their aspiration. Should student projects aim for less?

Think about the sorts of projects that parents love and cherish. The best projects endure in the minds of students and on their parents' refrigerator door.

Making things provides a powerful context for learning. An authentic, or real-world audience for one's work is a mighty motivator. As teachers, we often promote the idea that process is more important than the end product, yet it is often the product itself that provides context and motivates students to learn. Knowledge is a consequence of experience, and open-ended creativity tools expand opportunities for such knowledge construction.

Emphasizing the process – the "doing" part of project work – should not cause us to lower our expectations for the final product. Sometimes we overlook shortcomings in a final product because the result is… well… cute. While cuteness may be a desirable attribute of student projects, good is even more desirable. There is no reason why student products cannot be both cute and good. Interesting, timely, relevant, sophisticated, moving, whimsical, charming, thoughtful, original, clever, imaginative, and innovative are all attributes that contribute to a good project.

While every project may not generate an objet d'art, we should assume that every project we undertake has the potential to do so. We must operate from a perspective that children are competent, talented, and capable. Imagine if what they produced in school was great!

MAKING MEMORIES

Ever wake up late on a Saturday morning and realize that you have no milk for the coffee so critical to starting the weekend? You pull a coat over your pajamas, pull on a floppy hat, and run to the local Kwickie Mart. Just as you are leaving the store congratulating yourself for having gone unrecognized, a former student sees you from across the parking lot.

She comes rushing towards you with outstretched arms and just as you turn your head away because you haven't brushed your teeth yet or are having a bad hair day, the former student gives you a big awkward hug.

The former student wants to reminisce. She enthusiastically begins a sentence, "Remember that time we..." The rest of the sentence is never "crammed for the standardized test," or "used all of our spelling words in a sentence." The student's reminiscence always concludes with a description of a project created in your classroom.

Projects are what students remember long after the bell rings. Great teachers know that their highest calling is to make memories.

Chapter 5 - Teaching

I think it's an exaggeration, but there's a lot of truth in saying that when you go to school, the trauma is that you must stop learning and you must now accept being taught. — Seymour Papert

This chapter is about teaching and how to put the lessons of history and modern learning theory into practice. What does the teacher do to encourage invention, tinkering, and making?

Education policy often confuses teaching and learning. Learning is not the direct result of having been taught. If you have spent any time working with learners, you know that you can't simply talk at them, or do something to them, and expect that they have learned anything. A robot can deliver curriculum; great teachers provide much more.

In spite of research (see the Making the Case chapter) that shows that experiential classrooms and long-term projects are effective in teaching higher-order thinking skills and deep content knowledge, such pedagogical methods are not widespread. This may be a result of the current focus on standardized testing and the acceptance of teaching to the test as never before.

In addition to the current political climate, the kind of teaching required by making must be learned and practiced. Studies show that teachers have concerns about their own ability to provide the required scaffolding for students that can't be found in the back of the textbook. In addition, their "habitus," meaning expectations created by one's own experiences, interferes with this process. (Belland, 2012) Teachers fall back on their own experiences as learners when teaching. We will talk more about how to break this cycle in the upcoming chapter, Do Unto Ourselves.

A TEACHING MANTRA: LESS US, MORE THEM

Anytime an adult feels it necessary to intervene in an educational transaction, they should take a deep breath and ask, "Is there some way I can do less and grant more authority, responsibility, or agency to the learner?"

Understanding is the result of existing knowledge accommodating and explaining new experiences. If we focus on a handful of powerful ideas and create experiences where students naturally need to stretch their understanding, students learn more. The role of the teacher is to create and facilitate these powerful, productive contexts for learning.

One simple way to do this is to make your teaching mantra, "Less Us, More Them." Piaget suggests that it is not the role of the teacher to correct a child from the outside, but to create conditions in which the student corrects himself. Whenever you are about to intervene on behalf of a teachable moment, pause and ask yourself, "Is there a way I can shift more agency to the learner?"

Less Us, More Them (LUMT) doesn't exempt teachers from the learning process, or minimize the importance of their expertise within the learning environment. LUMT raises expectations and standards in our classrooms by granting more responsibility to the learner. In this environment, it is natural to expect kids to look up unfamiliar words, proofread, and contribute resources for class discussion without prodding from the teacher.

To start making your classroom more student-centered, demonstrate a concept and then ask students to do something.

Walk around and support them when asked. Bring the group together to celebrate an accomplishment or seize the next teachable moment. We need to operate as if students own the time in our classrooms, not us. Kids rise to the occasion if we let them. When students own the learning process, they also own the knowledge they construct. Self-reliance results when we relinquish control and power to our students.

Fetishizing Failure

Less Us, More Them may result in students sometimes making mistakes or pursuing paths that may lead to unanticipated results. Such stumbles are natural and worthwhile.

Many current books and articles celebrate the value of mistakes and failure as keys to innovative thinking. Educators are told that the mantra of Silicon Valley is "Fail early, fail often," implying that what's good for venture capitalists is good for kids. Failure is judgment. It is punitive and high-stakes.

The current failure fetish is more sloganeering than progress. It confuses iteration with failure, when in fact any iterative design cycle is about continuous improvement, keeping what works, and dealing with what doesn't. This is learning, not failure.

It is certainly important to eliminate the fear of failure as a driving factor in the classroom, but it is crucial that teachers avoid the trap of thinking they have to artificially produce failure. Mistakes are natural enough and occur without teacher intervention. In most cases, if a project is authentic, mistakes and failure are self-correcting. A mistake in measuring will result in a wire that is too short or a wall that is crooked. You don't have to wait a week for the teacher to grade it to know it's wrong. When the student is given agency over the task, they can decide for themselves if something is a mistake, a detour, or maybe a new path.

> Creativity is allowing yourself to make mistakes. Art is knowing which ones to keep. — Scott Adams, cartoonist

When children are allowed to think through problems, they may invent different paths to a suitable answer. The purpose of school should be to encourage children to develop such skills. Instead, we spend a lot of time telling children they are wrong, and then expecting them to accept that rejection and cheerfully try again. A teacher who allows a child time and support to rethink and revise gives a child autonomy and the ability to trust themselves to be problem solvers, even if their path to success is different than everyone else's.

It's crucial to determine who has the agency in the equation. If the teacher is the source of all judgment, this impedes student learning. The student will simply learn to wait to be told the right answer. We certainly do not need to add "failure" to the curriculum.

Researchers have found what they call "the double-edged sword of pedagogy." Instruction causes students to narrow the scope of exploration. Children given a toy and shown how to use it will "learn" how the toy works, but will not explore beyond what they are shown. This is true even if they simply overhear instructions being given to a child in the same room. Children not given instruction will explore the same toy with a wider range of investigations and will find things the first group of children do not find. (Bonawitz et al., 2011)

This is not to say that teachers should just stand back and watch children struggle fruitlessly. Wise teachers know when to dispense the smallest dose of information possible to ensure forward progress. The constructionist learning inherent in making, tinkering, and invention offers a way to approach teaching that is purposeful without direct instruction.

DOING CONSTRUCTIONISM

Constructivism is a theory of learning that doesn't mandate a specific method of teaching. It is most often associated with teaching models that are progressive, child-centered, open-ended, project-based, inquiry-based, and other similar models. Most of these teaching models have at the heart an active, social view of learning with the learner as the center of attention.

Constructionism is a theory of teaching. We believe that constructionism is the best way to implement constructivist learning.

However, the teaching theory underlying most of American education is *instructionism,* or direct instruction – the idea that math, history, or any subject is best taught by explicitly teaching facts or showing students how to solve problems, and then having students practice similar problems or memorize historical facts and dates. Direct instruction seems logical when you believe that math is comprised of sequential skills, history is made up of facts, and language arts is learning grammatical rules. Most textbooks are based on this didactic model and most teachers follow a textbook.

The distinction between instructionism and constructionism is quite clear. If you believe that learning is the direct result of having been taught, then you are an instructionist. If you seek to "reform" education by buying a new textbook, administering a new test, or tweaking teacher practice, then you are an instructionist. Instructionists rely on a treatment model to explain learning. "I did X and they learned Y." If only the transmission of knowledge worked so reliably.

Constructionists believe that learning results from experience and that understanding is constructed inside the head of the student, often in a social context. Constructionist teachers look for ways to create experiences for students that value the student's existing knowledge and have the potential to expose the student to big ideas and "aha" moments.

> Teaching involves linking associations and experiences. If a student has experience with control of body temperature and of the motion of a computer-controlled car, then, when the question arises, she may be able to grasp the common concept of feedback that spans these two disparate experiences. The problem for the teacher is to help the student make that link at just the right time – not too soon, or the concept will be meaningless, but not too late, or the student may be bored or frustrated. This kind of teaching is far different from more common direct instruction in which the teacher would tell students that these two situations were examples of feedback.

> Raw experience is of limited intrinsic value – the time it takes for a specific racecar to descend a particular ramp is better forgotten. What is important is what is retained from the experience, how it is codified and integrated with other experience. This implies that the learner be immediately and actively involved on an abstract plane. (Tinker, 1992)

Constructionism should not be misunderstood as being "against" any instruction. There is nothing wrong with instruction. Being shown how to use a tool or told a useful bit of information is fine. There is no reason to discover the date of Thanksgiving when you can ask someone. Instruction is useful for learning things that would take an instant or when little benefit would be gained by investigating it yourself.

We refrain from using the term "discovery learning," since conservative critics use the term to lampoon or dismiss the efforts of thoughtful educators sympathetic to constructivism or constructionism. To critics, "discovery" implies that learning is accidental and confirms their suspicion that teachers are lazy, or at least laisser-faire. Neither case may be true, but why waste energy defending sound classroom practice? Discoveries are made all of the time while learning. There is no reason to segregate a specific type of learning from natural cognitive processes.

Unlearning some of the habits of instructionism and resisting what seems to be a cultural imperative to lecture and test as the "right" way to teach may be the most difficult part of adopting a tinkering mindset for the classroom. Once you make the transition, you will be in good company. The world is filled with closet constructionists. Makers are out, loud, and proud constructionists, even if unfamiliar with the term.

Lessons From the Constructionist Learning Lab

In 1999, Seymour Papert embarked on his last ambitious institutional research project when he created the constructionist, technology-rich, project-based, multi-aged Constructionist Learning Laboratory inside of Maine's troubled prison for teens, The Maine Youth Center.

The story of the Constructionist Learning Laboratory is documented in Gary Stager's doctoral dissertation, *An Investigation of Constructionism in the Maine Youth Center.* (Stager, 2006)

Shortly after the start of the 3-year project, Papert outlined the "Eight Big Ideas Behind the Constructionist Learning Laboratory." This one-page document was designed for visitors to the classroom. Although non-exhaustive, this list does a good job of explaining constructionism to the general population.

Eight Big Ideas Behind the Constructionist Learning Lab

By Dr. Seymour Papert

The first big idea is learning by doing. We all learn better when learning is part of doing something we find really interesting. We learn best of all when we use what we learn to make something we really want.

The second big idea is technology as building material. If you can use technology to make things you can make a lot more interesting things. And you can learn a lot more by making them. This is especially true of digital technology: computers of all sorts including the computer-controlled LEGO in our Lab.

The third big idea is hard fun. We learn best and we work best if we enjoy what we are doing. But fun and enjoying doesn't mean "easy." The best fun is hard fun. Our sports heroes work very hard at getting better at their sports. The most successful carpenter enjoys doing carpentry. The successful businessman enjoys working hard at making deals.

The fourth big idea is learning to learn. Many students get the idea that "the only way to learn is by being taught." This is what makes them fail in school and in life. Nobody can teach you everything you need to know. You have to take charge of your own learning.

The fifth big idea is taking time – the proper time for the job. Many students at school get used to being told every five minutes or every hour: do this, then do that, now do the next thing. If someone isn't telling them what to do they get bored. Life is not like that. To do anything important you have to learn to manage time for yourself. This is the hardest lesson for many of our students.

The sixth big idea is the biggest of all: you can't get it right without getting it wrong. Nothing important works the first time. The only way to get it right is to look carefully at what happened when it went wrong. To succeed you need the freedom to goof on the way.

The seventh big idea is do unto ourselves what we do unto our students. We are learning all the time. We have a lot of experience of other similar projects but each one is different. We do not have a pre-conceived idea of exactly how this will work out. We enjoy what we are doing but we expect it to be hard. We expect to take the time we need to get this right. Every difficulty we run into is an opportunity to learn. The best lesson we can give our students is to let them see us struggle to learn.

The eighth big idea is we are entering a digital world where knowing about digital technology is as important as reading and writing. So learning about computers is essential for our students' futures BUT the most important purpose is using them NOW to learn about everything else. (Stager, 2006)

Jaymes Dec is a teacher and Innovation Specialist at the Marymount School of New York. He has taught digital design and fabrication classes in kindergarten through graduate school since 2007. That makes Jaymes the closest thing to an old pro in the exciting new world of school makerspaces. Jaymes calls his maker approach to teaching "applied constructionism."

Instead of standing in front of a class and lecturing, I prefer to encourage tinkering and exploration with technology. I introduce a tool and let kids explore and figure things out on their own. It's more like an art class, where students are learning how to use digital tools (computers, microcontrollers, soldering irons, laser cutters, 3D printers, etc.) as creative media. In my classes, there is very little emphasis on learning facts. It's more about learning processes – how to tinker or experiment with digital technologies; how to troubleshoot a problem; how to repurpose an existing computer program for your means. I really want students to lose their fear of failure. My goals are to get the students to ask questions. To help each other. To experiment. To break things. If someone shorts a circuit, or blows up an LED, that's a great class.

Playing the Whole Game

In his book, *Making Learning Whole: How Seven Principles of Teaching Can Transform Education*, David Perkins outlines teaching strategies to do what he calls, "playing the whole game." His favorite metaphor is baseball, and he asks teachers to put themselves in the context of teaching children this popular sport. Would you start with the rules of the game, and after rigorous testing, move on to baseball vocabulary words, and perhaps eventually let children actually touch a bat and pass a ball around the classroom? Of course not! That sounds ridiculous, but in fact it is close to how many school subjects are taught.

When teaching baseball to children, adults or older peers will often help children play a version of baseball, but something that is recognizable to all as baseball. The difference is that it includes crucial accommodations for younger players. You might put the ball on a tee, adjust rules, or any number of changes. But the children are still playing baseball.

Translating this idea into the classroom requires teachers to figure out what an equivalent version of the whole game is for math, science, history, or any other aspect of the curriculum. What Perkins recommends is consistent with this book: an emphasis on real-world, hands-on, cross-curricular work, giving student agency, and most of all, *time* – time for reflection, editing, and working on projects that matter.

Perkins also recommends that teachers lessen these common aspects of schooling:

- **Elementitis** – Pre-loading basic skill instruction, learning facts with no purpose, and memorizing vocabulary without context
- **Aboutitis** – Learning "about" things rather than doing or creating anything beyond a report
- **Lecture** – Relying on whole class lecture to deliver information

If You Aren't Lecturing, What Are You Doing?

It's very common for a non-educator to see a teacher lecturing and think, "That's teaching." It's the most obvious, visible thing a teacher does.

Talking should not be the primary work of teachers – learning about their students should be. A teacher who is mindful and involved with student work without being the center of attention can teach without lecturing. Teacher roles in a constructionist classroom may include:

Ethnographer – Find out what children already know

Documentarian – Collect evidence of learning that makes the invisible thinking of children visible

Studio manager – Make appropriate tools, materials, and resources available so children can make their ideas come to life

Wise leader – Guide children's inquiry towards big ideas without coercion

TEACHING USING ITERATIVE DESIGN CYCLES

Arriving at one goal is the starting point to another. — John Dewey

Any design model starts with an idea and cycles through planning, making, testing/feedback, adjusting, and then back around to making again. You may have a design model you like or one that your school has chosen to use. You may prefer our TMI model. We urge you to use caution in how much time you spend talking about the design process with your students before you actually "do" the design process.

It's the teacher's responsibility to ensure these stages occur naturally. Don't add unnecessary vocabulary or imposed structure to the cognitive workload of students. Do not interrupt their learning to monitor student progress "through" the cycles. Do not ask them which part of the cycle they are in or tell them how many cycles they should complete. Each student will be in different places, and that's a good thing. Some may cycle around twice, some 20 times. Counting cycles is not important. The important thing is that they keep making and moving forward, even if an occasional detour emerges.

When starting projects, employ Stager's Hypothesis to make sure you have the conditions for success in place: sufficient time, materials, and a culture of support. Use good project prompts that allow for a wide variety of projects and incorporate student's interests. Then get going.

When you ask students to produce something such as a 3D object or a movie, you may need to jettison some tried and true practices during the first cycles. The movie can be done without a storyboard or script, the 3D object may not be the most perfectly planned out, but the point is to create something that can be shared and talked about.

Then do it again. Each iteration of the project will "teach" students more about the materials and tools they are using. Every time they take a step forward, backwards, or sideways they gain confidence in their own ability to decide what is worth keeping and what needs to be tweaked.

Allow sufficient time for meaningful experiences. Encourage students to get totally involved in ideas. Keep an eye out for students who are off task, but allow those who are on task to continue to work independently.

Skip the Preload

It's tempting to take "just a minute" to show students every feature or menu option as you explain your final curricular objectives. However, information dumps are counterproductive in the long run. Less is more when it comes to instruction. If you need to teach something new, make the demonstration as quick as possible. Try limiting an instruction to a minute or two before asking students to use that knowledge.

If this sounds like an impossible challenge, consider the following iterative process yourself:

- If you lecture for 45 minutes, try 22
- If you lecture for 22 minutes, try 11
- Repeat until instruction is reduced to two minutes

Focus on the big ideas and what students need to know *now*, followed by an opportunity for them to gain experience with that idea or technique.

Don't Overteach Planning

The lessons of tinkering and making occur in the construction, not the planning.

This means letting students approach problems "the wrong way" without stepping in with "corrections." For example, a mindmap or a storyboard is a great tool, but only when a student needs a way to organize their thoughts. Imposing your planning framework, even with the best of intentions, deprives the child of the experience of solving their own problems and makes them dependent on you.

Every teacher knows the student who writes the required outline after completing a fabulous essay. Outlining becomes an end, rather than a means to an end. The goal of outlining, sketching, flowcharting, and other forms of planning is to help a person get unstuck. If a student is already clear or confident in their direction, forcing formulaic planning may be counterproductive and unpleasant.

Some programming classes begin with flowcharting or drawing logic diagrams. This may create a hurdle that may get in the way of students actually writing a program. Most early programming attempts are simple enough to do without a flowchart. If a student naturally draws something that looks like a flowchart, that's fine – just tell them that professional programmers use flowcharts to organize their work.

During electronic projects, use similar judgment in determining how much planning is necessary. Let the students decide if they need a sketch or circuit diagram to help organize their thoughts. The longer you delay students from getting to the "making" part of the design cycle, the more students will disengage and the longer it will take to learn the lessons.

If your curriculum requires lab notebooks, outlining, visual organizers, journaling, and similar techniques, try to maintain perspective on their relative importance. These techniques are intended to help some styles of learners at certain times solve particular problems. They should neither be viewed as a silver bullet or as a straightjacket imposed on students.

Encouraging Continuous Improvement

Tinkering is an iterative process. Learning and work quality should improve with each iteration of a design cycle. Encourage students who are frustrated or stuck to keep trying new strategies. Ask a student who is "done" what else they could add to their project, or how to make it more reliable, stable, useful, beautiful, valuable, or flexible. Use peer mentoring and encourage peer support. Sometimes simply asking a student to explain a problem to someone else is the first step in solving it. Explaining your problem orally, online, or in other forms of written communication may bring a solution into focus. Occasionally, the solution to a vexing project comes to you as soon as you get up to walk away and get some fresh air.

Allow students to solve problems their own way. Some students may find that talking to others helps. Some may need alone time. Some may need to get up and walk around the classroom to help get the "feel" of programming the onscreen action. Some may draw maps, logic diagrams, or flowcharts. There is no one right way to help students debug a program, design a 3D object, or build an invention. Asking a well-timed question and walking away may be most effective.

Tinkering is a mindset that is contagious. Encourage an atmosphere in your classroom where ideas and creativity are in the air.

One of the goals of preschool is to develop language abilities in young children. Without becoming didactic, teachers can revitalize interest by asking students questions about their activities. Example: "That's a beautiful square you made. What do you think would happen if you changed the angle to a different number?"

Build time in your schedule for sharing and collaboration. A short closing activity where students (and teachers) voluntarily share something they learned that day can be a lead-in to cleaning up.

In learning to program, design 3D objects, or make breadboards, copying is not cheating. A great way to learn is to take existing programs or projects and modify it slightly. Each iterative change makes the program or design more your own. In the real world, an engineer's most important skill is being able to find appropriate things to borrow. Fortunately, there are many online communities where learners of all ages share hardware, software, code libraries, images, and ideas.

In the classroom, students should be able to see and hear ideas from others and borrow liberally. In fact, most children will collaborate and share ideas quickly, almost instantly if they are allowed free access to each other. A non-competitive, sharing atmosphere supports innovation, creativity, and the iterative design process.

Reflection

Reflection is an important part of the learning process, and in iterative design, there are natural opportunities to ask students to be reflective. Short sharing sessions can be woven into the daily or weekly class schedule. Ask students to document their work to decorate the classroom and provide guides and ideas for others. Talk about the design cycle after the students have had a chance to experience it and live with it. Projects that are worth sharing will provide opportunities for students to share them authentically.

Teaching Students to Face Complexity

Students are quite skilled at figuring out what teachers want so they can get through their day as efficiently as possible. Coaching students out of this complacency will take time and will be a challenge. Take care that you are not telegraphing your expectations.

Andrew Carle, a maker and middle school teacher in Virginia, talks about realizing this:

> My daily challenge in our Makers group is cajoling eighth graders to face complexity honestly.
>
> It took me a few years of teaching to realize that kids would fake "a-ha!" moments for me in class, either to force some confirmation response from me or just to end the conversation. In Makers, these are vocalized as "I know what's wrong!" and often enacted by a grab for the soldering iron. Because when you're actively using tools, then you don't have to acknowledge the problems in your thinking and the flaws in your design. Just do stuff for a while, and then if it doesn't work, you can shrug it off as a good try. That mess of wire and PCB is just one of those "productive failures" Mr. Carle seems to love.
>
> Except it's not. It's a stall and a con.
>
> To be productive, you need to leave the "whoops!" moment with something new, some confirmation or new bit of knowledge that you lacked at the outset. When kids reach for tools out of frustration, they're not bringing in a plan or hypothesis to test. They're killing time, staging a performance for me, the class, or themselves.
>
> For the last year, I had focused much maker-teacher energy on troubleshooting after the project was built.
>
> But I'm realizing that when the driving force behind the initial build isn't passion or personal enthusiasm, when they're just looking for *something* to do in the moment, then the post-mortem is too late. They've been disconnected from the project throughout and haven't paid enough attention in the build to allow for meaningful reflection.
>
> Recently, I've pushed more on students to find a solid place from which to begin. I struggle every day to balance arbitrary "process" requirements in the limited time I have with students and their unwillingness to face complex tasks.

MOUTH UP, MOUTH DOWN FRUSTRATION

Many educators profess a concern about frustration that a child might feel when faced with undefined tasks or projects that take unexpected turns. Sometimes, worrying that a student might become frustrated is a projection of the teacher's own fear. Occasionally, it is a legitimate risk. Most often, kids will exceed our expectations, especially if exceeding our expectations *is* our expectation.

There really are two forms of frustration. Mouth up and mouth down. Mouth down frustration is when your hard drive crashes or you miss your bus. Your situation has deteriorated due to circumstances beyond your control.

Mouth up frustration occurs when you get stuck while solving a problem or learning something you care about. Kids often smile during such tests of will and are ecstatic once they outsmart the temporary speed bump. Great satisfaction and self-efficacy results from these momentary spells of mouth up frustration. Brian Silverman reminds us that powerful learning results from realizing that the way you got unstuck can keep you from ever getting stuck again. (Silverman & Kay, 2013)

> Never help a child with a task at which he feels he can succeed.
> — Maria Montessori

TEACHING THAT PROMOTES CREATIVITY

For the first time in decades, American children show less creativity in specialized tests than previous generations. Creativity researchers point to the contradiction of America's "standards-obsessed" schools, what we know about how children learn, and businesses that say that creativity is the number one attribute they need in new employees. (Bronson & Merryman, 2010)

Creation is the heart of creativity and is only meaningful when grounded in action – it's not a feeling, a mindset, or an outcome. But it can be developed, contrary to conventional wisdom; it's not an inborn talent that you are either born with or not.

Affective qualities like creativity, collaboration, passion, curiosity, perseverance, and teamwork are certainly desirable for teachers and students. However, these traits are developed while engaged in real pursuits, even within the existing curriculum. All that is required is a meaningful project. This is why we question the use of "meta" activities like ropes courses, ice-breakers, or trust-building exercises as a separate curriculum. The affective skills should be byproducts of meaningful learning experiences. Those meaningful experiences may be embedded in the existing curriculum and point towards a more modern pluralistic perspective on what students "should learn and do."

Some educators have recognized that schools are too impersonal and that teachers should get to know their students. We could not agree more. However, the prescription is often to create advisory courses or extend homeroom to deal with pastoral care issues. The result is one teacher who gets to "know" students while time is borrowed from other courses where teachers should get to know their students formally and informally in the process of constructing knowledge together.

Students learn creativity by being creative. They can develop self-esteem by engaging in satisfying work. Classroom management is not required when teachers don't view themselves as managers. Students learn perseverance by working on projects that make them want to stick with them. Kids can learn "digital citizenship" while learning to program, sharing code, and interacting online. They can feel safe at school by forming relationships with each of their teachers. Study skills are best gained within a context of meaningful inquiry.

When educators create a productive context for learning, achievement improves, students feel more connected, and behavioral problems evaporate. When the needs, interests, passions, talents, and curiosity of students are put ahead of a random list of stuff, they are capable of demonstrating remarkable competence.

ASSESSMENT

Gary has been known to say, "Assessment always interrupts the learning process." Even asking a child, "Hey, watcha doin?" is disruptive. It is up to each and every reasonable educator to determine the appropriate level of disruption.

Assessment is the work of teachers. It is judgment. We wish we could wave a magic wand and free teachers from all formal assessment responsibilities so they could use their time working with students. However, as long as teachers are required to assess, it should be as nonintrusive as possible and not distract students from the learning process.

Reflection and other metacognitive processes are part of the learning process and should not be used as justification for impinging on learning time.

Grades and Rubrics

Making, tinkering, or engineering are inconsistent with typical school schedules. Quality work takes time, disobeys bell schedules, doesn't result in neat projects that work with canned rubrics, and might not have any impact on test scores. Author Alfie Kohn says:

> As for the research studies: Collectively, they make it clear that students who are graded tend to differ from those who aren't in three basic ways. They're more likely to lose interest in the learning itself. They're more likely to prefer the easiest possible task. And they're more likely to think in a superficial fashion as well as to forget what they were taught. (Kohn, 2010)

Grading student work is likely to result in students being less willing to challenge themselves and to search for the easiest path to "done" rather than risk taking on another iteration of their projects.

Many advocates of project-based learning are firm believers in rubrics as being a path to grading that is less likely to destroy student motivation. Rubrics are tables that tell students how many points they will get for doing specific parts of the project using a scale, usually from 1–5, and explaining what constitutes good vs. not so good work.

The rubric is intended to provide firm guidelines about what the student is supposed to do, and the credit (grade) they will earn. It sets expectations so there is no mistake or misunderstanding about how the teacher expects the project to turn out.

However, there are reasons rubrics may be counterproductive:

- A rubric imposes the teacher's vision of what the student work should look like at the end.
- A rubric becomes the checklist for the project. It is difficult to argue that students will be creative when the rubric is very clear about how many words, how many slides, or how many photos need to be included in the student's work.
- Rubrics reinforce student dependency on how a teacher defines their work.
- Serendipity is impossible when the rubric requires a predetermined outcome.
- Human nature dictates that a student will expend minimum effort to receive a desired grade.
- In too many cases, the 4 on a rubric is really just a B. This not only continues behaviorist forms of extrinsic motivation, but is intellectually dishonest. Grades are grades.
- "Failure" is not an option. Making an interesting discovery or realizing that I need to learn more penalizes a student judged against a rubric.

School should not be about creating winners and losers through schemes designed to rank, sort, or "catch" kids not knowing something at a specific moment in time.

The politics of accountability have caused many to take leave of their senses. The best project a teacher can engage in is finding ways to justify the projects undertaken in their classroom. How can you demonstrate what a student knows besides an arbitrary grade or comparing one shoebox diorama to another?

Teaching is not testing. Deep learning is possible even when adults abandon prejudices about the outcome of a project. The emphasis should be on process and creating the conditions in which learners grow.

TEACHER SATISFACTION

Here is a semi-selfish (but healthy) reason for teaching making and invention. Research suggests that teachers who use more progressive or project-based learning techniques are more satisfied in their roles than teachers who use traditional instructional techniques. (Kalchik & Oertle, 2010) It stands to reason, it is just more interesting and fun to be a teacher if you are learning new things that interest you and sharing them with engaged, motivated students.

Chapter 6 – Making Today

We are all designers now. It's time to get good at it.
— Chris Anderson

Maker classrooms are active classrooms. In active classrooms one will find engaged students, often working on multiple projects simultaneously, and teachers unafraid of relinquishing their authoritarian role. Collaboration between students is flexible and teachers experience a seamless metamorphosis between mentor, student, colleague, expert, and personal shopper, all in service of their learners.

The best way to activate your classroom is for your students to make something. This might include one of the amazing high-tech inventions we'll explore shortly, or it might take the form of costumes for a historical reenactment, homemade math manipulatives, a new curtain for the local auditorium, toys, a pet habitat, a messy science experiment, or a zillion other things. Best of all, you don't need expensive hardware, or to start by mastering a programming language. You can begin with found materials: buttons, bottle caps, string, clay, construction paper, broken toys, popsicle sticks, or tape (hint: Google "tapigami" or "duck tape projects"). Reusing materials is consistent with kids' passion for environmentalism and is an ideal of the maker movement.

Educators should honor and nurture many forms of expression. Different students may demonstrate understanding and satisfy an assignment with a presentation, written paper, video, shoebox diorama, or deep-sea Yugoslavian folk dance. The tool(s) used are a whole lot less important than what is produced and the intellectual processes employed. By now, our expectations should be high regarding the quality of what students produce with these tools.

We want students to enjoy the greatest range of high quality experiences regardless of the tool, activity, or place where the learning occurs.

YOU ARE BETTER PREPARED THAN YOU THINK

The growing ubiquity of 1:1 computing, where every child has a personal computer for use at school and home, provides every student with a portable movie studio, art atelier, writer's grotto, printing press, practice room, and recording studio. This should democratize access to a more expansive range of high quality experiences and the quality of work to improve with dramatically increased access to digital tools.

If you don't yet have a fab lab or laptop per student, you already have lots of tools and materials suitable for making!

The last technological revolution allowed amateurs, even children, to manipulate words and images in unprecedented ways. We may take word processing, desktop publishing, and Web publishing for granted, but they each had a greater impact on communication in a few years than the sharing of information had experienced in the last several hundred years. Blogging, podcasting, and digital media editing allows anyone to share knowledge regardless of quality or an audience. These advances have upended several industries while giving the world both the Arab Spring and kitten videos.

Word processing has revolutionized the writing process. Any of today's word processing programs may be used for writing, editing, and publishing one's output on paper or the Web. Most also have layout features that allow your work to look attractive in any form you choose. Editing is now continuous when it used to be arduous and intermittent. The potential also exists for your work, or that of your students, to reach an infinitely large audience. Audience is a key element in motivating a person to write, and informs what they write as well. Motivation also increases when the product of student writing is attractive and valued by others.

There is no reason whatsoever why students should not be much better writers as a result of the word processing revolution. Their expression should not be limited to the five-paragraph essay or a PowerPoint presentation on a topic they don't care about for an audience they will never meet. Kids can and should produce poetry anthologies, magazines, and literary anthologies they can be proud of. They can even be novelists!

There are other ways to tell stories using computers. Inexpensive digital cameras, cell phones, graphics software, and video editing tools turn anyone into a photographer or filmmaker. This expands the palette of ways in which students may tell their stories to the world. You do not need expensive hardware or software to share your message in a compelling fashion. YouTube filmmaker Casey Neistat is turning the worlds of journalism, advertising, television, and storytelling upside down with the cameras many of us have in our pockets. Malik Bendjelloul, the director of the Academy Award winning documentary, "Searching for Sugar Man," used a $1.99 iPhone app to simulate 8mm film when that film proved too costly. (CNN, 2013)

Writing, filmmaking, and presenting information are the low-hanging fruit of creative expression in the digital age. Computers not only bring the collections of the world's great art galleries to kids' screens, but simple painting, drawing, and animation programs allow kids to create great art too. Crayons and paint can and should co-exist with digital tools. Old media can be digitized and merged with computer graphics in new forms of visual art. Low-cost drawing tablets bring precision and tactile aspects of hand-held tools to the creation of digital images.

Animation, once the property of highly skilled artists at well-equipped studios, is now an accessible way for students to tell stories or simulate dynamic phenomena. Ubiquitous digital cameras create free images that stand on their own or may be incorporated into projects. Students can share their photographs for others to use in searchable royalty-free online databases like http://Pics4Learning.com that add to the collective "intelligence" of the Web.

Imagine if students could create their own musical productions, not just perform in them. Today they can, allowing many more students to participate and expanding the range of opportunities for creativity. Kids can write a script, compose music, and design animated sets to be projected into their own musical theatre productions.

Radio production (or podcasting) is a great reason to write well and is a powerful context for developing oral language skills. Recording software, like Audacity and Garageband, allows kids to record, edit, and publish podcasts and digital radio productions.

All of these creative uses of new technology are well within the reach of almost any school with a few computers. Making is not just about the cool new stuff, but a way to look at all materials as learning opportunities.

Composition vs. Consumption – Gary

Music is such an important part of childhood and integral part of what it means to be human, but until recently its creation was reserved for the very few.

In addition to learning to program computers in junior high, I was blessed with four years of daily music theory class while in high school. In addition to such opportunities being extremely rare, the quality of the learning experiences was constrained by a lack of technology readily available to students today.

If I wrote a piece of music for bassoon and French horn and there were no students in class who could play those instruments, I never got to hear my work performed. Aside from disappointment, not hearing my music led to fewer opportunities to edit or improve the work. Composition, arranging, and orchestration remained an abstraction.

If I wrote a piece of music that was too difficult for my teacher to perform on the piano (which pretty much describes every piece of music composed by 15-year-olds), then the music went unheard. The sin of unheard music is now behind us due to computers equipped with notation software and low-cost MIDI keyboards that bring the world of composition to any child, when only prodigies may have been treated to composition experiences in the past.

Imagine a laptop orchestra where each student is a trombonist or cellist because that's the instrument they tell their laptop to sound like when they play one note at a time on a $50 MIDI keyboard connected to their personal computer. Every kid can now learn to read music and perform seemingly complex pieces from any genre. Playing together in an orchestral setting leads to a number of well-documented social and academic benefits. Plus, kids can make great music.

USING FAMILIAR MATERIALS TO LEARN IN UNFAMILIAR WAYS

Conventional materials familiar to both children and adults are now being used to create unconventional projects. Such materials expand the range of creative possibilities dramatically when they meet electronics or computers.

Feeling Squishy

One great new idea is Squishy Circuits – edible conductive and non-conductive dough that you mold just like regular modeling clay, but with one important difference. The conductive dough allows electricity to flow through it and the non-conductive dough is an insulator. Clever kids can make little creatures with eyes made of LEDs. When a battery is connected to a proper clay circuit, the spooky eyes can light up. You might even add buzzers or motors to your clay creation. Kids can learn fundamentals of electricity, including circuits, switches, and resistance while playing with dough! Scrounge for electronic parts to experiment with, or buy a Squishy Circuits kit, complete with enormous LEDs.

Best of all, recipes for Squishy Circuits dough may be found online and made with the kids at almost no cost. Need a fresh batch? The kids can whip some up for themselves and learn to follow a recipe! No oven is required and there is zero danger of electrocution.

Squishy Circuits http://courseweb.stthomas.edu/apthomas/SquishyCircuits/

Conductive Paint

If you like Squishy Circuits, you will love conductive paint. Conductive paint and conductive foil allow you to create electrical circuits on paper. Imagine drawing a piano on paper and then playing it! Leah Buechley, Director of the MIT Media Lab's High-Low Tech research group, shares exciting work in embedding electronics and interactivity into paper, cloth, ceramics, and other household items. Check out her amazing TED talk and prepare to have your mind blown by origami that folds itself, and light-up pop-up books!

Bare (conductive) Paint. Paint pens and interactive card kits can be found at this UK-based company; some of their materials are available at ThinkGeek and Amazon. http://bareconductive.com

Leah Buechley's TED Talk, "How to Sketch with Electronics" http://bit.ly/sketchwith

The Hot New Material

While 3D printing and microcontrollers were capturing the hearts and minds of the maker community, an old favorite was staging a big comeback – cardboard!

Caine was a nine-year-old boy who had to spend his summer hanging out at his father's used auto parts store in the Boyle Heights section of Los Angeles. There wasn't much for Caine to do while his dad worked, so he accepted a challenge from his father to try and make an arcade game. Caine loved arcade games. Before long, the front of his dad's shop was filled with various games made entirely out of cardboard and tape. In between inventing new games and refining existing ones, Caine waited for customers to play in his arcade. He designed prize tickets and constructed a makeshift office out of cardboard, naturally. One day, a man pulled-up at the auto parts store to buy something, asked Caine about what he had created, and bought a "fun pass" to play the games.

The gentleman fell in love with Caine's ingenuity and asked his father if he could make a video about the arcade. Not long after, Caine's Arcade lit up YouTube. Caine and his arcade

Caine engaged in cardboard construction

inspired millions of people around the world. He received invitations to visit other countries, a scholarship fund was created for his college education, and a foundation was created to nurture creativity in kids across the globe. Los Angeles Mayor Antonio Villaraigosa even gave Caine a cardboard key to the city!

You have some cardboard boxes lying around, right? Why not have kids build a cardboard city to accompany the reading of *A Cricket in Times Square*? How about a cardboard Alamo or puppet theatre? Since your students may not have as much time as Caine to construct their cardboard masterpieces, there are some low-cost reusable products to help.

Makedo is a collection of kid-safe and reusable plastic saws, hinges, and connectors for inventing with cardboard. Even kindergarteners can use MakeDo independently. The Makedo website has an online community that shares project ideas to inspire your constructions. Rolobox is a set of reusable wheels you can fasten to cardboard items that need to move. The super cool thing is that you can add items like lights, sounds, and robotics elements to your cardboard inventions.

The Story of Caine's Arcade http://cainesarcade.com

Makedo http://mymakedo.com

Rolobox http://www.rolobox.com.au

DECISIONS, DECISIONS

A well-equipped modern makerspace can feature flexible, computer-controlled manufacturing equipment for creating, cutting, and forming plastics, metal, plaster, and other common materials, including:

- **3D printers** that are capable of producing three-dimensional objects.
- **Cutting machines** that cut a variety of materials with precision. The cutting element can be a laser, water jet, knife, or other material.
- **Milling and routing machines** that drill and shape complex parts.
- **Joining machines** that use computer control to sew, weld or bond in other ways.
- **Traditional hand and power tools**, including soldering irons.
- **Decorative materials** for painting, embroidery, and embellishing projects.

Deciding what to focus on first may seem like a daunting task. There are new tools being announced every day as these technologies get better and prices drop dramatically. As we wrote this book, we scrambled to keep up as technology changed and new products were introduced. It's a guarantee that this will continue.

There is no absolute shopping list of must haves. There is nothing that is a fatal flaw if it's missing. Making do with what you have is a virtue. If you can't afford a 3D printer, don't have a perfect space, or are a bit fearful of electricity, you can still create an experience that is comfortable, creative, and fun for your students.

Don't be afraid to tailor this to your own space, interests, and experiences. There are no rules that gluing is less creative than soldering, but be willing to experiment with new tools and materials. Give yourself credit for what you already know. You may be surprised to discover that a 3D printer is actually simpler to use than most sewing machines.

Do something, get going, and refine as you see what works in your classroom. Don't let shopping get in the way of action. Use the lessons of the previous chapters to introduce iterative design, increase student agency, and honor a wide variety of problem-solving styles to amplify the learning potential of these new materials.

Find Allies, Advocates, and Mentors

Makers tend to be passionate about what they do. Like other artists and craftspeople, makers are happy to share their expertise with the next generation. Google "makerspace" or "fab lab" and your city name. Follow the hashtags #makerspace, #makered, #edumaker, #youngmaker, #k12fab, or #fablab on Twitter or Google Plus.

Reach out to local makerspaces, hackerspaces, tech shops and individual makers to find volunteers who would be willing to help out in your classroom. Museums, science centers, and libraries are adding makerspaces to their venues. Parents can volunteer too! These new collaborators may bring more than expertise to your school. Local maker mentors may also share materials and tools you need.

Makerspace directory makerspace.com/makerspace-directory

Hackerspace directory hackerspaces.org/wiki/List_of_Hacker_Spaces

K–12 Digital Fabrication Labs Discussion Google Group http://bit.ly/k12fablabgroup

Good Ideas Are Timeless, but It's up to You

Student imaginations will soar when you open your mind to an awesome world of possibilities. There is little risk involved in trying new things or being open to the world of the kids you serve. There have never been cooler things to learn and create with than today.

Think outside of the box. Mike Eisenberg of the University of Colorado Craft Tech Lab reminds us how making things to enhance the places, activities, and events so important in the lives of children may result in greater learning outcomes. Why not encourage youngsters to invent new gadgets for their bedroom, program videogames, choreograph a music video, make a high-tech birthday party piñata, or manufacture cell phone chargers for Father's Day gifts? Great teachers know how to connect the curricular requirements found in such learner-centered activities and can document what students learned in the process.

High-quality collaborative and creative experiences are a cornerstone of a sound 21st century education. Great construction projects are possible with low-tech, inexpensive, and found materials. Best of all, the new game-changing technologies are enhanced by the addition of such low-tech treasure. The old and the new, high- and low-tech make such beautiful music!

The last technological revolution allowed children to be writers, journalists, filmmakers, composers, photographers, and broadcasters. The next technology revolution will provide kids with expanded opportunities to be mathematicians, engineers, computer scientists, game designers, and more. There is no reason for adults to choose. Kids should be invited to explore as many domains as possible. You are the key ingredient to making this happen.

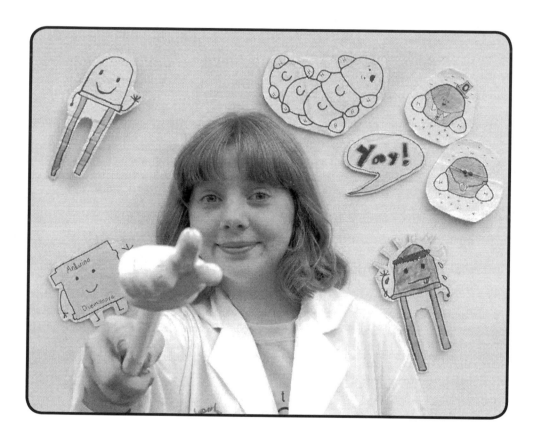

Sylvia's Super-Awesome Maker Show!

Chapter 7 – The Game Changers

The best way to predict the future is to invent it. —
Alan Kay

While there are many options for creativity in the classroom, we believe there are three technologies that have the most potential to provide the kinds of learning experiences that change children's views of themselves as competent learners. When choosing to equip your young makers, we urge you to include one or more of these revolutionary technologies in your planning.

THE GAME CHANGERS: FABRICATION, PHYSICAL COMPUTING, AND PROGRAMMING

- **Fabrication** – Technology for creating customized products is becoming affordable and easy to use. Computer-aided design, three-dimensional printing, laser and other cutters, and other tools allow students to design and build real-life objects.
- **Physical computing** – The ability to create machines that interact with their environment. Affordable hardware choices, robotics, Arduino, and innovative interfaces connect the computer to the real world.
- **Programming** – The key to controlling the digital world is understanding how computers are controlled by precise instructions. Programming is an act of mastery over the machine, an amplification of one's thinking, and the lingua franca of computer science.

FABRICATION

Just a few decades ago, having a printer in your home was unthinkable. Today it's commonplace. Similarly, three-dimensional, or 3D printing is a rapidly emerging technology now available to hobbyists. In just a few years, more and more 3D printers with better and better capabilities will burst onto the scene.

The use of 3D printers is expanding rapidly in industrial applications to create precise one-of-a-kind parts. In healthcare, 3D printers are being used to create prosthetics, body parts, or other medical devices that need to be custom fit. Cornell University scientists are experimenting with printing out human ears from cow cartilage. NASA is researching ways that 3D printer technology could take rocks from the surface of the Moon, refine them, and use the material to print out parts for robots and machines that could be built on the Moon. A little more down to earth, in a few years from now, buying a simple consumer product online like a watch or phone case could be transformed into buying the *design* of the product, transforming it the way you want, and then printing it out on your home 3D fabricator.

Chris Anderson, former editor-in-chief of *Wired* magazine, makes a sweeping claim that "3D printing will be bigger than the Web." (Foremski, 2012) This may be an understatement.

There is every reason to believe that fabrication technology will change the world even more than the information technology revolution has. We are at the forefront of a revolution, where every part of the global economy will be disrupted. Manufacturing items in massive factories and then spending a fortune transporting those items to stores will be replaced by emailing a digital file to be printed close to the customer. Think of the millions of dollars in fuel costs that will be saved. The planet will be grateful for the dramatic reduction in toxic waste and pollution. Best of all, customers will have greater control over the design of the products they desire. (Campbell, Williams, Ivanova, & Garrett, 2011)

3D printing is no longer the stuff of science fiction. A desktop 3D printer can be in your home or classroom today. As more uses are found, the technology gets better and less expensive. **This is the perfect time for classrooms to explore the idea of personal fabrication.**

A 3D printer is a machine that builds a three-dimensional object under computer control. Fabrication machines are sometimes categorized with other "additive" machines. These machines add materials together to create new and different shapes and products. Other useful machines are subtractive, meaning they take away material to create the final product. Computer-controlled milling machines, laser cutters, and other subtractive machines can add a lot of capability to the high-end machine shop, and are gradually making their way to classroom makerspaces. In this book we focus on 3D printers, but there are certainly lessons to be learned if you are in the position to acquire a subtractive device.

Additive and subtractive machines exist without computer control. Students gluing popsicle sticks together to make a 3D object is "additive." You might purchase a vinyl cutter or use scissors for the "subtractive" element.

The game-changing aspect of 3D printing extends beyond the ability to print something cool. The iterative *tinkering* process is employed while users continuously improve upon digital designs. The ease with which students can *make* real objects of their own design, with precision, expands the possibilities for *engineering* in the classroom.

How Does a 3D Printer Work?

To understand how a 3D printer works, think about a common desktop printer that prints on a flat, two-dimensional piece of paper. 2D printers print one dot at a time. The dots blend to make a line, and then line after line blends to make a full page of text or graphics. In a similar way, a 3D printer prints a small dot of material in a line, and adds more lines to make a flat layer of material. Then it builds upwards into the third dimension, layer after layer, one on top of the other, just like adding layers to a layer cake.

By changing the pattern of solid and empty space in each layer, you can build complex three-dimensional objects.

The cost of 3D printers can range from $1,000 to tens or even hundreds of thousands of dollars. There are many different options based on quality, size, speed, and the raw material used to create objects. You can build your own 3D printer from freely available plans, assemble a kit, or purchase one pre-assembled. At the time of this publication, most 3D printers used in K–12 classrooms are in the range of $1,000 to $4,000 and can create small, single color plastic items about the size of a cupcake.

Most 3D printers within reach of the classroom budget use a method called "fused deposition modeling," or "molten polymer deposition." These printers feed in plastic cable called filament to be melted (the "molten" part) and squirted out in computer-controlled patterns (the "deposition" part). The material quickly fuses together and cools to create the finished object.

There are other methods used in industrial settings that produce higher quality products, and naturally, cost more. These printers use lasers to melt the material, and are able to print materials other than plastic, and in many colors. Other printers start with a liquid resin that is fused with greater precision than the filament-based systems. Over time, these advances will become affordable and accessible for classroom use.

Typically, the old saying is correct: "You get what you pay for." The more you pay for a printer, the better it tends to work. The objects are created with more precision and the mechanisms are more robust. But, don't feel that you have to wait to purchase a 3D printer. The great should not be the enemy of the good. Students will be able to design and build interesting objects with today's 3D printers. Learning is in the process of designing the objects, not in the perfection of the product.

3D Printer Primer

A 3D printer has a lot of moving parts that you will become familiar with as you design and print objects. Printers vary quite a bit in design and how they work, but in general, the most important parts to know are:

- **Case/structure:** Printers can be made of metal, wood, or plastic. Some are open on all sides, which is good for letting heat out, but also lets fumes out and little hands in.
- **Print head:** The print head is the mechanism that controls where the molten filament squirts out. Most small 3D printers move the print head back and forth and side to side in an X, Y grid using a gantry system. The print bed moves down in the Z direction as the object is created. A few reverse this and move the print bed in the X, Y space and the print head up and down in the Z direction.
- **Print bed or build platform:** This is the flat platform on which the printed object is built. Some printers use heated print beds so that the warm molten plastic hitting a cold surface doesn't warp the object.
- **Extruder:** The extruder is the part that grabs the filament and feeds it through the printer to the hot-end. It's like the trigger mechanism on a glue gun feeding the glue stick towards the metal nozzle.
- **Hot-end or print nozzle:** This is the hottest part of the printer, where the filament is melted into molten plastic and deposited onto the print bed or the partially completed object.

An early hobbyist 3D printer – MakerBot Thing-O-Matic

Filament Fundamentals

The filament used in 3D printers is the equivalent of ink in a 2D printer. In a 2D printer, the ink comes already in liquid form, but in a 3D printer, the filament must be melted. At publication time, there are two types of plastic filament primarily used with low-cost 3D printers:

- **ABS (Acrylonitrile butadiene styrene)** – ABS is what LEGOs are made of. It is generally sturdier but more expensive than PLA and melts at a higher temperature.
- **PLA (Polylactide)** – PLA is made of cornstarch or sugar, so it is potentially biodegradable. However, it requires a composting process, so just throwing it in the trash or recycle bin isn't really saving the planet. Some types of PLA are more flexible than ABS, while others are more rigid.

Some printers can switch between different filament types. Use the filament that your printer manufacturer recommends for best results.

Either of these kinds of filaments are fed into the 3D printer, melted until soft and pliable, and formed into an object. There are pros and cons of each of these materials, so if your printer can use both, you can do some tests to see what works best before you commit to a whole year's worth of supplies.

Safety First!

- Students must keep their hands and other parts out of the 3D printer. Don't ever try to adjust an object or poke at the printer parts while the printer is printing, even if the printer seems stuck.
- When heated, there are fumes released from ABS plastic, so ventilation around these printers is a must. Children with breathing issues and birds should not breathe these fumes.

The 3D Printer Workflow

Step 1: Design: Ideas and existing designs → CAD (design) → STL files

Step 2: Prepare for print: STL → CAM (slicing) → G-code

Step 3: Print: G-code → Software printer control panel → 3D object

3D printers generally have a workflow starting with a design and going through several steps before your object is printed. However, these steps will vary widely depending on your printer and choice of software.

This book does not include options for high-end design and very expensive 3D printers. The options for desktop fabrication are rapidly changing as the software and hardware is developed to make the workflow faster and easier. It is easily conceivable that in a few short years, it will be possible to complete a design online that will wirelessly transfer to a 3D printer without the need for any intermediate steps.

At the time of writing this book, the following workflow is the most common way that printing 3D objects in a classroom-based makerspace is accomplished.

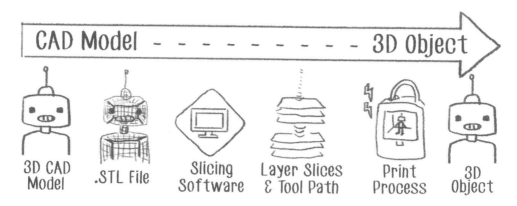

The 3D printer process

Step 1: Design: Ideas and Existing Designs → CAD (Design) → STL Files

The first step of designing a 3D printable object is the idea. When students are introduced to 3D printing, they will have many ideas about what they can print. Some of them may actually be practical and possible. Some will not. Luckily, there are many steps between the idea and the printing, and these steps will help the students narrow down their choices.

Many designs for 3D printable objects start from a library of existing designs. These collections of designs can be found online, with contributions from people all around the world who share their designs. One such website is Thingiverse (http://www.thingiverse.com). Other websites collect designs from people using similar software or printers. For example, if you use the free CAD program SketchUp, there is a library of designs shared by other SketchUp users on the SketchUp site.

In today's world, such design sharing is not copying or stealing. These sites have clear terms of use that allow anyone to download and use the designs. In many cases, they ask users who upload designs to specify whether other people can use the design and if there are limitations on that use. Some people may share their designs, for example, but ask that their designs not be used for commercial products. On the Thingiverse website, each design has a designation of the rights the owner asks other people to respect when using the design. It also shows any other designers who contributed to the design. In this way, the community benefits from the designs of others and gives credit to all contributors.

Many design collection sites use Creative Commons (CC) licenses (http://www.creativecommons.org) to explain the rights to share, remix, and reuse the designs. Creative Commons licenses provide a simple, standardized way to give the public permission to share and use your creative work with conditions of your choice.

If your students have been learning about copyright and intellectual property, learning about these licenses can reinforce those lessons. Creative Commons licenses do not replace copyright. The original author of a design still owns the design. But the Creative Commons licenses make it easier to feel comfortable about sharing your designs with others.

Warning – Any site that offers user uploading will potentially have designs with adult themes such as body parts and nude sculpture.

STL Files

The digital DNA of 3D objects are stored in digital files called STL (Stereolithography) files. These STL files are the output of software programs called CAD (Computer Aided Design) programs. These design programs range from high-end industrial CAD programs that cost thousands of dollars to programs designed for hobbyists or even some that run completely in the browser.

A CAD program allows the user to design a 3D object and then save the results in an STL file that any 3D printer can use. From Wikipedia:

> STL (STereoLithography) is a file format native to the stereolithography CAD software created by 3D Systems. STL is also known as Standard Tessellation Language. This file format is supported by many other software packages; it is widely used for rapid prototyping and computer-aided manufacturing. STL files describe only the surface geometry of a three dimensional object without any representation of color, texture or other common CAD model attributes.

> An STL file describes a raw unstructured triangulated surface by the unit normal and vertices (ordered by the right-hand rule) of the triangles using a three-dimensional Cartesian coordinate system.

Breaking this definition down, the STL file contains all of the data necessary to build a 3D object. Inside the file are the X, Y, and Z coordinate values for the many little triangles that make up your object. It is not necessary to understand the math behind this file format, because the design programs take care of the details for you.

For some teachers, working past these kinds of intimidating definitions will take some courage, especially if math anxiety is an issue. Don't worry, print happy!

Computer Aided Design (CAD) Programs

To create the STL file, you will use a Computer Aided Design (CAD) program. CAD programs are useful in many areas beyond designing objects for 3D printing. Just because a program claims to be for CAD, it doesn't mean it's the best choice for designing simple objects for 3D printing.

Many CAD programs are very complex tools for industrial designers. These almost always present too high a learning curve even for high school students.

CAD programs such as **Maya** or **Blender** are used by video game animators to create the creatures and landscapes that populate virtual worlds. These programs were not originally intended to produce real objects, but can be used for 3D printing if you are careful. Learning them will also require a steep learning curve. However, these programs are within reach of a highly motivated high school student. **Blender** is free, and you may have some students who are interested in video game design who will be willing to put in the time to learn it.

CAD programs called "solid modeling programs" are best for learning how to design 3D printable objects. **SketchUp, Shapesmith, 3DTin**, and **Autodesk's 123D** are all free solid modeling programs suitable for classroom use. They use simple shapes like boxes and cylinders that are dragged onto a design grid and combined together. These shapes can be added to each other, like putting a sphere on a box to start a robot. The shapes can also be subtracted, like putting a smaller square inside a bigger square to make an empty box. The CAD program lets you define all of the sizes and allows you to position these shapes to make complex objects. Once the design is complete, you save a file in STL format.

The most common CAD program currently in use in K–12 classrooms for 3D printing design is SketchUp.

SketchUp (http://www.sketchup.com) (Mac/Windows) was developed by Google but was recently sold to Trimble, a modeling software company. At the time of publication, they continue to offer a free basic version of SketchUp on their website and have committed to continued support for a free version. The program must be downloaded and installed on a computer. SketchUp was originally developed as a 3D modeling tool to create buildings, cars, and other realistic digital objects that could be placed in Google Earth. However, it is an easy-to-use option for students to use for designing objects for 3D printing.

There is a huge library of digital objects for SketchUp created by people from around the globe, but many are not meant to be printed out in the real world. Since SketchUp was originally designed for virtual objects, you may find many objects that have walls with no thickness and other impossible creations that will not hold up when printed. If you want to use SketchUp as your CAD program, search the Internet and you will find websites that offer tutorials and design help for printable objects.

One further issue with SketchUp: there is no option to save your designs in STL format, which you will need for the next step of the 3D printing process. If you choose SketchUp, you will also need to download and install one of the free plugins that allows SketchUp to output STL files.

Other CAD Options

Autodesk's 123D. Free 3D modeling program, available both browser-based and as a downloadable app. Options include creating paper sliced or folded creations. http://www.123dapp.com/

Shapesmith. Free, open source, browser-based. http://www.shapesmith.net

3DTin. Free use, charges for storage. Browser-based (WebGL enabled browser required). http://www.3dtin.com

Check your printer manufacturer's recommendations and test these programs yourself to see which ones will work best with your students and your hardware.

Step 2: Prepare for Print: STL → CAM (Slicing) → G-code

The next step in the 3D printing process is preparing the STL file you just saved from your CAD program and turning it into something the printer can read and print successfully.

Computer Aided Manufacturing (CAM) programs do this step for you. CAM programs do several things:

- **Find errors.** Just because you have an STL file doesn't mean you can actually print an object. Designs can contain fatal errors such as the legs of a table not actually reaching the bottom of the tabletop, disconnections between parts, or insides that end up on the outside by accident.
- **Slice your design.** The STL file describes a solid object, but the printer needs to print it one layer, or slice, at a time.
- **Output printer commands.** The CAM program will create instructions for the printer that tells it where to start and stop and where to put the plastic in each layer. These digital instructions are called G-code.
- **Set printer controls.** CAM software also allows you to set controls like print speed and quality.

This is an area that is changing rapidly and will depend on which printer you are using. Many printers include CAM functionality in the control software that comes with the printer.

Step 3: Print: G-code → Software Printer Control Panel → 3D Object

This step completes the workflow of printing a 3D object. The G-code is transferred to the printer and you print your object.

The steps to make this happen are best found in the printer manual that comes with your printer. Features typically found in this software allow you to stop, start, and pause the printer, and choose other settings that will affect print quality. You will be able to adjust the printer head position and the printer bed so that it is level and calibrated. If your printer is not calibrated properly, your object may start printing in midair and will not print properly.

Many affordable, classroom-friendly 3D printers use the open source CAM program ReplicatorG (http://replicat.org). ReplicatorG directly connects with printers such as MakerBot Replicator, Thing-O-Matic, and RepRap printers. This combines Steps 2 and 3, making the process a bit easier.

Using an Iterative Design Cycle

There are several opportunities to use iterative design principles when using a fabrication device.

- **Design cycle** – Students can come up with multiple ideas and start to design on paper, modeling clay, or using a CAD program. Students can share ideas and check each other's work. This peer review has the advantage of not only catching mistakes, but also spreading ideas and techniques quickly through the whole class.
- **CAD and CAM software** – Depending on your tools, the CAD and CAM software will generate error messages that will have to be addressed before moving on to the next step.
- **Printing and redesign** – When students print out their object, they may find flaws or just want to make improvements. This is natural and hopefully can be accommodated in spite of the extra time and cost of materials.

Choosing Your Printer

Choosing a printer can be challenging. There are choices at every price level, many overlapping features, and new printers coming on the market every day. Three useful resources to help the decision-making process are:

The Edutech Wiki – http://edutechwiki.unige.ch/en/3D_printing

Instructables Introduction to 3D printing – http://www.instructables.com/id/3D-Printing-1/

Make Magazine (Winter 2013) – 3D Printer Buyer's Guide http://amzn.to/17ccaGR

Sorting your "must haves" from your "nice to haves" list is an ongoing process. One suggestion is to find educator colleagues and communities to give you advice. Sharing ideas and tips with people who understand the logistics of working with students is as least as valuable as finding the perfect printer. You will find that features valued by educators are often not the same as the typical hardcore DIYers who are writing most of the online reviews of new printers.

Once you narrow down your choices, do an extensive search online for the printer model. You should be able to find several reviews, forum posts, and comments on reviews that will help you decide if the printer is right for you.

Printer Considerations

- **Budget** – Check different suppliers for the total cost of the printer and filament, as well as the availability. Does the supplier accept school purchase orders?
- **Setup and documentation** – You can save money by building a 3D printer from a kit, but do you have time and the expertise necessary? Are you willing to "get under the hood" to keep a printer running? Many printers

have their documentation online – does it look comprehensive and easy to understand?

- **Materials** – What kind and size of filament does it use, and can it use different types? Can you get that easily? Make sure the printer you choose does not need special filament or filament cartridges that may be more expensive.
- **Features** – What is the size of the printer? What is the size of largest printable object? What software is included?
- **Performance** – Check out the printer's speed, precision, quality of printed objects, and printing consistency.
- **Convenience** – Some printers require leaving a computer connected to it while the printing is going on (tethered), while others can complete a printing job even if you take your computer away (untethered). Some even have slots for inserting a USB drive or SD card. There are a few printers that are battery-powered and some that are more easily portable than others – a consideration if you do not have a permanent home for your printer.
- **Reliability** – Does the printer have a reputation for reliability? Does it look like it will survive classroom use? Is there support offered by the manufacturer? Is the support forum up to date? Do people who post questions get answers?
- **Community** – Are there people online (especially other educators) who use the printer and can offer support?
- **Open source** – Some printer manufacturers release their hardware designs into the open source community. This allows others to copy the hardware and make improvements that are also shared with others. This may be a valuable feature if you are the type of person who will tinker with the printer to make it work better. If not, open source hardware may not matter as much to you.

For even more criteria, *Make* magazine offers a rubric of over 60 questions used in their Winter 2013 printer roundup. http://blog.makezine.com/make-ultimate-guide-to-3d-printing/grading-rubric/

3D Printer Projects

Karen Blumberg, Technology Integrator at The School at Columbia University says:

> We use SketchUp and Tinkercad[1] to draw our designs. Then we print them using one of our available printers (a Makerbot, a Bits From Bytes 3DTouch, or a Replicator 2.). Sample projects have involved third graders re-designing an everyday object (tissue box, pencil box, Xbox console...), fifth graders designing Greek temples and outsourcing their designs to be tweaked and printed at a nearby school, and sixth graders

1   Tinkercad is no longer available.

studying surface area and volume in math designed complex shapes for each other to measure.

Project Ideas

- Toys, game pieces, dice, action figures, small statues, pencil toppers
- Items that show use of ratio, measurement, scaling, geometry
- Bling out your makerspace: wall mounts, tool holders, spacers, drawer labels
- Needed parts for other inventions; replacing missing or broken parts – cranks, knobs, cases, latches, holders, and stands
- Building tools useful in other school activities – simple machine samples or math manipulatives for another teacher to use
- Small decorative items and gifts – names in 3D, desk accessories, plaques, bottle openers, keychain fobs, cell phone cases, beads, and medallions for making jewelry

Connecting your students' projects to big ideas expands your makerspace from just being a factory. The eight elements of good projects and the concept of simple prompts can be tailored for your students at any age.

Look for opportunities to add precision and measurement to the designs the students are working on. This doesn't have to be "school math" – you don't have to work hard to introduce dividing fractions into student work. In 3D printing, as in the real world, the result of miscalculation or misunderstanding the coordinate system is quite evident when you build an object that doesn't work.

Ideas can come from everywhere: real life needs, what students are studying in other classes, and making math come to life. Students are often interested in ecology and may ask about the wisdom of making things that are going to just end up in a landfill. These and other interests are prime for further inquiry:

- PLA filament is made from organic materials – does this automatically make it more environmentally friendly? Is it really biodegradable? Can we prove it?
- Find out about the latest advances in 3D printers – there are people working on printers that print food and candy, some that could print artificial human organs, etc. What are the implications of these inventions?
- What would be the environmental impact of not having to ship physical products around the world? Can students find data on how much pollution is caused by shipping products such as toys thousands of miles?
- What jobs in the future might be lost and which ones might be gained by 3D printing becoming more widespread?
- Is it OK to print copyrighted objects, like LEGO blocks or a statue that looks like Bart Simpson?
- Is it legal to print something dangerous, like a gun?

Avoiding the "Keychain Syndrome"

In a new book on FabLabs, Paulo Blikstein of Stanford University, who started the FabLab@School project, writes about lessons learned in running early digital fabrication workshops in partnership with K–12 schools. Students quickly learned how to use the fabrication equipment, but once they learned how to make a simple object like a keychain, they would make endless versions of the same thing.

> The workshop became a keychain factory, and students would not engage in anything else. The plan worked too well – it backfired. Students found an activity that was personally meaningful, produced professional-looking products that were admired and envied, and used a high-tech device. However, as much as it was a very effective solution to engage them in digital fabrication, it offered a too big reward for a relatively small effort, to produce an object that did not include any computation or complex constructive challenges. Ironically, it is as if students had discovered exactly what manufacturing is about – mass-producing with little effort – and were making the best of it. Students "cracked" digital fabrication and were using the lab as a fabrication facility, rather than a place for invention. (Blikstein, 2013)

The incentives to continue to make a trivial object were stronger than the incentives to move onward to more complex, challenging work. This dilemma is amplified by typical school curriculum tendencies to emphasize product over process and to value pre-planned activities with no surprises.

This is an ongoing conflict for makerspace teachers. Both students and the status quo must be challenged simultaneously.

> The "keychain syndrome," therefore, revealed two of the crucial elements of learning environments based on digital fabrication. First, the equipment is capable of easily generating aesthetically attractive objects and products. Second, this generates an incentive system in which there is a disproportionate payoff in staying at a 'local minimum' where the projects are very simple but at the same time very admired by external observers. Settling for simple projects is a temptation that educators have to avoid at all cost. (Blikstein, 2013)

Being mindful of the keychain syndrome might help teachers envision the invention-oriented classroom as a continually evolving quest for what to do next, rather than settling into a folder full of weekly activities that get repeated class after class, semester after semester. It will not only be the students who are tempted by the keychain syndrome, but the teacher as well.

Fabrication and Learning

Andrew B. Watt is the Director of the Design Lab at the Independent Day School in Middlefield, Connecticut. Andrew teaches the students in grades 1–8 graphic design, some programming, some architectural and structural engineering, and a few bits and pieces of mechanical engineering.

This is what I get for going to the bathroom while a print job is in progress in the Design Lab: a bad print.

I don't know: maybe my feet on the floor of the lab bounced the print head. Maybe a parent, or a kid, touched the printer in the middle of the build, and shook it just slight off its rocker — an accidental daemonic possession. A gremlin fussed with the code along the way perhaps, or the code just isn't that well written. Whatever it is... This kid's design is ruined. And it's an hour-long print job. It will be Thursday before I can try again.

Under ordinary circumstances, in an ordinary classroom, I'd have to tell this kid he failed the class. He didn't produce a model that was worthy of the name. It doesn't matter that it wasn't his fault: he didn't produce a model and get it to me before the end of the day; he didn't supervise the printer all the way through his build. All kinds of things went wrong or could have gone wrong, that he couldn't control and aren't his fault. All I know is that the top part of his model is offset, and the bottom is sort of sloppy... And isn't that worth a C or a C+?

Except.

Except when was the last time you taught a fourth grader to use a 3D printer?

When was the last time you taught a fourth grader to use a 3D printer while you were still learning to use it yourself?

The typical 3D printer is a Frankenstein's monster of wires and gears and heating elements. It has controls written and explained in X, Y and Z, on a Cartesian grid most of my students won't learn until seventh or eighth grade. It's far too easy to tell a student, you're no good at this, or, this is beyond you.

But none of that is true. It's the falsest falsity there is.

I told a mother today, "We give no grades in the Design Lab." I think we dare not. Artists and architects and engineers, and for that matter, great writers like Hemingway and Tolkien and Austen learned their crafts and their artistry not from being graded — but from selfish, constant, almost obsessive trial and error.

There's no way to replicate that with a grade on one project. There's no way to tell if their grade should be a C+, or a graduation magna cum laude until you know if they give up after a failure, or if they instead simply move on to the next version.

It's here, I think, that modern educators need to learn something from the medieval alchemists. For the product is not the thing of utmost seriousness in school. Rather, it is the child — to become physically strong through sports, mentally alert through study, creative and imaginative through the arts, empowered through distillation and refinement — that is, the discovery of errors and their gradual removal.

Getting to Know Your Printer

Teachers who have never used a 3D printer may naturally have some reservations about their own ability to understand how to use it, teach students how to use it, and keep it up and running. The hobbyist level of 3D printer that most schools will be able to afford may not be the most robust of devices. However, you may be surprised to find out that you can learn to handle that. Karen Blumberg and her students were using a 3D printer that wasn't working well, so she went to her boss to find out what to do. He told her that she should figure it out, so that's what she set out to do:

> While I consider myself handy, I would never fool myself into describing myself as an engineer, and I really didn't need to be weighed down with the possibility of breaking a $4000 machine. However, I do what my boss tells me, so I went forth unafraid. It took many hours over many days, but I think I know what I'm doing now.
>
> I looked at pages and pages of information and FAQ from the manufacturer's website. First I learned how to replace a delivery tube and load new filament. Then I experimented with raising/lowering the extruder nozzles and leveling the printer tray in order to print a successful raft. Once I had items printing regularly, I saw that we were running out of ABS filament and only had PLA left in our stash of replacement spools. So, I learned about the difference between ABS and PLA (ABS is more robust, PLA is cheaper), and learned how to change the target print temperature and RPM for each nozzle.

Karen's investigation of the printer didn't happen before she let her students use it, it occurred naturally when there was a problem. This is exactly the kind of behavior you want to model for students.

Just like you hope students develop the confidence to jump in with both feet, so must teachers develop similar habits. The worst thing that can happen is waiting for the teacher to figure everything out perfectly ahead of time. Often this turns into unboxed equipment locked in the closet waiting for that day when a teacher has extra time to read all directions, follow the online tutorials to the letter, and feel 100% confident that he or she can teach a lesson, answer all student questions, troubleshoot any problem along the way, and do it all before the bell rings. The trouble is, that day never comes.

Printing Without a Printer

Staples, the office superstore chain, has announced it will be equipping stores with 3D printers in the near future. These printers will be able to read files that you upload to their website, which will have the object mailed to you or ready for pick up at your local Staples store. The printers use a method based on laminated paper, which when cut, stacked, and glued together, will create a 3D object made of paper, but extremely hard paper.

There are companies that offer 3D printing services right here and now. These companies will take STL files, print out your object, and mail it back to you. This is a way to have objects made with different materials, more colors, or in larger sizes than the creations you can print on your own printer.

These sites offer a variety of features and different pricing plans. Most allow you to price out your object in different sizes and materials and get an instant price quote. Make sure you carefully read the shipping policies and timelines; some of these sites use global manufacturing facilities that can add weeks to a delivery date. Some of them have marketplaces where you can sell your designs.

Shapeways http://shapeways.com

Ponoko http://ponoko.com

Sculpteo http://sculpteo.com

Controversy With Fabrication Devices

The ability of fabrication devices to create "anything" challenges some long-standing legal and moral barriers. These challenges are making their way to courts around the world right now and the full implications are yet to be known. There are two areas that have the most implication for your students: creating objects that can cause harm (like guns) and the laws surrounding copyright, patent, and trademark.

Printing Guns and Other Dangerous Things

Printing guns is not far-out science fiction. There have already been guns and gun parts printed and fired successfully. (Farivar, 2013) So far, completely plastic guns are not sturdy enough to compete with metal guns, but in the not too distant future, the materials will get better and the controversy deeper. Current United States gun laws control manufacture and sales of guns, yet it is not illegal to make a gun at home, nor is it illegal to publish instructions for homemade guns or gun parts. For your students, anything dangerous like guns or other weapons should be off limits, but this one case offers an interesting peek into the future of the disruptive potential of personal fabrication.

Something a little closer to home for students might be to discuss if it is unethical to copy a car key, for example. It might be fine if it's your car, but not if it's someone else's and especially if the intent is to steal the car.

Intellectual Property

In the United States, there are three main ways that people and companies protect their inventions and creations, called intellectual property: copyright, trademark, and patent. All of these are under challenge with fabrication technology.

Copyright protects the designs that are expressions of ideas – but not the ideas themselves. For example, recipes are rarely copyrightable, but a cookbook is. Copyright also does not typically cover functional objects, such as a vase, but can cover the design on the vase. In 3D printing, the collections of user designs found online have specific instructions on them regarding use. They may ask that if you use their CAD file, you not sell it commercially, for example. Students should be made aware of these requirements when they download files from these sites.

Trademarks are legal protections that protect a company so that their "mark" such as a logo, brand name, or distinctive design can't be used by anyone else. Trademark law exists to protect the consumer from being deceived by look-alike products, and to protect the company's reputation from being harmed by low-quality copies. In amateur 3D printing, there is little likelihood that anyone would mistake your bust of Darth Vader for a licensed Star Wars product. Use the same care with trademarked items as you would with an assignment to build scaled-up models of household items like giant packs of gum.

Patents are expensive and time-consuming for manufacturers and inventors to get, but provide the most protection for an invention. The law was created to protect people who have put a lot of effort into a new invention only to be undercut by someone else who just copies their design. A patent covers entire inventions, and copying that invention, even inadvertently, violates the patent. However, making a part of an invention, such as a replacement part, does not infringe on the patent.

Under current law you could, for example, create look-alike building blocks that are exactly like LEGO, but you could not sell them, call them LEGO, or even say that your blocks connect with LEGO. If you uploaded your design to a community website, it might be possible that the LEGO company could request that your files be removed. There are, in fact, designs for blocks that connect different building kits together available on many fabrication project websites. So far, none of the building kit manufacturers have made claims that these designs violate the law. As 3D printers become more capable and widespread, this may change.

Given this ever-changing and somewhat confusing legal landscape, we believe that the best way to teach students to respect intellectual property is to use common sense. Don't make dangerous things. Respect the requests of authors when you use their designs and underlying code, and if you aren't sure, ask. Make your own designs when possible. Don't try to make money using someone else's ideas and hard work. Always give credit where credit is due.

The Future

There is no doubt that 3D printers will continue to become more affordable as time goes on. They will also become more reliable, create better objects, be easier to use, and use more varied and colorful materials. The software will become simpler, and the steps from design to object will be consolidated into more user-friendly applications, or even be embedded directly into some printers. Some printers may be designed to simply deliver products designed by others. There are already scanning programs that allow you to take a 360-degree scan of an object with a camera and automatically create the files needed to recreate the object.

It is not out of the realm of possibility that Amazon will make a printer that exclusively prints products purchased and customized on the Amazon website. Considering that a Kindle exists only to enable book purchases from Amazon, this is not a far-fetched prediction.

These inevitable advances will make 3D printing easier and more affordable, but also diminish the value of having students use 3D printers. As an analogy, you would hardly make a lot of claims for the learning benefits of using a 2D printer, but you can make a case for the writing process. It would be a mistake to replace English class with Laserprinting.

A printer that is part of design process should allow maximum student agency. A yet-to-be invented printer that automatically prints out designs found on the Web might be a useful appliance, but is not as intellectually nutritious.

We are not advocating that all students make their own printers from parts, tolerate unreliable equipment, or write G-code by hand. While it is true that today's 3D printers are buggier than they should be, one should not confuse tweaking the machine with learning something valuable. Struggling with bad tools doesn't make you a better carpenter. The sooner 3D printing becomes a seamless part of the creative process the better.

There are already educators nostalgic for the days when students had to build the 3D printers from scratch. A handful of kids may have enjoyed a maker experience overcoming the quirkiness of printer mechanics, but the activity was essentially limited to assembling a kit. Using a 3D printer purposefully is likely more important than the resulting physical artifact.

There is every reason to suspect that as 3D printing becomes more widespread in schools, you will start to hear sales pitches for products "designed for learning." Be wary of such claims. Attempts will be made to turn 3D printing into a teaching technology. There will be claims that teachers can print out "learning objects" for students such as 3D models of the human skeleton, molecules, or historic buildings. There will be professional learning workshops where teachers will be taught how to use a 3D printer and given a list of how to integrate 3D objects into their classroom. These efforts should be banished from the building. 3D printing is a creative learning tool only in the hands of the learner.

PHYSICAL COMPUTING

Aside from blowing stuff up, kids' next favorite activity is making things go. Physical computing is the game changer that allows kids to invent working machines. Learners design, construct, and program "smart" machines to live outside of the computer and interact with the world. Some of these machines just do as they are told, while others are programmed to accept stimuli and make decisions determining a physical response.

Physical computing provides a tactile context for STEM, complete with all of the messiness, surprise, and occasional frustration associated with real science and engineering. Students can have an idea, build, debug, improve, and embellish a three dimensional operational machine. Physical computing supports a wide range of learning styles and offers a part of the process that appeals to kids who have different attitudes, interests, or expertise. Debugging now takes two forms: hardware *and* software. Physical computing projects require learners to overcome mechanical obstacles and alleviate programming bugs in order to achieve their goals or test a hypothesis.

Toys, parts of broken appliances, and other found materials enhance the DIY computers, robotics, whimsical interfaces, and microcontrollers that encompass physical computing. This high- and low-tech gumbo helps to make cutting-edge technologies accessible to even the youngest learners and is consistent with the playfulness of childhood.

> In today's world, Interaction Design is concerned with the creation of meaningful experiences between us (humans) and objects. It is a good way to explore the creation of beautiful – and maybe even controversial – experiences between us and technology. Interaction Design encourages design through an iterative process based on prototypes of ever-increasing fidelity. This approach – also part of some types of "conventional" design – can be extended to include prototyping with technology; in particular, prototyping with electronics. The specific field of Interaction Design involved with Arduino is Physical Computing (or Physical Interaction Design). (Monk, 2012)

There are three truths associated with the exciting new world of physical computing:

1. Technology is improving and changing constantly. It may even become cheaper the day after you buy it.
2. There are helpful people and resources available online.
3. The answer to the question, "Will X work with the new Y?" is almost always, "Yes, somehow." People online have undoubtedly done what you are thinking about and are willing to share their wisdom.

A Truly Personal Computer

Since the 1960s, Seymour Papert was frustrated by the fact that kids could not make their own computer for a variety of practical and commercial reasons. They could program a computer, connect a science probe, or control a robot, but building the whole thing was impossible. Some piece of agency over the machine was always out of reach.

Hardware manufacturers limited the availability of parts, the costs were prohibitive, or policy makers just didn't trust kids with building school computers. Even in cases where kids did assemble PCs, it was more like completing a jigsaw puzzle than inventing. Snap the pieces together and voilà! Computer!

Raspberry Pi changes all of that and encourages computer programming.

Around six years ago, Eben Upton was the Director of Studies of Computer Science at Cambridge University in England. Upton shared the sort of concerns we have expressed in this volume about a generation of young people becoming passive users of technology they neither understand nor control. Even worse, the computers and game systems in the bedrooms of kids were difficult or impossible to program. Upton knew how much fun programming was, as well as the economic benefits of computer fluency, and was concerned about the decreasing interest in the study of computer science by students lacking any experience in the subject. He and a group of colleagues had an idea to produce an inexpensive and small computer they could give to perspective students at their university's open day. When those students returned to campus a few months later for their admissions interview, they could show what they had programmed with the computer.

The Raspberry Pi was born. "Raspberry" paid homage to the naming of computers after fruit, and "Pi" is an abbreviation of Python, a programming language they liked for beginners. As the non-profit Raspberry Pi Foundation continued its development work, it became evident that even an incredibly low-cost computer could offer a great deal of power and functionality. It could be the brains of a media center, gaming machine, Internet appliance, and a whole lot more. In May 2011, a British technology journalist used his phone to shoot a video of the Raspberry Pi prototype in action and posted the video on his blog. The video became an instant viral sensation and the Raspberry Pi folks had inadvertently promised the world a $25 PC! (Upton & Halfacree, 2012)

Producing a general-purpose computer at a retail price of $25 required lots of ingenuity and compromises, and it had to work with peripherals people might already own, such as a TV, mouse, keyboard, and power supply. Using peripherals you have lying around not only makes the Raspberry Pi inexpensive, but also is consistent with the DIY, tinkering, recycling, and re-use values of the maker community.

> The Raspberry Pi is cheap enough to buy with a few weeks' pocket money, and you probably have all of the equipment you need to make it work: a TV, an SD card that can come from an old camera, a mobile phone charger, a keyboard and a mouse. It's not shared with the family, it belongs to the kid, and it's small enough to put in a pocket and take to a friend's house. If something goes wrong, it's no big deal – you just swap out a new SD card and your Raspberry Pi is factory new again. And all the tools, environments and learning materials that you need to get

smarted on the long, smooth curve to learn to program your Raspberry Pi are right there, waiting for you as soon as you turn it on. (Upton & Halfacree, 2012)

The first day that the Raspberry Pi was available for sale online, 100,000 orders were placed, crashing the servers of the two companies manufacturing and distributing it. Folks like us waited the better part of a year for the invitation to buy a Raspberry Pi and then waited for it to arrive. The good news is that production is now sufficient to meet demand and you can buy as many as you'd like from a variety of sources.

Once again, the maker movement has brought things full circle. In the early days of personal computing, hobbyists built and programmed their own computers. The Raspberry Pi makes that exciting prospect available to a new generation.

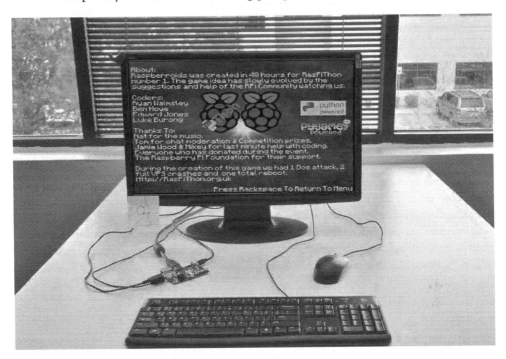

Raspberry Pi (yes, that's the whole computer on the desk)

What Can It Do?

The Raspberry Pi is a computer, like your iMac or Dell, except it doesn't have a hard drive, monitor, keyboard, mouse, CD/DVD drive, or even a case to house itself in. What did you expect for $25? However, the Raspberry Pi is roughly the size of a credit card; it stores its operating system, programs, and files on an SD card; it has two USB ports for a mouse and keyboard; and it may be connected to a TV via composite RCA plugs or power your high-definition flat screen via the built-in HDMI port! The $35 Raspberry Pi version B includes an Ethernet port for connecting to the Internet. However, you can use one of the USB ports and a Wifi dongle for wireless access too.

You can power the Raspberry Pi with the sort of Mini-USB power supply commonly used to charge cellphones, and with devices like the GoPro video cameras. Best of all, the Raspberry Pi contains 17 General Purpose Input/Output ports (GPIO), in addition to pins providing power to connected electronics. The GPIO ports allow the Raspberry Pi to receive feedback from sensors or to power things like lights, motors, and buzzers. These GPIO ports are digital in that they can be turned on or off or read True and False. (The GPIO ports on an Arduino are more versatile).

The Raspberry Pi runs the open source Linux operating system and can do most of the things you can do on any other much more expensive PC running Linux. Web surfing, image editing, media playing (in HD), office applications via Open Office or Google Apps, controlling appliances, and robotics and programming – especially programming – are some of the things your Raspberry Pi computer can do. The programming languages, Scratch and Python, work great on a Raspberry Pi!

The operating system, software, and user files for the Raspberry Pi are stored on a common SD card, typically capable of holding 4GB or more of data. Linux is quite small, but software and your media files may benefit from the extra RAM on a larger SD card.

Once your Raspberry Pi is up and running and you dive deep into the world of Arduino, you may find ways to use both to create otherwise impossible projects. Your Raspberry Pi can be used as a home entertainment system, Web server, home automation controller, and a whole lot more! There are websites, blogs, YouTube videos, books, and an eager community of users available to help you get started and inspire you as you use your Raspberry Pi.

Don't Buy It Because It's Cheap!

The Raspberry Pi may appear inexpensive, but remember that you need to buy (or build) a case for it. You also need cables for connecting it to a television or HDMI-compatible monitor, plus an SD card and power supply. Hopefully, you have a mouse and keyboard lying around, because you'll need those too. That can easily bring the cost of the $25 computer to over $100. That's still not bad, but not so cheap. When you consider that you may be able to purchase a tablet computer or netbook for a hundred dollars more, the Raspberry Pi begins to look like a bad idea.

That is, unless you understand the potential of the Raspberry Pi as an open-ended computer built, programmed, and owned by its user that can be modified, hacked, and extended in ways we may not yet have imagined. The price of freedom in this case is quite low. The creative potential of the Raspberry Pi makes it a very wise investment indeed.

Raspberry Pi Resources

Raspberry Pi Foundation http://www.raspberrypi.org/

Make Magazine Raspberry Pi
http://blog.makezine.com/category/electronics/raspberry-pi/

LEGO

Mechanical building sets have offered add-on motors, lights, switches, and buzzers for decades, but in the mid-1980s, LEGO produced the first robotics construction kits that allowed kids to build "smart" machines that could interact with the users and their environment. Outputs (motors, lights, and buzzers) were met by inputs (sensors for temperature, light, rotation, touch, and later sound) for the first time. By programming your machines, you teach them to respond to external stimuli and events. Let's think of robotics as the act of giving behaviors to machines.

LEGO has dominated the educational robotics market since 1987, and hobbyists have embraced the materials for the elegance and snap-together simplicity, even if they go on to modify their kits. The ability to snap together an invention, test it, and make modifications quickly and easily without tools makes LEGO an excellent vehicle for learning through robotics construction. The familiarity and trusted brand of LEGO made robotics accessible by educators who might other-

LEGO digital gingerbread house

wise have shied away from engineering. Like LEGO itself, LEGO robotics has a wonderful playful quality.

The original LEGO robotics sets were programmed in a version of Logo. This made perfect sense since Papert and his colleagues at the MIT Media Lab invented the materials for LEGO. On a deeper level, the building of complexity out of simple elements with LEGO mirrored the cognitive processes involved in Logo programming. Kids loved LEGO and Logo. It was a match made in epistemological heaven. Since the early 1990's, LEGO has abandoned Logo as the language for programming its bricks and embraced RoboLab[2], a version of the LabView software used by scientists to control monitoring equipment. LEGO programs are created by connecting screen icons to one another. LEGO likes to tout the lack of words in the environment as a virtue, but debugging may be more difficult, especially for children, since there is no obvious vocabulary or grammar at hand for talking about your program. Unlike Logo, it's difficult to act out a LEGO program created with their proprietary software. LEGO has also created robotics elements, like a wheel assembly with a gear train hidden inside that makes the mechanics of a machine much more opaque. As a result, kids are less likely to play with the mathematics and physics of gears as much as they used to.

In our opinion, the trend away from Logo-like languages and the addition of mysterious "black box" building elements leads to a narrower range of projects created by kids. At times, cleaning up and creating a robot slightly more efficient than your opponent have been favored over celebrating the creativity of a learner or of powerful ideas. There is no reason why robotics materials cannot be treated in the same spirit as any other arts and crafts supply. Classes of students don't all need to reproduce the same truck with two lights and a touch sensor that causes it to change direction. They should use robotics materials to support a spirit of kinetic sculpture, solving real problems, controlling experiments, puppetry, and anything else a kid can dream up. Robotics materials should be unconstrained by the imagination of toy designers. They should have a low threshold and high ceiling. The wider range of artifacts students create, the more they will learn.

LEGO currently offers two robotics sets, WeDo and NxT (both Mac and PC). Both sets use a version of the LabView software, but focus on different ends of the K–12 spectrum. WeDo is intended for grades K–2, and augments traditional LEGO bricks, plus some gears and wheels, with a USB interface that connects to the computer and a motor, tilt, and motion sensors. The sets come with step-by-step building plans – whimsical project ideas that will inspire kids to create their own inventions. However, all of the machines must be tethered to a computer via the USB interface. So your car can't race around the classroom and most inventions have limited mobility. This was to keep costs down and to add simplicity to the system. Debugging your machine is literally a game of "wrist bone connected

---

2   Over time, LEGO has called its LabView-based software by the following names: Robolab, Mindstorms, WeDo Software, NxT Software, or EV3 Software. When we refer to Robolab, we are talking about the current version of LEGO's icon-based robotics controller software.

to the arm bone." When your robot is tethered to the computer, communication issues disappear from the debugging process.

LEGO's Mindstorms NxT system, more expensive than WeDo, is intended for upper elementary through high school and has become a staple of robotics competitions, such as the FIRST LEGO League. It uses its own version of the LabView software and features a number of sensors, including ones that touch, measure rotation, calculate acceleration, hear sounds, and "see" via ultrasonic waves or infrared. It is even possible to connect or make non-LEGO sensors work with the system. The NxT brick, approximately the size of a few decks of cards stacked on top of one another, is the brains of the system and controls all inputs and outputs. NxT robotics have programs uploaded to them and are then capable of operating untethered from the computer.

In addition to gears and pulleys common in LEGO's Technic sets, Mindstorms NxT introduces many new special-purpose building elements that, while still compatible with traditional LEGO bricks and beams, impose a new building vocabulary.

By late 2013, LEGO will begin replacing the NxT with the Mindstorms EV3 set. The intelligent brick will look a lot like the NxT, but will be capable of being controlled from a smartphone or computer over USB. New sensors and upgrades to LEGO's software are inevitable. There are software options for users of LEGO robotics materials. WeDo may be controlled by Scratch, and the NxT elements may be programmed via Enchanting.

The elegance, simplicity, and popularity of LEGO puts it on the pricier side, although the non-consumable, interchangeable parts last a lifetime. The relatively closed ecosystem provided by LEGO make certain kinds of projects possible within the constraints of a traditional classroom without dealing with tools or electronics, but the future of robotics and learning will likely be more open-ended, complex, and messier. That said, LEGO offers students great learning opportunities while engaged in engineering and robotics. It may also serve as a great introduction to the wild world of microcontroller programming.

LEGO Education http://legoeducation.us

Scratch http://scratch.mit.edu

Enchanting http://enchanting.robotclub.ab.ca/

Arduino: The Future of Robotics

Physical Computing uses electronics to prototype new materials for designers and artists. It involves the design of interactive objects that can communicate with humans using sensors and actuators controlled by a behavior implemented as software running inside a microcontroller (a small computer on a single chip).

In the past, using electronics meant having to deal with engineers all the time, and building circuits one small component at a time; these issues

> kept creative people from playing around with the medium directly. Most of the tools were meant for engineers and required extensive knowledge.
>
> In recent years, microcontrollers have become cheaper and easier to use, allowing the creation of better tools. The progress that we have made with Arduino is to bring these tools one step closer to the novice, allowing people to start building stuff after only two or three days of a workshop. With Arduino, a designer or artist can get to know the basics of electronics. (Monk, 2012)

Arduino is an open source electronic microcontroller based on flexible, easy-to-use hardware and software. It is the Apollo Project of the maker movement. No other "maker" technology generates more excitement or uses than Arduino. It was released in 2005 by Massimo Banzi and David Cuartielles, and like the Raspberry Pi, was originally developed for use by students. (Banzi, 2008)

Think of the guts or brains of your programmable LEGO brick or personal computer without the nice plastic case, USB ports, drives, keyboard, mouse, or monitor and you'll understand what a microcontroller is. The Arduino is the brains of a computer, disinterested in word processing or social networking. It has RAM for running programs and a small amount of EPROM flash memory for storing your programs, even if the Arduino is turned off. The Arduino also features a variety of input/output pins for connecting other electronics to the board. The USB port on the Arduino is not only used to download programs to the microcontroller[3], but also allows the Arduino to serve as an interface between the computer and the electronics connected to the board.

Arduino is in fact a small microcomputer that can receive input from sensors, use that information in a computer program, and take action by controlling lights, motors, buzzers, or other output devices. Many physical computing projects don't really need a whole PC-like computer. They only need a little bit of processing power. Using the Arduino means that you have just enough computing power to do what you need in a lightweight, easy-to-deal-with form.

There is a growing range of microcontrollers in the Arduino family used to embed intelligence or interactivity into an invention. Some are more general purpose and suited for a wide range of applications, while others are smaller, cheaper, and targeted to performing one or two functions reliably. Your watch or toothbrush may each contain a microprocessor, but they do not need to be as powerful or flexible as the one in your laptop.

Arduino and its variants are intended to be embedded in machines, control external devices, or serve the prototyping process. Arduino is intended for artists, designers, hobbyists, and anyone interested in creating interactive objects or environments. Despite its small size and low cost, Arduino is used by children to

---

3   Some Arduino-compatible microcontrollers use Bluetooth for wireless communication between the computer and board. Similar standards will likely become more commonplace in the future although such functionality will drain a battery much more quickly.

explore simple circuits, control a lawn sprinkler system, or to automate a factory assembly line. It slices. It dices. It's Arduino.

Building and programming robots with Arduino may be messier than using LEGO, but Arduino is infinitely more flexible and powerful. A whole new world of sensors, motors, lights, and peripherals can be made to obey.

The open source nature of Arduino means that the design of the microcontroller is available to anyone who wants it. Those who change or improve upon the design promise to share their changes with the public, so ideas are shared and everyone profits from the innovation. If you are really ambitious, you can download plans to build Arduino boards from scratch. Since today's most popular Arduino microcontrollers only cost around $25, readers of this book are likely to buy the latest version preassembled and ready to go.

Extensibility is a hallmark of Arduino. That means that the creators of the Arduino standard left the system open enough to allow others to invent new functionality. This is often accomplished via "shields" – additional electronics boards that stack on the Arduino to allow it to perform new tricks, like receiving wireless information, playing music, driving motors, controlling video games, or powering a display. In some ways, the Arduino does less than a Raspberry Pi, but shields give Arduino super powers.

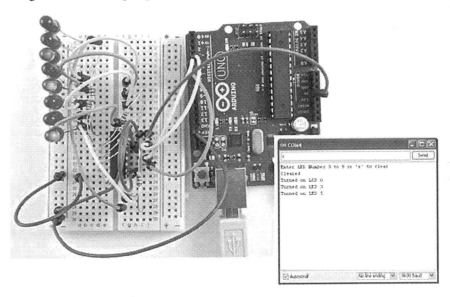

Arduino blinking LEDs on a breadboard

Prototyping and Messing About With Arduino

Prototyping is one way to use Arduino. Scientists and engineers build models and test them before manufacturing or building upon a concept. If you sew, it's like making a muslin dress pattern to get the perfect fit before you make the real dress. The prototype of the Arduino-controlled electronic circuit is put together in a way that is quick and easy to change, test, and change again until you achieve the desired result. This makes Arduino excellent for tinkering with electronics and using iterative design methodology.

Arduino prototyping typically uses a breadboard connected with wires to the microcontroller. A breadboard is a small plastic board with many electronic connectors for making and modifying circuits without the need for solder. If you look at the bottom of a circuit board, you see how all of the components are connected to one another. The breadboard allows you to experiment with the proper placement and use of components without committing to a soldered circuit board.

Arduino boards are also very small, lightweight, and don't use a lot of electricity, making them perfect for small, battery-powered projects. Once you have perfected your invention with a breadboard, you may solder together a robust machine and release it into the wild.

How It Works

The Arduino standard is powered by an ATmega328 microcontroller produced by Atmel. It controls all of the memory, processor, and input/outputs on the Arduino board. Outputs and inputs may be digital or analog. In other words, you can turn an LED on or off, or you can set its brightness. A switch is digital, a dimmer is analog.

The software that runs on the Arduino computer is also open source. This means it is free, and that many people are adapting and resharing the software. You will find that there are many variations on what software you can run, and how to interface it to your computer. The name "Arduino" is trademarked, but the board designs are all open source and freely distributed under a Creative Commons license. That's why you'll see any number of different microcontroller boards being sold with the suffix "–duino" at the end of them. The official Arduino boards are well distributed, reliable, and sell quite well.

Because it is open source, there are many variations of the Arduino hardware and software. This is both a blessing and a curse. The good news is that there is a large community of users and a large library of shared code, hardware additions, ideas, blogs, and resources. The bad news is that it seems like there are *too* many options, and this can be overwhelming.

All you really need to get started with Arduino is the microcontroller, a computer, the free IDE software, a USB cable to connect the Arduino, and your computer. That should be sufficient to write a program to flash the LED built into most Arduino-style microcontrollers. A bit of solid core (one metal strand) wire, a small DC motor, a few LEDs, and a push button switch are all you need to go wild.

We strongly recommend purchasing one of the low-cost Arduino kits on the market. Less than $100 usually gets you a kit complete with an Arduino, breadboard, wire, and an assortment of motors, lights, switches, and sensors to support a wide range of projects. Most kits contain simple project ideas too. Once you get the hang of Arduino engineering and programming, you can scrounge for parts or buy the parts you need in bulk.

Electronics Makes a Comeback

You won't get very far with physical computing, especially Arduino, without dealing with principles of electricity and simple electronics components. Although that might sound daunting, it is actually very good news. Electronics is central to our lives but disappeared from our consciousness. We have taken electronics for granted for too long in our consumer society. Physical computing brings the fun, creativity, and problem solving of electronics back into the lives of kids.

There is no reason to be afraid of being electrocuted while tinkering with Arduino or Raspberry Pi! They use a maximum of 9 volts. You should, however, be careful around electrical outlets, sharp tools, and soldering irons.

Kits are a great place to start your Arduino adventures, because frankly, there are not enough electronics books written for children (and teachers) that are visually attractive, clear, and intended to support tinkering. We recommend a few of our favorite electronics books that should be in your library, but more kid-friendly texts are needed. The Web is filled with tips, tricks, reference manuals, and tutorial videos, but there is nothing quite like curling up with a good book. eBook versions are quite handy to have in your workspace while tinkering, too. They take up little space, lie flat, and pages are easily turned with a swipe.

Kits allow you to learn about Arduino and physical computing through direct experience. Kits also ensure that you have all of the needed bits and pieces to get started creating Arduino-powered projects. It won't take long before working with resistors, LEDs, switches, sensors, potentiometers, motors, and microcontrollers becomes second nature. Once you have some experience with the training wheels that kits provide, it's time to go freestyle!

Getting To Know the Arduino

Arduino is constantly evolving and there are lots of different compatible microcontroller boards on the market. However, most of those boards share the same features, including:

- A USB port for connecting to the computer
- A power supply for connecting to a battery pack or AC power source
- A voltage regulator to serve the Arduino with the correct amount of electricity
- The microprocessor chip containing the Arduino's operating system and non-volatile RAM for storing your programs, even when the board is turned off.
- A reset button
- One each 3.5 volt, 5 volt, 9 volt, and ground power connections
- 14 digital input/output pins (pins 0–13) that may be used either as inputs or outputs, depending on your sketch
- 6 analog input pins (pins 0–5) used to receive a range of values from 0–1023
- 6 analog output pins (pins 3, 5, 6, 9, 10, and 11) programmed by your sketch

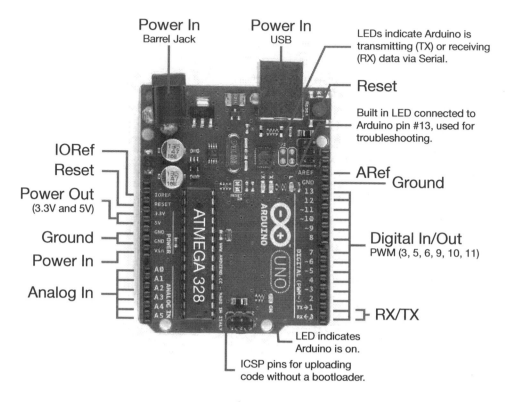

Power In
Barrel Jack

Power In
USB

LEDs indicate Arduino is
transmitting (TX) or receiving
(RX) data via Serial.

Reset

Built in LED connected to
Arduino pin #13, used for
troubleshooting.

IORef
Reset
Power Out
(3.3V and 5V)
Ground
Power In
Analog In

AREf Ground

Digital In/Out
PWM (3, 5, 6, 9, 10, 11)

RX/TX

LED indicates
Arduino is on.

ICSP pins for uploading
code without a bootloader.

Arduino Uno

You can plug wires or even LEDs directly into ports. It may be possible to burn out an LED if it is connected to a pin sending out too much voltage. This is not typically dangerous, but still annoying. The short leg of an LED is negative and connected to ground (labeled GND) while the long leg is positive and connected to one of the other ports. Pin 13 contains a resistor limiting its voltage to 5 volts, perfectly safe for most LEDs.

The breadboard becomes handy when you need to connect components that don't reach the pins on the Arduino or will cross over one another in potentially confusing or short-circuiting ways.

Some Handy Definitions

Motor – An electronic device that transfers electrical energy into rotational energy by spinning a shaft that may be connected to gears, pulleys, or belts to do work. You can turn the motor on, off, and usually control its rotational speed, but not with great precision.

Servo Motor – A motor that may be precisely controlled with pulses of electricity equivalent to specific motion or speed. In other words, servo motors are more accurate if you wish to turn by a specific fractional rotation or maintain a specific speed.

Sensors – Electronic circuits that provide feedback to the microcontroller. Common sensors give machines "senses" like touch, sight, hearing, or determining the temperature. The combination of sophisticated sensors and software programs allows machines to behave more "intelligently," and seemingly make decisions while interacting with the world outside of the computer.

Sensors are divided into two categories: analog and digital. Some sensors are digital and report only two values: True/False, On/Off, or in the parlance of Arduino, Low/High. Analog sensors report a numerical range via tiny variances in voltage. A light switch is a digital sensor as is the button in your snooze alarm. The temperature sensor in your thermostat is analog. The volume control on your stereo is analog. As you turn the potentiometer, a value is sent to the stereo telling it how to adjust the volume.

Shield – A special purpose circuit board that adds functionality to the Arduino by snapping into it. This eliminates the need for soldering, even to perform many complex tasks. Shields may be stacked one on top of another when necessary.

IDE – An abbreviation for Integrated Design Environment or Integrated Development Environment. The IDE is a software tool that creates the on-screen interface you will use to program the Arduino. In the IDE, you write sketches in a version of the C programming language, borrow code libraries to use in your project, debug, and compile your programs for use by the Arduino.

Sketch – The term used to describe an Arduino project created in the IDE.

Programming the Arduino

The first thing you need to do is download and install the IDE for your personal computer (Mac/Windows/Linux). The IDE is the programming interface you will use to run, write, and save the Arduino programs you write. In the world of Arduino, those programs are called sketches. Write the program, click the upload button, and your program is now compiled into the machine code used by the Arduino. If programmed correctly, it should perform as you expected. If you receive an error message or the Arduino misbehaves, it's time for some debugging.

Sketches are written in a version of the C programming language. C is finicky about punctuation, capitalization, and formatting. That's why it is a good idea to start by experimenting with other people's sketches or installing "libraries," the pieces of code that already perform a series of functions. Read those sketches, run the programs, make modifications, and observe the changes in your machine's behavior. The Arduino website offers lots of step-by-step tutorials for simple projects to get you started. We highly recommend that you buy a copy of the book, *Programming Arduino: Getting Started with Sketches* by Simon Monk. (Monk, 2012) This inexpensive book is a priceless resource we can't live without.

One online discussion suggested that if you or a student is really interested in learning more about C programming, get a copy of the oldest, cheapest C programming text you can find. You don't want a new book or one on C++ programming since the C used in Arduino programming is fairly primitive. Don't forget to join online communities or local user groups to find people who can help you along your learning path.

Modkit

Former MIT Media Lab students concerned with supporting childhood programming and engineering have created Modkit, an iconic programming environment for controlling Arduino, Lilypad, and a number of other popular microcontrollers. Modkit (http://modk.it) offers a snap-together interface familiar to anyone who has used the Scratch programming language. Robotics is a perfect application for iconic programming languages since programs tend to be concise.

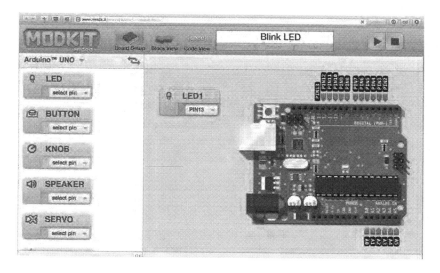

Modkit microcontroller selection interface

The genius of Modkit is that you select the microcontroller you are using in a graphical fashion without having to worry about port specifications. The snap-together blocks make it easy to write programs that have a high probability of working as you intended. Modkit also lets you toggle back and forth between the graphical block program and the C code it creates. This may not only aid the debugging process, but also provide a transition to the standard IDE for beginners.

Modkit offers a desktop version for desktop computers and laptops (Mac/Windows/Linux) for a fee, and a free browser-based version that runs right in your favorite Web browser. Tutorials and activities are designed with learners in mind and there is a commitment to supporting new hardware as it becomes available. Modkit may be the best friend Arduino (and you) have ever had.

Using the free browser-based version means your students will always be using the most recent version of the software. However, it increases your dependence on the Internet, and you may spend more time dealing with logins and passwords. At the time of publication, cloud storage for projects was being released.

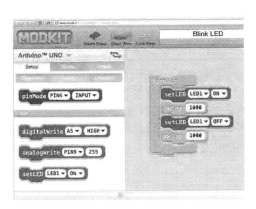

Modkit program to flash an LED   Arduino program in the IDE to flash an LED

Wearable Computing

Imagine making a sweatshirt with turn signals sewn into the back that flash while peddling your bike home from school, a backpack that detects intruders, or a T-shirt with LEDs that dance in a pattern that you've choreographed. What was science fiction a few years ago is now a classroom project.

Lilypad is a variation of Arduino, specially designed to be used in clothing and other textile objects. Designed by Leah Buechley at the MIT Media Lab, the board is machine washable and flexible. Sewing with conductive thread, rather than wire, creates circuits. Lilypad works with switches, sensors, lights, buzzers, battery holders, and other electronic components used with traditional Arduino microcontrollers. Smaller, flatter, sewable versions of these components are also available from the companies selling Lilypad. One major difference between Arduino and Lilypad is that Lilypad does not have a USB interface built-in. An FTDi connector is used to connect the Lilypad board to a USB cable from the computer.

Lilypad is programmed in the same way as Arduino, via the Arduino C IDE or alternative software like Modkit. Lilypad kits are a great way to get started with all of the bits and pieces you need.

Lilypad http://www.arduino.cc/en/Main/ArduinoBoardLilyPad

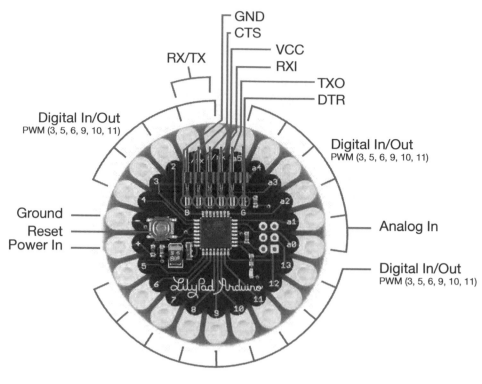

Lilypad Arduino

In 2013, Adafruit Industries released **Flora**, the next generation in wearable computing construction materials. Flora is quite similar to Lilypad, but is smaller, has built-in USB, and can control up to 4,000 chainable LEDs and even a tiny GPS module. Imagine your jacket lighting up as you approach the Apple Store, or alerting you that you only have another mile to run during your workout!

The Flora board itself is quite attractive. Adafruit sells a magnetic back for the Flora that can turn it into a piece of interactive jewelry.

Oh No You Didn't!

While doing the research for this chapter, a new microcontroller called PCDuino hit the market. PCDuino costs $60, promises more power than Arduino, and can run Linux or Android operating systems. PCDuino may be the greatest thing since sliced bread, but rest assured that tomorrow there will be an even better microcontroller available. That's the very nature of technology. Get used to it and get busy with the materials you have. A little microcontroller, even a slightly older one, can go a very long way and power exciting projects.

The DIY, reuse, and recycling values of the maker movement urge you to squeeze every last drop out of the technology you already have.

Where to Start With Arduino

The Arduino website has information you need to get started, including instructions for beginners, software downloads, lists of where to buy parts and kits around the world, and a community forum to meet other Arduino users. These forums are very useful and you can find answers to a lot of questions just by looking through the archives. Almost all of the online stores that sell Arduino also have project ideas and tutorials. http://www.arduino.cc/

Arduino Project Collections

Make Magazine Arduino – Videos, project ideas, how-tos, kits, parts, and blog posts about what people are doing around the world with the Arduino. http://blog.makezine.com/arduino/

Super Awesome Sylvia's Simple Arduino Projects – 11-year-old Super Awesome Sylvia presents video tutorials for two simple Arduino projects. http://sylviashow.com/episodes/s1/e3/full/arduino

Instructables – This site offers a number of Arduino projects at varying levels of complexity. http://www.instructables.com/id/Arduino-Projects/

Arduino Books

Programming Arduino: Getting Started with Sketches by Simon Monk

Getting Started with Arduino by Massimo Banzi

OTHER PHYSICAL COMPUTING OPTIONS

MaKey MaKey

The MaKey MaKey, an "invention kit for everyone," should be a part of any tinkering classroom. http://www.makeymakey.com/

MaKey MaKey creates a simple alligator clip-based interface between the computer and everyday objects. It plugs into the USB port of any computer, even a Raspberry Pi, and turns household objects into a keyboard or joystick. Play a piano made of bananas, a drum solo on your best friend's head, a xylophone made of flowers, or a video game with a controller made of paper and Play-Doh. The MaKey MaKey simplifies the input so you don't have to worry about resistance or capacitance – just attach the alligator clips to any real world object.

The "neat phenomena" and playfulness of the MaKey MaKey makes it a great introduction to physical computing prior to tackling Raspberry Pi or Arduino.

Professor Marvin Minsky and MaKey MaKey inventor Eric Rosenbaum use cupcakes as a computer interface at Constructing Modern Knowledge 2012

Fun With Electronics

You and your students can enjoy making things with electronics, even when the projects don't use a computer. Learning your way around a circuit board and developing soldering skills will pay big dividends in other projects. Here are three popular and inexpensive kits any fourth grader can tackle with adult supervision. All three are available from adafruit.com.

Drawdio allows you to turn a pencil into a simple music synthesizer. You can play music while you write!

Minty Boost is a small kit that lets you create a battery-powered cellphone charger that fits inside a tiny gum tin. The kit doesn't come with the tins, so you might wish to purchase those too.

TV-B-Gone is a tiny contraption that turns off (or back on) any television in your vicinity. This has serious mischief potential and can make your colleagues want to kill you, but kids love it and learn a bit about electronics too (before being chased from the mall).

Why Physical Computing for Learning?

Chris Champion, a Computer Science teacher at Cumberland Perry Area Vocational Technical School in Mechanicsburg, Pennsylvania says:

> One of the challenges I face at a vocational school is that many times, students who are deemed "not college prep" are sent to me – yet I teach college prep-level material. One of the most challenging things to teach a student who doesn't have good math or writing skills is programming. Programming is pretty much full of math and writing – it's a foreign language with a dose of algebra. For years I would struggle with a subset of kids who traditionally didn't do well at "theoretical" learning, but who excelled at hands-on tasks. When it came time to learn how to program, their grades went over a cliff.
>
> Then I learned about programmable robotics. For a few hundred dollars, I could get a LEGO robot with a robust, Carnegie Mellon Robotics designed C programming environment. I tried it with my students and it broke through the "what does it mean?" barrier because they could see the physical manifestation of their programs.
>
> This year I added Adafruit's Arduino ARDX kit for the same reason, and I've had incredible results. I'll give you one example. Michael (not his real name) came to me with delayed learning problems – specifically math. Once I had a discussion about buying things in the store and he said that he couldn't add all of the items up in his head, so when he got to the register, he often had to leave items behind because he didn't bring enough money. Michael struggled when we got to writing programming code. Simple "less than" or "greater than" comparisons confused him. The final programming project (a point of sale computer program) was beyond his ability. He got lots of help from me and the special education aide, but frankly, he often just waited to be told the right answer.
>
> However, when I put an Arduino in Michael's hand it was different. He could see the results of his program and correct it to meet the assignment's specification. For instance, I asked students to create a rubber band shooter using a ruler and a hobby servo. The servo was programmed to slowly move to the arming position (a programming loop that runs from "center" 90 degrees to 0 degrees), pause for 3,000 milliseconds (3 seconds) to allow the human operator to load it, then rapidly move to fire the rubber band (move from 0 to 180 degrees). He grasped it rapidly, especially since extra points were assigned if a student could hit me at my desk with the rubber band.
>
> I'm sure Michael's geometry teacher had concluded that he could not determine angles and would be astounded to see Michael use angles accurately and deliberately in the physical world. But it wasn't nearly as hard as if I had asked him to write an angle on paper. It was just intuitive.

A Bazillion Robotics Prompts

- Plan and construct a city of the future including robotic elements.
- Construct and give behaviors to a robotic animal.
- Build and program a robot to write your name.
- Construct and choreograph a robotic ballerina.
- Invent a machine that can paint a picture. **Extreme Challenge:** Can you make your paintings reproducible? In other words, can the machine make a similar painting over and over again?
- Build and program a robotic athlete to kick, throw, or bat an object. **Extreme Challenge:** Create a robotic defense or score-keeping goal!
- Construct and perform a machine to do a chore you dislike doing.
- Bring a stuffed animal to life with robotic components. **Extreme Challenge:** Make the creature dance and/or sing.
- Construct and program a supermarket scanner.
- Build a robot toy factory.
- Build a bird feeder that will snap a photo of a bird when it comes to feed. **Extreme Challenge**: Alert a human after a photo has been taken.
- Invent a robotic musical instrument.
- Build a robot that can play a xylophone. It should not just bang keys, but also play a repeatable melody. **Extreme Challenge**: Add additional percussion instruments to your robot orchestra.
- Construct a machine to send or receive Morse code.
- Build a better robotic "smart" mousetrap.
- Organize a robot truck or tractor pull. How much can your machine lift, push, or pull?
- Create robot sumo wrestlers.
- Build a machine to play a vinyl record. There should be some sort of comprehensible sound uttered by the machine. A variation could be a machine that simulates playing a CD.
- Construct the world's slowest vehicle.
- Construct a machine to climb a hill.
- Construct a machine that will blow soap bubbles. **Extreme Challenge:** Can you make the bubble machine mobile?
- Build a machine that will deal a hand of cards. **Extreme Challenge:** Program the machine to play blackjack or another card game against a human opponent. You may wish to use some sort of code on the back to mark each card.
- Design a kinetic sculpture with robotic elements.
- Build a system that will automatically deliver luggage to two different planes, represented by either different color LEGO bricks, or by barcodes on the sides of the bricks. **Extreme Challenge:** Delivering luggage to four, six, eight, or 92 different planes is even better!
- Design, construct, and program a house of the future.

- In the fall of 1999, the Coca-Cola company announced that they would be commercially testing a soda machine that would charge thirsty patrons more for a can on a hot day than on a cold day. Build a temperature-sensitive vending machine that charges the user more money on a hot day. **Extreme Challenge:** Total the value of coins deposited and store them inside the machine.
- Monitor the behavior of a mouse, gerbil, or hamster using robotic elements.
- Construct a robotic dog-walking machine.
- Build a robot that will pour a drink.
- Invent a new robotic vending machine. **Extreme Challenge:** Program the machine to dispense a precise quantity of M&Ms or gumballs when a coin is deposited. Can your machine make change?
- Build and program a robot slot machine or other game of chance.
- Construct a robotic toll collector.
- Build and program a fax machine.
- Control or monitor a science experiment with a robotic lab assistant.
- Build a chairlift, cable car, or gondola capable of pulling itself along a string. **Extreme Challenge**: Program the machine to drop a paratrooper when instructed by your homemade remote control.
- Build a vehicle that will climb to the top of the steepest possible incline and then automatically roll down the incline without falling. **Extreme Challenge**: Design the vehicle to turn before it heads back down the ramp.
- Build a robot creature that follows a flashlight or goes towards the lightest part of a room. You might try to make another vehicle that runs away from light or one that goes towards a beacon being sent by another robot (perhaps a game of tag). **Extreme Challenge**: Find a way to solve the problem of the robot finding an obstacle between itself and the light source.
- Design a can holder that alerts you when your drink gets unacceptably warm.
- Invent something never thought of before!

PROGRAMMING

> Too many of the computing devices a child will interact with daily are so locked down that they can't be used creatively as a tool... Try using your iPhone to act as the brains of a robot, or getting your PS3 to play a game you've written. – Eben Upton

The computer is perhaps the most important invention of the 20th century. In the 21st century, children do not know a world without computers. Yet today, programming computers still finds little acceptance in schools. If there is a programming class, it is too often reserved for a small minority of students at the end of their high school careers. 90% of American schools do not teach programming, and only nine states consider computer science a legitimate math or science course. (Code.org)

Computer science is one of the jewels of human ingenuity. It is a legitimate branch of science that has influenced nearly every aspect of daily life over the past half-century. This field allows us to solve problems, communicate, create, and invent in ways impossible for much of recorded history. Computer science is dependent on one's ability to program the computer – to teach a machine to do what it doesn't already know how to do.

Learning to program a computer is an act of intellectual mastery that empowers children and teaches them that they have control of a piece of powerful technology. Students quickly learn that *they* are the most important part of the computer program. The computer is really quite dumb unless you tell it what to do in a precise fashion the machine understands.

> Programming a computer means nothing more or less than communicating to it in a language that it and the human user can both "understand." And learning languages is one of the things children do best. Every normal child learns to talk. Why then should a child not learn to "talk" to a computer? – Seymour Papert, *Mindstorms* (Papert, 1980)

Like in many science and math courses, students rarely get to experience the art of the discipline. School computer science courses with an emphasis on memorizing sorting routines and recreating programs one can easily download from the Web are no exception. The art, beauty, and power of computer science eludes most children without rich programming experiences.

Poor school computer science experiences would be bad enough, but most students have no such opportunities at all. This disempowers learners by depriving them of agency over the technology so central to their lives and narrows their career options. Computer science is a pathway to a plethora of career options that extend well beyond obvious high-tech jobs.

Despite a dystopian depiction of social isolation and inaccessibility in the popular culture, all children should enjoy computer science experiences. It is simply unacceptable to celebrate the occasional kid who makes a fortune programming an iPhone app when his classmates are relegated to keyboarding instruction. Communicating a formal idea to the computer is also a powerful way to think about thinking. Debugging, meaning eliminating a "bug" (error) or overcoming an obstacle in a computer program, develops habits of mind and systemic thinking skills beneficial for a lifetime.

If mathematics is the language of science, then computer programming is a great way to construct mathematical understanding. Much of the typical school math curriculum has little relevant context in the real world while exciting new branches of mathematics, including fractals, number theory, chaos, and topography are dependent on computing.

Computer Science – Gary

In 1975, the junior high school I went to taught every seventh grader, including me, how to program. It now only expects 12-year-old children to identify the space bar and return key. This is clearly a lowering of standards.

In high school just a few years later, I took a course imaginatively titled, "Algebra II with Computer Programming." The course used the same textbook as other Algebra II classes, but we wrote computer programs to help solve the assigned problems. Such a "radical" course is impossible to find 35 years later, despite the ubiquity of computers.

In the late 1980s, the education community stopped speaking of computing as a verb and shifted emphasis towards "technology" as a far less specific subject of study. This shift requires less of teachers and pays fewer dividends for learners. Replacing computing fluency with computer literacy is like sacrificing orchestra for music appreciation.

Things were not always so bleak. For the first decade or so of the PC, computer owners were programmers too. There were hundreds of thousands of hobbyist programmers in the United States alone. Steve Jobs and Steve Wozniak, the founders of Apple Computer, were two of them. Over time, the growth of the consumer software industry and more user-friendly operating systems dwarfed amateur computer programming with more passive computer use. But today, new languages, new options for microprocessors, and new places to share work have revitalized programming as something within the reach of everyone. Like other aspects of the maker movement, computer programming has been given new life.

Through the 1980s, education publications, books, and conferences taught hundreds of thousands of teachers to teach programming to children. Magazines such as *Creative Computing, Compute,* and *Byte* catered to the interests of hobbyist programmers. "Hobbyist programmer" might sound oxymoronic to folks with no programming experience. Yet, like any good hobby, programming can be rewarding, continuously challenging, and fun. The better you get at programming, the more challenges await.

We used to tell teachers, "Computers should be used transparently across the curriculum, and formal computer science opportunities should be available for those students who desire it." Today, we believe that and more. The transparent use of computers across the curriculum is inseparable from the responsibility of teaching computer science K–12 to every child by every teacher. Maximum agency over the computer is critical for modern knowledge construction.

In 2012, the UK government announced that their national ICT (information and communication technology) curriculum was being scrapped because it is "harmful and dull" and recommended that it be replaced by computer science K–12. This followed Google Chairman Eric Schmidt castigating the British school system for not teaching computer science. In recent days, President Obama, Mark Zuckerberg, and Microsoft have all advocated for kids to learn "coding." Although there are few specifics to be found in these proclamations, progress may be on the horizon.

Programming is the nervous system of the maker revolution. Not only can new virtual products be invented, but programming is required to bring life and intelligence to the physical artifacts a tinkerer or engineer makes.

Math and Video Game Programming – Sylvia

When I was in charge of video game development at a game publishing company, I hired many programmers who didn't have computer science degrees. Now, there are arguments about whether having a computer science degree is essential to be a great programmer, but in my experience, many programmers never had the chance to make that decision. Many of them had been told that they were "bad at math" and had been steadily placed in lower and lower-level math classes until they simply gave up. More than a few dropped out of high school because there was nothing that interested them at school. Many had already found their passion in programming video games and taught themselves at home. Often, as I listened to intense conversations about the complex mathematical problems that need to be solved in developing high-end video games, I would wonder why school systems had the need to label kids with deficiencies. These programmers were obviously not "bad at math" as long as the kind of math involved played into their passions.

Programming Projects

The quality and sophistication of your students' programming projects will be highly dependent on the language they use, their age, and the time devoted to programming. It may take several iterations of projects to become proficient at guiding students to successful programming projects.

There are many resources to help narrow down the list of potential projects that students can choose. Use the recommendations for project planning found in the Projects chapter and focus on developing some good prompts for students. Explore the programming challenges and project ideas found on the websites that support your programming language. Try to move away from the pre-planned tutorials as quickly as possible. Some students will work on tutorials permanently as a way to stay in a comfort zone.

Students often focus on programming games or interactive stories, but also encourage students to find ways to solve simple problems using programming. Math problems, codebreaking, or art projects can also be good programming projects.

It is difficult to include a detailed list of programming project ideas since they are quite specific to the language you use. While Scratch is good at animation and video game programming, it's not as strong at data manipulation, text, or mathematics. MicroWorlds excels at user interaction, word and list processing, and complex computation, but is not very good at sharing via the Web. Text-based languages are better for longer, more complex programs. Block-based icon languages are great for robotics where programs tend to be shorter and less text-intensive.

As you gain experience with a language, you will be better able to judge your student project ideas and help your students tackle the parts of their ideas that are achievable. This takes time and experience with the language.

Programming in the Curriculum

Some of you may be thinking, "All of this talk of invention and robots and wearable computers is fine and dandy, but I have a curriculum to cover." Although teachers have more flexibility in how curriculum is "covered" than some like to admit, you are indeed responsible for students learning specific things. Making, tinkering, and engineering can lead to greater understanding of traditional topics too.

For example, take fractions (please)! Fractions are taught to kids all over the world, often over multiple years and with great disparity in achievement. Fractions are one of the things we teach kids over and over again, yet they don't stay taught. Idit Harel-Caperton's American Educational Research Association award-winning research demonstrated that if you ask fourth graders to program a computer "game" to teach younger children fractions, the programmers gain a much deeper understanding of fractions, plus a host of other skills, than children who were taught fractions in a more traditional fashion. (Harel, 1991)

Asking 10-year-olds to write a computer program that represents any fraction as a part of a circle leads to a greater understanding of fractions, as well as a working knowledge of variables, division, the geometry of a circle, and the knowledge that comes from engineering and debugging.

Devoting several class periods to one project may be much more efficient than spending several years of instruction on the same topic.

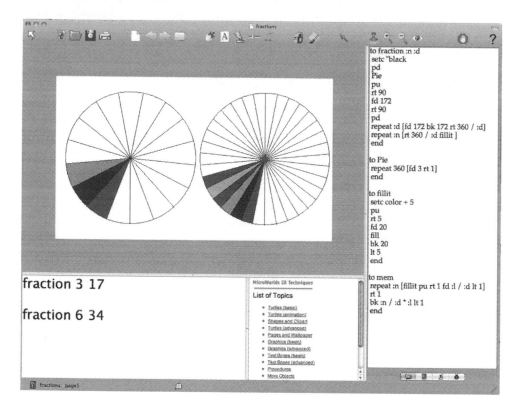

Fraction program written by 4th graders in Logo using MicroWorlds (LCSI)

A seventh grade girl completing an assignment to write a program to solve a linear equation will come to understand the math topic, perhaps better or quicker because she was able to add computer graphics or an animated story or musical composition to her program. Programming supports a range of expression and learning styles. Therefore, a willingness to engage with someone else's assignment may become more palatable when motivated to do so in your own voice.

Look for opportunities to enhance even the most traditional school subjects in the spirit of making. This approach may be a more efficient way of ensuring understanding and lead to learning outcomes that exceed your curricular expectations.

Choosing a Language

Educators interested in teaching programming need to select a language. Programming languages differ in their structure, user interface, grammar, syntax, and functionality. Some languages are created to perform a narrow range of tasks while general-purpose languages offer more extensive opportunities for messing about with ideas and personal expression.

There is something to learn while using any programming language, although some of that learning may be accidental or tied to navigating the particular language. Many programming languages were invented for the purpose of getting work done. Some programming languages were created for children to use and focus on product creation, such as simple video games or controlling LEGO. Other programming languages place a greater emphasis on process rather than product and were designed to provide deliberate learning experiences for the child engaged in programming.

There are even programming languages appropriate for 5-year-olds. Like any written or spoken language, the permutations of a programing language are infinite. The best programming languages support both "baby talk" and the expression of complex ideas. Words combine to become poetry.

Don't assume that simple programming languages teach less or are only for younger students. Logo programming is an excellent example of "less is more." With only a couple of commands, like Forward and Right, a child can program the computer to draw absolutely anything. Complexity may be composed of simple elements, and engineering is about solving problems within constraints. We add confusion and reduce learning opportunities when we teach intricacies of the software to children at the expense of the time required to become proficient programmers.

We recommend you choose one language and stick with it. Programming fluency is developed over time. Students will gain much more proficiency and confidence if they are able to grow with one language. Don't worry about "covering" programming. The big ideas of computer programming are consistent across languages.

Unless you are teaching a job-training course there is no reason to select a programming language based on the idea that it is used in industry. You should choose a language that satisfies your educational objectives or works with the peripherals (robots, printers, etc.) your students need to control.

The choice of programming language is wrought with tradeoffs and new languages emerge all of the time. Therefore, we will just discuss a few of the most popular options in this chapter. Pick one and get started!

Logo

Logo is distinct from other programming languages in that it was designed for learning. For over 40 years, a great deal of research has led to insights into how best to design a programming language capable of creating artifacts attractive to youngsters while leading them to explore powerful ideas in the process. While versions of Logo have evolved over the decades to keep pace with technological advances, the structure and principles of the language remain consistent with its roots.

Seymour Papert, Cynthia Solomon, and Wally Feurzeig developed Logo at the Cambridge, Massachusetts research lab – Bolt, Baranek, and Newman – and raised it since infancy at MIT. Logo is a dialect of LISP (list processing), the language of artificial intelligence research for 50 years. The goal was to create a computer programming language that would allow children to be immersed in a "mathland" where one would learn math naturally through use, just as a child growing up in France learns French. Early versions of Logo focused on manipulation of words, lists, and numbers since graphical computer displays were in their infancy and programming required teletypes connected to remote mainframe computers. Despite these limitations, Alan Kay was so excited by the mathematics he saw young children engaged in during a 1968 visit to Papert at MIT that, on his flight home, he sketched the "dynabook," the prototype for modern laptops and tablet computers. Kay viewed the "personal" computer first and foremost as a child's machine.

Cynthia Solomon teaching Logo programming (1971)

Logo is a procedural language in which students combine commands and operations into procedures they name. Naming is incredibly important in that programs are created in the same way a human develops language. New words are defined based on combining existing ones created by the user or the primitives built into the language. The computer only "runs" the "words" or procedures it already knows. Variables may be named with words that connote their function. You call things X and Y in math class because it's a pain to handwrite *length* and *width*. That is not a problem while typing or interconnecting blocks, so a level of abstraction associated with variable is eliminated.

Not long after the invention of Logo, a robot that looked like a small trash can on wheels was added to the system, tethered via cable to the computer. This "turtle" could be placed on a large sheet of paper and given instructions for moving about on the floor with a pen in its center that could be raised and lowered to leave a trail.

The turtle moved about in space like a child does, and through formal commands could draw on sheets of paper placed under the robot. Children could "play turtle" and practice giving each other commands to follow, such as "forward," "back," "right," and "left." Doing so and correcting the bugs in their drawings led to the construction of powerful mathematical ideas. The turtle concretized abstract concepts of number, measurement, angle, and much more. When graphical displays became widely available, the turtle left 3D space and became a triangle on the screen that could be commanded to move and draw like it did on the floor.

Logo soon became synonymous with "turtle geometry" as microcomputers entered schools in the early 1980s. Every new computer system had its own version of Logo. In fact, Apple Logo was the first licensed and bundled software, quickly followed by Atari Logo. For several years, schools could not purchase a microcomputer without Logo on it and as a result, countless teachers taught Logo at every grade level. Over 100 Logo books for educators were published and some sold extraordinarily well.

As computers gained processing power and memory, some Logo variations featured multiple turtles that could be dressed in customizable costumes and used in animation projects as well as for drawing. These turtles, or sprites, not only had linear motion, but they could be given velocity as well. This added aspects of physics as an "object to think with" to turtle geometry.

In 1986, LogoWriter added word processing to the programming environment and four customizable turtles to the system. This allowed students to tell digital stories complete with animation and create simple video games for the first time. One year later, the LEGO TC Logo was released, allowing children to build and program their own robotic creations. When LogoWriter and LEGO TC Logo were combined, student projects could live on and off the screen at the same time. The widespread adoption of graphical user interfaces and digital media led to MicroWorlds in 1993. MicroWorlds had a theoretically unlimited number of customizable turtles and an ability to control media elements with the same ease that one moved the turtle. In 1990, schools embraced 1:1 laptop computing for the first time, primarily as a way of using LogoWriter and then MicroWorlds across the curriculum in a way that produced maximum benefit for children.

Things had come full circle. The children's machine was at long last a reality and it was a computer for using Logo. Logo makes simple things easy to do, but more importantly, it makes complexity possible. Such complexity was only realized if students had the time and flexibility required to develop fluency – to make their computer dance by amplifying their individual potential.

The late 1990s saw the arrival of free Logo versions designed for more specialized purposes like modeling and simulation, including the massively parallel StarLogo and NetLogo. Berkeley Logo and MSWLogo were also free, but were more traditional general-purpose versions of Logo focused on turtle graphics, usually with one turtle, and list processing. Then Logo development went in an entirely new direction with the creation of Scratch.

Scratch is an open source dialect of Logo that borrowed the turtle animation functionality from its cousin MicroWorlds, replaced text-based programming with snap-together blocks, and made Web-based collaboration, sharing, and "remixing" of projects simple. Kids use it to tell animated stories, create music videos, and design video games.

By design, Scratch is limited in functionality. The software environment was intended for students to learn at home or in afterschool clubhouses without expert teacher intervention. Adding too much functionality to the system would be the ruin of Scratch. To date, more than three million projects are shared on the Scratch website.

If kids are programming in Scratch at home, teachers should leverage their skills and seize upon the opportunity to teach more sophisticated computer science concepts.

The Logo language is much more than turtle geometry. It is incredibly powerful and suitable for a wide range of projects. Like a real language, Logo is not just for children, but is usable for a lifetime. Logo is a programming language with a "low threshold" (easy to learn) but a "high ceiling" (powerful when you gain fluency). Student fluency with the language takes time and deserves more than to be treated as a novelty covered quickly in an overstuffed technology curriculum.

Logo offers learners a powerful intellectual laboratory and vehicle for self-expression. It provides teachers with a catalyst for rethinking the nature of teaching and learning. Logo is an object to think with, both for the learner and for the people who are thinking about the thinking of the learner. By making thinking visible, Logo inspires teachers who gain a greater insight into the minds of their students while observing the thought processes used while programming and evaluating the artifacts created.

Logo Variations

Logo Computer Systems, Inc. is a company founded by Seymour Papert that has designed and published the majority of Logo versions available since the advent of microcomputers. **MicroWorlds EX** (Mac and Windows) is commercial software that may be purchased as a cost-effective site license (an invention of LCSI back in the 1980s). Kids may also purchase the software for home use. MicroWorlds may be the most full-featured version of Logo available today and is the personal favorite of Gary who has been involved in its development over the years.

MicroWorlds features unlimited turtles, a robust programming language complete with words, lists and multiple variable types, painting tools, animation, multimedia integration, online help, tutorials, and sample projects to deconstruct. You program MicroWorlds through text, although simple animations may be created with the mouse. MicroWorlds is great for storytelling, math and science simulations, modeling, geometry, text manipulation, and game design. It supports a wide variety of learning styles and programming strategies. Problems can often be solved in many ways at any age. http://microworlds.com

MicroWorlds EX Robotics, also from LCSI, allows tethered control of the LEGO NxT materials. If you're serious about teaching computer programming or exploring powerful mathematical ideas, MicroWorlds will not disappoint. Its only major weakness is that it does not play well with the Web like Scratch does.

MicroWorlds is used around the world, particularly in Latin America, and is available in several languages.

StarLogo, **StarLogo TNG** (The Next Generation), and **NetLogo** are all free cross-platform massively parallel versions of Logo intended for complex systems modeling, simulations, and problem solving. StarLogo TNG features elements for the creation of games, 3D graphics, and virtual worlds. NetLogo focuses more heavily on mathematical explorations and scientific simulations that may be run on computers across the globe. Each has a large library of projects you can download and remix.

StarLogo http://education.mit.edu/starlogo/

StarLogo TNG http://education.mit.edu/projects/starlogo-tng

NetLogo http://ccl.northwestern.edu/netlogo/

Scratch (Mac and Windows) was developed by the MIT Media Lab and is hands-down the most popular programming language ever created for kids. It's free, features multiple turtles for turtle geometry, supports digital media integration, and projects may be published on the Web with the click of a mouse. Once published, other users may explore your creations, borrow some code or a cool sprite for use in their project, or remix the project. Scratch even keeps track of where each idea in a project came from so that authors are credited for their efforts. A user can create a program in one of more than a dozen languages and share it on the secure and supervised Scratch website, and a kid in another part of the world can download the project and read its programs in their native language, which has been automatically translated for them. That's right, download a project created in Hebrew, improve upon it in English, and share it with a friend in Japan.

Scratch also may be used to program LEGO's early childhood robotics set called WeDo. Plug the WeDo into your computer, boot Scratch, and new blocks appear for robotics control.

The new version of Scratch (2.0) to be released around the time of this book's publication allows users to interact via gestures by using a laptop's camera or the Xbox Kinect. Scratch 2.0 projects will be able to be created, run, and edited on any Flash-capable device.

The simplicity of Scratch also reduces the range of projects it makes possible. It is not as strong as MicroWorlds for teaching mathematics or for dealing with text. You may also grow tired of programming by clicking and dragging the mouse and having your projects confined to a small "stage."

Scratch website: Download Scratch and explore projects
http://scratch.mit.edu

WeDo programming and Scratch: http://info.scratch.mit.edu/WeDo

Scratch educators: Teachers of Scratch may find camaraderie, assistance, and project ideas at the ScratchEd website. http://scratched.media.mit.edu/

Scratch Variations

The popularity, openess, and ease of use of Scratch has led others to create new versions with specific functionality added. Note that in order to avoid confusion with the "official" version of Scratch, projects created in these Scratch flavors cannot be shared on the Scratch website (at this time).

S4A (Scratch for Arduino) is just like its name suggests – a block-based version of Scratch intended for programming and controlling an Arduino microcontroller. S4A requires that the machine you invent be connected, or tethered, to the computer, at least for now. In the long run, ModKit may be a better option. http://seaside.citilab.eu/scratch/arduino

Snap! (formerly called BYOB) is Scratch with first-class objects added to make more complex programming projects possible. It was created by veteran Logo creator and educator, Brian Harvey, to be used in his Beauty and Joy of Computing (BJC) course at UC Berkeley, and is becoming increasingly popular in high school computer science courses.

One strength of Snap! is that it is clever enough to run on a Mac, PC, Android device, *and* iPad. Unfortunately, projects may not be shared via the Scratch website (at this time). http://bjc.berkeley.edu/

Enchanting (Mac, Windows, Linux) is a version of Snap! that allows users to program LEGO's popular NxT robotics elements in a "Logo-like" fashion. http://enchanting.robotclub.ab.ca/

Turtle Art (Mac and Windows) is a programming language intended to create beautiful images. It was created by Artemis Papert (Seymour Papert's daughter) and Brian Silverman, who has had a hand in nearly every version of Logo created since the 1970s, including MicroWorlds and Scratch. Turtle Art uses block programming like Scratch, but there is only one turtle, no multimedia, and projects are focused on the creation of art through the use of mathematics. The genius of Turtle Art is that you can drag and drop an image from the Turtle Art website into the software and the static picture includes the blocks that created it. Borrow a block or two, remix a project, and when you save or email it to a friend, it looks like a normal graphics file in PNG format. Open that same file in the Turtle Art program and its blocks reappear!

Turtle Art allows you to build a piece of art from scratch or by reassembling someone else's "painting." Young children and adult artists alike are amazed by how easy it is to create beautiful images out of mathematics.

Turtle Art is free, but not open source. Its creators like to know who has the software and do not wish to spend their time providing technical support. If you would like a copy of the software to use with students, send an email to info@turtleart.org after you explore the website. http://turtleart.org

Other Programming Language Options

If you choose not to teach using one of these Logo variations, there are other options. These options are best if you have a background in these languages or a specific interest that they match.

Java is the language used in AP Computer Science courses, and therefore may have some advocates if this is a course taught at your school. For robotics, Java is not quite as universal as C and other C based programming languages, but there are numerous sites, code libraries, and books available to make different microcontrollers work with Java.

C++ is a language used widely in business and industry, and you may hear things like, "… we should teach C++ because it's a real programming language," or "…our kids will be prepared for jobs in the real world." We suggest you ignore such reasons. Even if you are a C++ wizard, it is not the best language for teaching a wide variety of students. It will be a stumbling block instead of helping them become articulate computer users. You may also hear that C++ is similar to the Arduino programming language, so you should teach C++ instead and get the best of both. However, we feel this adds unnecessary complications. If you are using Arduino you should start by teaching the Arduino programming language. You could also opt for Scratch for Arduino or ModKit, which combines both the Arduino and a Scratch-like graphical interface.

Processing is a free, open source language for programming visual images and animations. There are excellent teaching resources available and a vibrant online support community, which means there are regular bug fixes and updates. Processing is compatible with any platform and moderately easy to learn.

Erin Mumford Glenn, Upper School Technology Integrator at Friends Seminary in New York, uses Processing with 7th–12th graders.

> Processing gives you instant visual output, which is much more compelling to students than a text box that says "Hello World." Because graphics and animation are so easy to achieve, the product of the work students do (even early on) is commensurate with their effort. Additionally, the software is free and compatible with any platform, there is no compiling, and the feedback it gives makes it easy to troubleshoot – yet the syntax is so similar to Java that students will be well situated to move on to AP or to collegiate level courses. It's very similar to the software for Arduino as well.

> I like Processing because the students can get immediate results. It's also beautiful, and it connects to geometry and science in a way that supports the interest many of my students have in art and animation. My students have started creating simulations of principles of physics (incorporating variables for gravity, using momentum, and using oscillation/sine/cosine functions).

> I didn't have a lot of programming experience before I started teaching it. I had taken some introductory classes in high school and college, but I'm

completely self-taught in Processing; I picked it up the summer before I started teaching it.

Processing website Be sure to explore both the "learning" and "reference" tabs. http://processing.org

Learning Processing by Daniel Shiffman http://www.learningprocessing.com/

BASIC has been a language popular with beginning programmers since the 1970s. There are many different versions of BASIC available for various operating systems. Therefore, programs may not be completely compatible across systems and dialects. BASIC is an easy language to learn and can be used to perform a wide variety of tasks. Visual BASIC (now called Visual Studio) may be used to control or add functionality to Microsoft Windows and Office applications.

BASIC-256 Free, easy to use BASIC designed to teach programming. (Windows) http://www.basic256.org/index_en

Small BASIC Microsoft-supported free BASIC and tutorials. (Windows) http://msdn.microsoft.com/en-us/beginner/ff384126.aspx

Python is known for ease of use and clean, simple code. A growing chorus of makers advocate Python as a programming language. It is free and well supported by online user groups, libraries, project examples, and tutorials. Python is also a popular programming language on the Raspberry Pi.

Download Python (Mac, Windows & Linux) http://www.python.org/

Introduction to Python V2.1 (Free PDF e-book) By Mark Clarkson http://bit.ly/intropythonpdf

Other Programming Environments

There are a multitude of programming platforms and creativity tools that are highly programmable that you may consider using under certain circumstances. This is a short list of a few that are most appropriate for students in middle grades or above.

Squeak. Alan Kay and his colleagues at Xerox PARC began developing Squeak in the 1970s, yet it remains a modern marvel today. Squeak is a modern, open source, full-featured implementation of the powerful Smalltalk programming language and environment. Squeak is highly-portable, easy to debug, analyze, and change. Squeak is the vehicle for a wide range of projects including multimedia applications, educational platforms, and commercial Web application development. You might think of Squeak as a computer operating system and set of applications, all of which are fully programmable. Squeak runs on Mac, Windows and Linux platforms.

The Etoys software created in Squeak provides microworlds for kids to explore powerful mathematical and scientific concepts. Scratch itself was created in Squeak. Get it? Scratch and Squeak?

Squeak system http://www.squeak.org/

Etoys http://www.squeakland.org/

Flash is often used to create graphics and animations for websites, and has a programming language that can be used to control the animations and to make games. If your school has a license for the Adobe Creative Suite, you may already have Flash. However, Flash is complex and suitable mostly for high school students. You may lose a lot of students with Flash. http://www.adobe.com/flash

AgentSheets was introduced in 1991 and pioneered drag and drop visual programming for kids. AgentSheets is part of the Scalable Game Design project to teach young people around the world about computer science and science. In 2013, AgentCubes, a 3D version of AgentSheets, introduced the ability to create web-publishable 3D games. AgentSheets and AgentCubes are targeted for children around 10–15 years old. http://www.agentsheets.com/

In the early days of the Apple Macintosh computers, Hypercard was a very popular programmable application used in many schools. It consisted of a "stack" of pages, or cards, that would each allow for some limited programming capability and interactivity as you moved from card to card. It was extremely easy to learn and use and could create some very sophisticated interactive experiences for its time. Unfortunately, Hypercard has not been available since 2004. The newly released **Live Code** is a "Hypercard on steroids" cross platform development engine. There is a free and open source version under development for non-commercial use. Site licenses and discounts for student use are offered. There are educator resources on the website and extensive documentation. http://www.runrev.com/

Mobile app makers are an option for students who are interested in programming iPhone, iPad, or Android apps, and there are several tools that allow this. However, it is easier to create apps for Android devices. This is because Apple has set some stringent restrictions about iOS programming tools and applications allowed on iTunes, which is the only way to get apps onto your iOS device. There are a few "drag and drop" app creators for iOS devices, such as **GameSalad Creator**, but we can't really recommend any iOS app creators at the time of this publication. If you are considering this route, be sure you have tested this completely on your own to understand the potential complications and expenses.

MIT App Inventor is software that allows you to create apps and games for Android devices. Code samples, tutorials, and extensive educator resources are on the MIT website. http://appinventor.mit.edu/

Game Design Tools
You may have students who are interested in programming primarily with game design in mind. There are some applications that cater directly to that desire. Keep

in mind that if you choose to teach using these tools, students who are not interested in making games may feel left out.

GameMaker is a commercial product used in many schools (mostly high schools) to teach programming through game design. It does have a free version that is usable, although the full versions are very reasonable. The website offers many tutorials and there is a worldwide community of teachers using GameMaker to teach design and programming concepts. http://www.yoyogames.com/make

Gamestar Mechanic is another commercial product designed to teach game development. It offers education pricing, lessons, tutorials, and an educator community. http://gamestarmechanic.com/

Kodu is a visual programming tool made for creating Xbox games. The programming environment runs on the Xbox and uses a game controller for input. http://research.microsoft.com/en-us/projects/kodu/

Teaching Programming

Computer programming may be something that you personally enjoy, or have no experience in. We would encourage you to approach teaching programming with an open mind in either situation.

Teachers With Little or No Experience With Computer Programming

The thought of teaching computer programming may seem scary and impossible. Don't worry!

Many associate computer programming with only the very smartest, math-oriented people. However, this is a misconception. There is a wide variation of different programming languages that people can learn, and a wide variety of styles that people use to program. It is not just for one type of person.

Students will pick up these skills more quickly than you think possible, and will be able to help each other. This supports a collaborative, project-based classroom environment. Give your students a chance and let them surprise you!

We aren't implying that you do not have to learn to program. Would you ask your students to do something that you wouldn't tackle yourself? It is valuable for your students to see the teacher model learning, and the experience will be valuable to you as you learn with and from your students. The more you use a programming language, the more you will understand what types of projects are possible. You will be better able to steer students away from complexities that will derail their projects and lead them towards success.

Teachers Who Are Experienced Programmers

Teachers who have experience with computer programming will have different issues and questions. Carefully consider whether your favorite computer language is appropriate for your students. You may love C++ or Java and feel very comfortable using and teaching it, but it will be a steep learning curve for most of your students.

There is a difference between languages designed for getting work done vs. languages designed for building thinking skills. Logo-like languages are designed for learning, and offer many different entrance paths for many different kinds of students. It may be frustrating to you to know that you could knock off a line or two of code to solve a problem, but it will be worth it when you see how many different kinds of students learn these languages, and how easy it is for them to add sound, animation, and music.

Do not impose professional programming techniques like flowcharts, sorting algorithms, or "correct" syntax on them. When babies learn to walk, you don't teach them walking rules or make them write walking plans. You let them walk, fall down, get up, and try, try again. Do not worry that your students will learn "bad" programming habits. Their first experience is simply to get them engaged and empowered. Channel the "Less Us, More Them" teaching mantra and allow students to find their own ways and learn their own lessons.

Supporting Student Learning

The four elements of Stager's Hypothesis – A Good Prompt is Worth a Thousand Words – are crucial as you give students programming projects: a motivating challenge, an appropriate programming language, sufficient time, and a supportive classroom culture.

Most programming languages, especially Logo-based languages, will easily fit into an iterative model. For early programming efforts, get going without requiring extensive design, storyboards, or logic diagrams. Almost all programmers learn by modifying existing code samples and playing around with changing little bits here and there. It's perfectly fine to start with an idea, search around for the closest example you can find, and tweak the code to get started.

Help students break down a programming challenge into steps that are achievable. They do not have to program everything at once. For example, if they want to make a Pacman game, start by figuring out how to get an object to move across the screen. Then add the animation of the mouth opening and closing. Then add obstacles that disappear when the character "eats" them. By tackling one improvement at a time, and making sure the new code works before moving on to the next, students will more easily find errors and make forward progress towards their goals.

Error messages and the outcome of the program will give instant feedback to your student. Challenge their notions of "done." Support them as they work through the challenges and encourage shared expertise and collaboration. As your students become more expert in their programming, you can introduce longer design cycles, better plans, and more efficient coding techniques.

Chapter 8 - Stuff

To invent, you need a good imagination and a pile of junk. — Thomas Edison

Engaging projects, recess, and the performing arts can break the humdrum nature of classroom life. So too can "stuff" (our highly scientific term of art). Great teachers are highly skilled hoarders! Well-stocked classroom libraries, supplies, gadgets, technology, tools, toys, recycled materials and other assorted stuff within an arm's reach of students are learning accelerants. Eleanor Duckworth reminds us, "If materials are slim, the only questions likely to be posed are the teacher's." (Duckworth, 2005) You never know what a learner might need and when, so within the parameters of space, tidiness, and good taste, fill your classroom with stuff.

BASIC STOCKS

Beyond the game-changing technologies discussed in the previous chapter, your makerspace should include a basic stock of supplies to keep your students challenged, inspired, and busy. Try to build basic stocks in these areas:

- Electronic parts and tools
- Computers, cameras, software
- Craft and art supplies
- Building materials and traditional tools
- Junk for recycling into new products
- A library

If you have a 3D printer or other fabrication tool, you should have a ready supply of the raw materials or consumable parts they use.

Electronic Parts and Tools

- Electronic tools such as: voltmeter, soldering iron, soldering supplies
- LEDs, buzzers, things that make light and sound
- Batteries of assorted sizes
- Wire, copper tape, conductive paint
- Resistors, capacitors and other small electronic parts
- Tools such as: wire cutter and strippers, small pliers, tweezers
- Magnifying glass
- Small vise for holding parts and circuit boards steady

Check the Resources chapter in this book for sources, or visit a local electronics store. Many online sites and stores offer teacher discounts. Some may be willing to donate items.

Soldering is the process of joining metal parts together by melting a filler metal (called solder) between the parts. Soldering will be a necessary skill to learn if using any kind of electronics. A soldering iron is a tool with an insulated grip and a metal tip that gets hot enough (700°F) to melt the solder to either fasten things together, or to remelt the solder and take them apart. Soldering irons get very hot and your students will have to learn not to touch the tip, and to carefully place the irons back in their holders.

Seven-year-old Tyler soldering

Soldering is a handy skill to learn because soldering parts together is much more robust than clipping, twisting, or taping wires together, or using a breadboard, yet it's easy to unsolder parts if things need to be changed.

Most soldering irons plug into an A/C outlet, but some run on butane gas, and these will minimize tangled cords or the possibility of someone getting caught in the wire and sending a hot iron flying. There are many soldering tutorial videos and tool recommendations to be found on the Web.

Instructables: How to Solder http://instructables.com/id/How-to-solder/

Sylvia's Super-Awesome Maker Show handout on how to solder with great tips and safety instructions. http://sylviashow.com/printables/how-solder

Computers, Software, and Cameras

Computers are the most versatile part of your makerspace. Make sure that you have enough computers and computer power to interface with 3D printers, Arduinos, controllers, or whatever you have planned. Build a collection of peripherals and parts that students can use whenever they need.

- Cables of various types
- Memory sticks, memory cards
- Blank CDs and DVDs
- Microphones, headsets, speakers, etc.
- Software

Software is at the core of what the computer can do. It doesn't make sense to spend a lot of money and have high expectations for your hardware, and then expect all software to be free. Free can come at a high price when the software is buggy and there is no tech support – or worse, the website you depend on disappears overnight. It's also no guarantee of quality to only use software that is browser-based. It may save you some hassle of installing software, but carefully consider the reliability and speed of your Internet connection, and whether your students can handle online logins and passwords to web-based accounts. In many cases, high-quality software that you own, supported by a company that is grateful for your business, is worth paying for.

Both still and video cameras can serve double duty as project tool and project documentation. Even very inexpensive cameras are usually good enough and you may be able to amass quite a collection for student use. Don't forget that many students have phones with cameras.

An indispensible computer peripheral is the Wacom tablet. This drawing tablet replaces a computer mouse and is a must for students to draw on the computer.

Besides the programming languages and 3D fabrication software covered previously, we recommend making open-ended creativity tools available to students. This should include movie-making, audio production (Audacity, Garageband), stop-motion, and other tools. Avoid software that promises "one-click" or "instant" results. Some of our creativity favorites are:

Hyperstudio is a creativity tool that allows the user to combine interactive media elements to create presentations, websites, audio, video, and more. http://www.mackiev.com/hyperstudio

Tech4Learning offers a suite of creativity tools designed for project-based learning. These are fully featured programs for drawing, animation, stop-motion, photo editors, website creation, audio and video, animation, and more. http://tech4learning.com/

Animationish is an entry-level animation program with interactive tutorials. http://fablevisionlearning.com/animationish

Craft and Art Supplies

Art supplies and electronics are perfect partners for high-tech invention. Be sure to think beyond the usual crayons, construction paper, and glue sticks that you probably already have. Look for items that are lightweight, small, and have a wide variety of uses. You want to have enough on hand so that students can use them in multiple projects.

- Glue gun and supplies
- Felt, fabric, sheets, card stock, plastic that can be cut, foam, carpet remnants, tile samples, vinyl
- Stickers
- Pipe cleaners, rubber bands, paper clips, brads, string, fishing line
- Sewing supplies, snaps, Velcro, grommets
- Tape and duct tape
- Scissors and utility knives
- Wooden dowels, popsicle sticks, wooden toothpicks
- Modeling clay
- Containers for housing inventions such as cookie tins, Altoids containers, oatmeal boxes, cigar boxes, film canisters

Exploring craft stores and office supply stores can be very fruitful. Don't miss the closeout area at toy stores or dollar stores. Ask parents to collect and donate objects like empty cardboard tubes, cardboard boxes, cleaned-out plastic containers, etc. You can never have enough stuff and you do not want to postpone a potential learning experience for lack of the right material.

Building Materials and Traditional Tools

- Tools – A variety of pliers, clippers, scissors, hammers, snips, clamps, measuring tapes, screwdrivers, punches, hacksaw. Be sure to get multiple screwdrivers, including Torx and ones small enough for use on electronics.
- Electric tools – Drills and electric screwdrivers. Should be used with caution.

- Scrap lumber and plywood – Use for projects and stable bases. Plywood cut into squares about 2x2 ft make nice worktables that can be moved around or put away for later.
- Vinyl floor samples – Use for handy work surfaces; not as rigid as wood.
- Cardboard – Cardboard fasteners such as Makedo http://makedo.com.au/
- Assembly – Nails, screws, nuts, bolts, washers, pins, clips, different kinds of tape, glue, brads, fasteners, hooks, etc.

A Dremel tool is an extremely useful and versatile tool with different attachments for drilling, grinding, sharpening, cutting, cleaning, polishing, sanding, routing, carving, and engraving. It is also easy to handle, especially the battery-powered versions.

Battery-powered tools in general have the advantage of being safer and more flexible with no cord to get in the way. However, they may be more expensive, will need to be charged, and eventually will require new battery packs.

Junk for Recycling Into New Products

Many mechanical or electronic parts can be brought from home. The electronics may be useful, but even if not, you can disassemble things and reuse the cases, knobs, and other parts. Sometimes these parts can be used for decoration on larger projects. Be sure you disassemble things with safety in mind.

Ask students to bring in:
- Old phones
- Calculators
- Remote controls
- Clock radios
- Televisions
- Unneeded tools

Recycling junk teaches students to open up and look at anything in their world as part of their problem-solving toolkit. Tracy Rudzitis at The Computer School in New York:

I love saving things in case they are ever needed for something else. One look at my own basement confirms this.

What has been a great making experience for my students is understanding how you can re-fabricate one part from another. Two of my students needed a 3" x 1" piece of flexible metal they could use to mount two motors on. I showed them the storage bin that held old computer parts, hard drives, super drives, and other assorted things from technology's recent past. They dove in with screwdrivers and pliers and called me over not too long after to show me a couple of parts they thought might work. We were able to cut three of the needed pieces from an old SuperDrive, enough for other students wanting to make a similar bot.

Yesterday the same students needed a small switch to use for their robot. We had larger switches, but nothing that would work for their use. Then I remembered the remote control car that other students had brought in to disassemble for parts, and that there was a small switch attached to the components. After a "deal" was made between the two groups of students, the boys who needed the switch got busy. My attention was pulled away (as happens when there are four or five simultaneous projects going on in the room) and before I knew it, the team had removed the switch from its old location, figured out where it needed to be attached in the new location, and soldered it together. The switch worked perfectly!

It is exciting to see the students look at things and start to realize and understand that they can make other things, that instructions can sometimes be altered, or changed, or revised, according to materials on hand or need. That there is never just "one way" to solve a problem or attempt to find a solution and that just the act of trying to figure stuff out like that can sometimes be the best part of a project.

Too many times within the constraints of school students are taught that there is only one correct answer, or perhaps that there isn't enough time to really explore many other possibilities. It is crucial to learning to have space for invention and innovation.

Library

For students of all ages, a well-equipped library is an essential part of the invention center. Students should have access to all kinds of books that will inspire them with ideas for projects, or just stretch their imaginations. Look for a variety of books at all levels:

- How-to books – digital photography tips, how to do special effects in movies, how to build things, crafting, sewing
- Books of projects for kids – invisible ink, origami, tangrams
- Puzzle books – codes, math tricks, logic puzzles
- Cross-cultural books – games from around the world, Islamic tile patterns, Aboriginal paintings, Native American weaving
- Artistic books for inspiration
- *Make* magazine
- Computer magazines

These are likely not books found in the school library. Used bookstores or closeout sales may have many things that will inspire. Books with step-by-step pictures are very useful.

PURCHASING/ACQUIRING STUFF

There are a number of ways you can collect the supplies and tools you need for your classroom makerspace. "Collect" is a good word for how this usually works, because it's unlikely you will purchase everything you need at once.

If you don't have the budget to get everything you need, consider these alternatives:

- **Parents and Parent-Teacher Organizations.** Create a list for parents of suggested donations to your classroom makerspace.
- **Local businesses.** Be specific and don't feel like you have to take anything. Reward your benefactors with photos of the finished projects, thank you notes, and mentions in school newsletters and parent letters.
- **Local hackerspaces/tech clubs.** These groups may be willing to let you have or borrow extra equipment, have other sources, or at the very least be sources of expertise in purchasing.

You (May) Only Live Once

Be a little greedy if you are lucky enough to have an administration, donor, or school board interested in funding your maker activities. The idiosyncratic nature of school funding is such that you may lack sufficient funds in the future. If you have a window of opportunity to kick things off on a sound footing, stock up on all of the consumable materials, parts, hardware, and software that you can. Buy whatever you can and save most of it for a rainy day. You may only get one golden ticket (or purchase order).

Donations

Create a specific list of what you need so that you get donations that are useful and will not just pass the burden to you of getting rid of useless or hazardous cast-offs. List what you need, and also things you do not need. For example, if you are letting students disassemble electronics for parts, you should be clear that you *do* need phones, remote controls, computers, clocks, radios, calculators, etc., but you *do not* need printers, televisions, microwave ovens, etc.

Your own experience should guide you – if you are not comfortable working with electronics yet, you should probably not accept anything that plugs into an A/C outlet.

Tracy Rudzitis shares this:

This fall I put together a basic Donor's Choose grant to purchase some basic supplies. I already had some supplies I could bring from home – a soldering iron, wires, tools, etc. The first time you put together something with Donor's Choose you must use their suppliers. This posed a small problem at first when I realized that I couldn't include any Arduino or LilyPad electronics or kits. But I soon realized that I could order switches, motors, LEDs, tools, hot glue guns, safety glasses, and solder to create the foundation for our makerspace.

My favorite purchase was the long folding table. My classroom is a computer lab with tables that are not moveable and have computers permanently attached to them. The table is "our makerspace," we pull it out and place chairs around it and we have our work area. I even wrote "The Computer School Makerspace" along the edges of it. It is a symbolic thing I guess.

Versions

Big expenses such as 3D printers can take a big bite out of your budget. Purchase the best hardware and software you can afford, and assume you will have to get at least two years' worth of use out of that investment. When you need to replace things, or have the opportunity to purchase additional hardware, you may find that you have a dilemma. Should you purchase the same model of what you already have, even if it is out of date? Or, should you continually upgrade to newer models?

There is no easy answer to this question. If you stick with purchasing the same model of 3D printer, or the same version of an Arduino board, it will match what you have and you will not need to keep track of different models, parts, instructions, etc. However, your printers or computers will slowly fall out of date and you may someday be faced with having to purchase a lot of new models at the same time. Worst of all, your students will miss out on using newer, and presumably better, tools or materials.

If you continually purchase new versions, it will be more difficult to keep track of the variations. You may find that you will have different instructions for many different versions of the same equipment, all just slightly different enough to confuse you and your students.

Your choice is going to depend on how comfortable you feel with managing different hardware versions and helping students understand these small distinctions. Some of your students may be able to help. Allow students to become experts in various aspects of the technology and you will have a crew of experts on hand when things get confusing or new versions need to be cracked.

Allocating Your Budget

Here's how MIT spent $70,000 to stock a FabLab: http://bit.ly/fablabinventory

If you have $70,000 to spend, congratulations! But if not, looking at the MIT FabLab budget yields some interesting observations.

Of the total, around 40% was allocated for major equipment purchases with another 10% for spare parts for that equipment. Consumable supplies and electronic parts each got about 10% of the budget. 10% was spent on tools and another 10% on computers. The remaining 10% covered books, safety equipment, cleaning supplies, office supplies, and storage.

This is a good reminder that when you purchase expensive equipment, it can't be your entire budget. You will need to budget for spare parts and the consumable supplies and parts your students will quickly use up as they start to use the equipment and build projects. You may need to purchase computers to control the 3D printers, interface to microprocessors and robots, or do design work. Think ahead and make sure you get what you need, just like the big boys and girls at MIT do!

Stocking Up

If you will be exploring physical computing or electronics in your classroom, you will want to be well-stocked so that students have all of the tools and components they need, when they need them. Kits are great because they tend to include what you need to create a number of projects. However, you are paying a premium for kits when less expensive parts may be available in bulk.

Besides being less expensive, buying in bulk is great because you probably teach lots of students.

The companies that sell the best kits, suitable for school use, also charge a premium for their expertise and high-quality components. Shipping is quick. Customer service is excellent and they may even take a school purchase order (a reality you may need to live with). However, you may save a bundle by purchasing consumable parts, like batteries and non-consumable reusable electronics components, in bulk from a variety of vendors.

When it comes to items used routinely in projects such as watch batteries, LEDs, switches, battery holders, motors, and buzzers, you can be sure a few pieces will fail, break, or be lost. Therefore, a wise shopper uses "the Google" to find the best deals. Once you know you have a better sense of the supplies you need in your classroom, look for bulk components on sites like eBay and even Ikea. For example, Ikea sells the Solvinden, their version of the popular CR2032 lithium watch battery used in e-textiles and a host of other projects for $1.99 (package of 8). That is just 25 cents per battery, and if you watch for sales you can stock up for even less! Many eBay vendors sell lots of electronics components from China in large quantities at a great price. Just be careful when it comes to shipping rates and time, so you don't spend too much or wait too long for your items to arrive. "Use the Google" and save money!

Online Stores

Sparkfun Electronics. Specializes in hobbyist electronic components, tools, and kits. The website features a project blog, buying guides, and tutorials from soldering to using a breadboard. Ask for educator discounts. http://www.sparkfun.com

Adafruit. "Unique and Fun DIY Electronics and Kits." Check the "Young Engineers" section for selections that are whimsical and fun, and the educator section for tutorials and badges. Ask for educator discounts. http://www.adafruit.com

Maker Shed. Vetted by *Make* magazine. Specializes in kits for learners of all ages. http://www.makershed.com/

Electronics Goldmine. Extensive supply of cheap electronic parts. Look for deals and bulk purchases, such as a container of 200 LEDs that costs $5.00. http://www.goldmine-elec.com/

Jameco Electronics. Another popular source of electronics parts and kits. http://www.jameco.com

Chapter 9 - Shaping the Learning Environment

The role of the teacher is to create the conditions for invention rather than provide ready-made knowledge. — Seymour Papert

Planning a creative design space and collecting the "stuff" are only a part of shaping the learning environment. Creating an "intellectual design space" is another. Your students need to believe that they can be inventors and creators. Materials, tools, and resources are crucial, but the teacher's job is to keep the spirit and mood of the space conducive to creativity. Young people need their teachers to craft learning environments that reduce stress levels, interruptions, and confusion. Teachers can signal that the makerspace is a different kind of learning space through visual and physical clues.

School may be a place where the daily expectation is for children to sit quietly, listen to lectures, and follow directions to produce identical output. It should come as no surprise if students are initially confused by the different expectations of a makerspace. Signal this change through visual and physical clues to help students understand that indeed, this is a space where their ideas are honored and the rules are different. If your makerspace is a shared space, or part of your classroom, the ritual of "opening" the makerspace signals this transition. This can take the form of banners that come out, door signs that turn over, or, as in Tracy Rudzitis's case, special furniture that is labeled as being just for the makerspace.

Seize any opportunity to turn responsibility for design, decoration, and space planning over to students. Weave brainstorming and project documentation into the space. In the Stanford FabLab, there are small dry erase boards on cabinet doors where students write their ideas, display photos of projects in progress, and post tips for successful projects using the contents of that cabinet.

Papert's "Eight Big Ideas Behind the Constructionist Learning Lab" from Chapter 5 is a great guide for the ethos of your makerspace. Find ways to make your space match your intentions for a vibrant learning environment where "hard fun" is expected and learner individuality is respected.

Andrew Carle, a maker and middle school teacher in Virginia says:

> I want a middle school space to be filled with things that intrigue and entice adolescents. Something needs to slow down traffic in the hallway and pull them through the door. This is a huge reason why I'm so in love with our pinball machine. Every pinball machine, every arcade cabinet, was designed to capture fleeting fascination of passing teenagers. 3D printers can do the same work, leaving a trail of ABS breadcrumbs throughout your school. Developing a maker-mindset means discovering ways that you can tweak, hack, or create new things that exist in and interact with the wider world. I'd argue that the same is true for a maker-space. To thrive, a middle school space has to generate something that's visible and exiting to the wider school community.
>
> But it's not enough to pull a few curious heads through the door. A maker-space needs to empower visitors and transform them into makers, not just provide specialized tools. Students should find something to touch and produce, something that provides a sense of accomplishment and reward on their timescale. I backed the MaKey MaKey Kickstarter project out of frustration with how our existing Arduinos failed this test. The time it took students to simply replicate a project they'd found on the Web, projects with the code and parts list provided, fell well outside that window. This doesn't mean that Arduino-based projects are "too hard" for middle school students, just that they're too complicated to serve as an initial incitement. It's still early days for the MaKey MaKey, but so far they fit far better into that space.
>
> An "ideal" tool allows kids to make/hack/play quickly enough to close the engagement loop, but still offers enough substance that it will feel qualitatively different than the pre-fab challenge of "normal" school.

HELP OR GET OUT OF THE WAY!

Children have always known things their parents and teachers didn't. What's different today is that what kids know, or think they know, is feared or coveted by adults. Teachers need to get over their "fear" of modernity and reject the simplistic notion that children are "much better at technology" than adults. If there is any truth to this myth, it is because children use the technology. Doing develops expertise. That should come as no surprise.

The best teachers know more about the game-changing technologies discussed in this book than their students. They may lack specific knowledge that can be co-constructed with students, but great teachers possess the curiosity, life experience, research skills, Rolodex, and habits of mind that lead to asking the right question at the moment a student requires motivation or debugging help. Asking the sorts of questions suggested in the "Improve" section of our TMI model (Chapter 3) can go a long way towards being a better teacher. Actual experience solving the sorts of problems our students may encounter is even better.

In case we have been too subtle, you should learn to program, solder, build a robot, or design a 3D object, especially if you expect children to. This journey may begin as simply as developing a greater awareness of what's possible.

Henry, Software Mogul

Our friend asked if there was any software his 10-year-old son Henry could use to program video games. We suggested Scratch. Within 48 hours, we received this update about Henry's adventures in software design.

> Henry and his friends think they can create an online multiplayer game. To hear him talk about it, he has such enthusiasm and grand ideas for music, graphics, plot. That's why I was hoping something like Scratch existed. Henry thinks he's Steve Wozniak. But he doesn't know what he's talking about, but is so confident he does.

> He's going to be a good salesman. He can talk about this "OMG" [not Massively Multiplayer Online Game, MMOG] for hours! He discusses the most technical of details using computer and programming jargon he's heard, but doesn't quite understand. Graphic formats, coding, OpenGL – you name it – he throws it out there! Whenever I question him about some specifics, he tells me not to worry, his friend Mike "knows how to code." Mike is ten.

> Henry spent about a half an hour drawing a sprite in Scratch, didn't save it, and then messed it up. He was a basket case because it was going to take "so long" to fix or redo. When I pointed out he's only had Scratch for 30 minutes, he didn't appreciate it. I made sure to show him how to save and to do it every few minutes.

> I'm trying to help him to develop some realistic expectations without squashing his enthusiasm. I think he likes it, but he's complaining Scratch is not 3D. Ha!

Alan Kay defines technology as "...anything that wasn't there when you were born." Henry and Mike assume they are video game designers, just like previous generations of children played doctor or nurse or fireman. The difference today is that the tools exist to let children *be* software designers, while playing at being a software designer. Such play and the ability to make digital artifacts of use or interest to others are significant. Teachers should play a substantive role in building upon their students' digital chutzpah.

When you don't know what is impossible, you are inclined to think that anything is possible. Along the way, students will develop fluencies that would be otherwise unavailable to them, as well as increased confidence. A wide range of experience and resulting knowledge leads to more informed decision making in the future.

It is incumbent upon educators to cherish the gifts that children bring to us, even if just an absence of fear, and help them build upon those gifts, to go farther than they could have gone on their own.

RIDING UP THE DOWN ESCALATOR

During our summer teacher institute, Constructing Modern Knowledge, we observed a teacher undergo a personal learning process that Gary describes as, "riding up the down escalator." The teacher had visited the MIT Media Laboratory with us the night before and was inspired by Leah Buechley's work with paper circuitry. The next morning she set out to create her own project that would turn a piece of paper into a musical instrument. Her plan was that her instrument could be played by touch and would generate sounds based on circuitry affixed to an ordinary sheet of paper. The fact that an educator could become fascinated by an MIT research project on Wednesday night and could attempt to create her own version on Thursday morning is a testament to the availability and accessibility of new construction materials. When the teacher presented her work in progress later that day, she described more about her intellectual process than the product itself.

The learning story went something like this:

I tried making what the MIT researchers had made, but I didn't have the special conductive tape. So, I tried a different material and that didn't work.

So I tried conductive paint, but that didn't work, so I tried aluminum foil cut with an X-Acto knife.

And when that worked a little bit, I tried something more complicated, but that didn't work.

So, I tried a subset of that strategy and that worked.

And then I tried to improve my project a bit more and that worked...

This educator "rode up the down escalator" because despite the complexity of the task, the limited resources, and incomplete knowledge pushing down like gravity upon her, progress was indeed achieved. We suspect that many adventures in making, tinkering, and engineering – in school and the outside world – follow a similar non-linear path. The classroom learning environment needs to support and welcome such pluralistic problem solving.

Irv's Troubleshooting Tips — Sylvia

My father was a mechanic and tinkerer who learned about cars and motorcycles by taking them apart. His father used to tell stories about coming home and finding 10-year-old Irving in the driveway with the parts of the family car surrounding him, and how most of the time the car was put back together successfully.

If my brother or I came to him with a problem, he would always ask, "What have you done already?" and remind us of his primary rule: "Use all your senses." Have you looked carefully at the problem? Does something look new or different? What sound is it making? Does it smell funny? Does it feel hot or cold? (And yes, when appropriate, taste it.)

If none of those questions provided any clues, the second rule was "wiggle it." Sometimes literally, but he also meant it figuratively. Change something a little, try something slightly different, or think about what other similar problems you've seen.

The final and most important rule was "Test drive it!" No car left Irv's garage without a thorough test drive. It was a measure of pride to never claim something was "fixed" when it wasn't.

GENDER FRIENDLY SPACES AND STYLES

Research on university students has shown that women rate themselves as less interested in computer science simply based on the room in which the survey takes place. Rooms decorated with "geek" décor – Star Trek posters, scattered cans of Mountain Dew, action figures, and discarded electronic parts – result in girls rating their interest in computer science lower than men; whereas girls taking the same survey in a neutrally decorated room scored about the same as men in the same room. (Cheryan, Plaut, Davies, & Steele, 2009)

When people enter a room, it is human nature to size it up and get a feeling of whether they belong or not. Does it feel familiar? Would I like the people who created and occupy this space? Your makerspace should have a gender-neutral answer. This is not about throwing a few Hello Kitty posters up on the walls. It's about making an effort to show that all kinds of interests and activities are valued.

Gender identity studies often show that girls have different problem-solving styles than boys. This does not mean that *all* girls or *all* boys solve problems in a single style, but that there is a wide range of styles. However, girls tend to use more collaborative techniques such as building consensus and adapting rules than boys do. Boys will more often take a problem as a personal challenge, and work on it to the point of obsession.

Both of these characteristics are helpful and worthy of monitoring. Tackling a problem with enthusiasm is a good thing, but allowing unbounded competition to harm the "losers" is a bad outcome, especially in a classroom. Building consensus is a good skill to master, but not being able to make a decision and get anything done is a bad habit.

What does your makerspace say about who belongs there? What kind of problem-solving styles are accommodated? If you aren't sure, ask some students.

DOCUMENTATION

Documentation, whether in the form of a lab report, inventor's notebook, video, podcast, design portfolio, blog, or wall poster, serves multiple functions and many masters. The crudest use of documentation is for grading. Documentation should be used to make private thinking public or invisible thinking visible. The early childhood educators of Reggio Emilia, Italy use documentation as a research artifact that teachers study, discuss, and interpret in order to prepare the environment for the next stage in a learner's development. Documentation can brighten up a school hallway, commemorate a significant moment in a learning adventure, inform teaching practice, and communicate a school's activities to the community.

Younger or reluctant students may document project progress by taking a digital photo, annotating it, and sticking it on a wall or blog. Such images in progress tell a child's learning story, invite others to engage with their thinking, and provide an artifact to refer to while reflecting on a project or remembering how to solve a similar problem in the future.

> Remember kids, the only difference between screwing around and science is writing it down. — Adam Savage, host of *Mythbusters*

You cannot have too many digital cameras or video cameras available for use in projects and for recording the story of a project. Cameras should be charged and widely available in order to capture powerful "Aha!" moments and record evidence of learning, even misconceptions or bugs, in a fashion impossible with pencil and paper.

Completing a simple to-do list at the start and finish of a making session may also be beneficial for the learner who needs help planning or for the teacher who requires documentation of progress.

THE TECHNOLOGY ECOLOGY

A funny thing happens when you make something, particularly something of a technological nature. You are inspired to learn something else. When you make a guitar from a cigar box or by handcrafting wood, you tend to want to learn to play it. You learn to read music, develop musical skills, and perhaps score the soundtrack for your next digital video. Invent a machine to graph fluctuations in temperature over a long period of time and you will want to conduct more complex experiments. Program your own software for performing geometric constructions, the better your program becomes, and the more geometry you will learn. Your newfound understanding of geometry will encourage you to make your software more sophisticated.

COLLABORATION AND GROUP WORK

Much has been written justifying classroom cooperation and cooperative learning. Most teachers have experience engaging students in group work. Our bias is towards flexibility. The purpose of working together is *interdependence*. Each member of the team gains benefit by working collaboratively. If there is no benefit to working together or if the collaboration is burdensome to the process, then why do it? When the collaboration is authentic, students will gain a greater appreciation for the benefits of collaborating and the result of the experience will be richer.

We recognize the complex social dynamics of a classroom and your desire to have students work together. However, flexibility may lead to even more collaboration and cooperation. Identifying expertise in others and knowing when collaboration best suits a situation is an important 21st century skill.

Students may need to collaborate in unpredictable ways for short periods of time. Students often engage in what education researcher Yasmin Kafai calls "collaborations through the air." Rich collaboration may occur in the hallway between classes, while looking over someone's shoulder, or in other informal settings. This may explain how a skill taught in 1st period on the west side of your campus is being used in 3rd period by another student in another grade on the east side of the campus. Kids are much more natural collaborators than we think.

When you do assign groups, be sure to keep each team to four or fewer members. Beyond that number, it is likely that some students are not participating.

REMEMBER LUMT

Remember the teaching mantra "Less Us, More Them" as you guide your students. Be careful not to be the classroom "guru." When students need help, ask questions that will steer them in the right direction. Allow them to write code that is not as efficient as you would like, or struggle with electronics for a while. If you step in too early and always solve their problems for them, they will not learn how to push past that early frustration on the road to solving tough problems.

That does not mean you can't help your students. At times, you will know more than they do about programming, or 3D design, or just be able to anticipate the problems that might derail a project. You may realize that a small snippet of code will be a useful project starter for the whole class. Lending a helping hand with a circuit that has a tricky design is a good idea. Just try not to anticipate so far in advance that you end up giving them solutions that lead them down a single path to "success." Watch for signs of "Mouth Up, Mouth Down" frustration levels and help students realize their capabilities.

Don't be Bob — Sylvia

When I worked in aerospace engineering, our lab was a fairly shop-like work environment. We were programming microprocessors and breadboarding the circuits that were going to become part of the GPS satellite research project. Bob was in charge of the lab where we worked. He was a veteran of many projects and the electronics lab was his baby. He knew every piece of equipment, every tool, every rule, and everybody. Despite only having one leg, he seemed to be everywhere at once and was able to make anything work. When Bob showed up, things magically got done.

But one day we arrived and Bob was not there. He had had a medical condition flare up and needed a few days off. No worries, we could struggle along without him. And we did struggle. No one knew where things were. No one knew how to make the equipment work. Bob was supposed to come back in a week, but a week stretched to two weeks, and then to months. We realized that "Go get Bob" had become our crutch, creating huge gaps in what we knew as individuals and thus in what we could accomplish as a team. We had been lulled into complacency by his competence and didn't realize it until we were forced to.

SHOW AND TELL?

Some teachers like to inspire students by showing the final products of former students before embarking on a project. Reasonable educators are free to disagree on this practice. It is clearly a close call.

We recommend against showing examples of completed projects for the following reasons:

- Some students may feel intimidated by the sophistication, complexity, or quality of a finished project. They may not be able to see a clear path from here to there.
- Some students will assume that the former project is the right answer and will embark on a process of imitation, not creation.
- Old projects assume no change in the quality of tools and materials that may now be available.
- Not every student needs to create a replica of every other student's project. Everyone benefits when many different projects are part of an active learning community.

Teachers should refrain from doing the same thing year after year or semester after semester. Keep it fresh. Keep learning and trying new things. Then examples of former student projects serve as inspirational examples of strategy or technique, rather than A+ work.

MAKING COMPLEXITY ACCESSIBLE

One day, a class of fifth graders was building interactive toys. Some students worked in teams while others worked alone. Hugo built a robot car out of LEGO and powered it with a PicoCricket[4]. He programmed the car to start moving forward when he clapped his hands once, and to stop when he clapped his hands a second time. This required the use of a sound sensor and a program that would act upon a noise the approximate volume of a handclap. Writing such a program requires the creation of a separate program to determine the numerical value of a handclap "heard" by a sensor. Since no two handclaps are exactly the same, Hugo needed to find a reliable range of sound reported from a sensor to indicate a clap. He also needed to control for ambient noise since he did not want his car to run away if someone closed the door or dropped a textbook on a nearby table.

In addition to building a working car powered by an "intelligent brick," by this point in the project Hugo had already encountered two powerful ideas:

1. In order to "teach" a machine to react reliably to outside stimuli, you need to write a program that lets you observe the data received by a sensor over several trials and under a range of conditions.

2. School is the only place in life where one thing equals something else. The world is a lot messier. Building an intelligent machine and many programming tasks requires the understanding of tolerances. The result you are testing for is usually "close enough" to a particular value. Determining the range of acceptable is a powerful idea throughout science and engineering. Absolute value, set theory, and plain old "greater than" or "less than" come in handy at times like this. Asking children to explain < or > outside of the context of computer programming frequently leads to much stammering, squinting, and desperate attempts to remember which way the alligator's mouth should face.

Satisfied that his car worked well enough, Hugo decided to improve it. He got a clipboard, piece of paper, pencil, calculator, and yardstick (because Americans are still taking a "wait and see" attitude on that whole metric deal). He modified his robot's program slightly so that instead of starting and stopping with each successive handclap, the car would now start on a handclap and stop exactly one second later. Hugo knew to record successive trials of his experiment and record how far the car traveled in one second (on that particular surface).

Gary observed what Hugo was doing and immediately realized why he changed his program. Hugo was trying to determine how fast his car goes. He

---

4   Sadly, the PicoCricket robotics kis are no longer available.

knew that he could increase the accuracy of his data by averaging the results of multiple trials. His car traveled 31 inches in 1 second.

That's not a measure of speed kids use for things that go fast. American kids use miles per hour. It is at this point that the fun and games usually come to a screeching halt and several years of torturous unit conversions commence. Asking a fifth grader (or their teacher) to convert 31 inches per second into X miles per hour will likely lead to screaming.

Gary took a chance and opened his laptop's browser to the computation engine, wolframalpha.com. He typed 31 inches per second into Wolfram Alpha and was instantly provided with:

787.4 mm/s (millimeters per second)

0.7874 m/s (meters per second)

1.761 mph (miles per hour)

Bingo! That's what Hugo was looking for! His car travels at a rate of 1.76 miles per hour!

That was followed by kilometers per hour and other conversions. A few lines lower, Wolfram Alpha provided a bit of trivia neither of us had expected:

Comparison as speed:

~~ 0.7 × typical human walking speed (2.5 mph)

Before Gary could finish reading that line, Hugo ran back to modify his car. Why? He wanted to see if he could make it move faster than the average human walks. In this case, success and a new discovery led to further inquiry.

We know that some readers might conclude that the use of Wolfram Alpha is cheating. 30%–40% of you are probably wearing eyeglasses. You cheaters! We use technology every day to assist us. We take technology like eyeglasses for granted even when we still argue about the use of calculators or computation engines in the classroom.

Seemingly reasonable adults still rationalize turning kids into poor replicas of $2 calculators by asking, "What happens if the batteries run dead or the solar calculator no longer works because the sun is blocked?" We suggest that if the sun is blocked for an abnormal period of time you should tend to the impending apocalypse. Your math homework can probably wait.

The real lesson of Hugo's project is that if you make simple things easy to do, you make complexity possible.

TAKING THE LAB OUT OF THE FAB LAB

Efforts are underway to bring fab labs and maker-style learning to K–12 schools. While these projects bring exciting new opportunities to learners, it would be a shame if the interdisciplinary power of making, tinkering, and invention were relegated to a specialized lab for occasional use. Microcomputers originally entered classrooms through the personal investment of an excited teacher. Before long, schools decided to expand computing opportunities to more students and invested in additional computers. They quickly realized that not every teacher shared the enthusiasm or expertise of the early-adopters and placed the computers in a special bunker called the computer lab. Once there, a formal schedule and curriculum was invented based less on the power of the computer to transform learning opportunities and more on the logistical demands of dividing scarce resources evenly across too many students. Frequently, the computer lab became the kingdom of a single specialist, leaving teachers dependent and restricting children from using computers in novel ways anytime anywhere.

We get it. Some of the new hardware for making is expensive, and perhaps even a bit dangerous. However, it would be more dangerous to relegate the learning opportunities afforded by making, tinkering, and engineering to one special 42-minute class period per week. To more fully realize its potential, making should be the primary activity across the curriculum, not a field trip.

Makerspace on the Move

Josh Burker is a specialist classroom teacher in a Connecticut K–5 school. He works with students in other teachers' classrooms for 45 minutes once a week, bringing the tools and equipment he needs with him. In Josh's case, his choices for materials and projects are influenced by this logistical challenge, but in reality, every teacher faces logistical challenges that need to be overcome. Josh also runs LEGO and LEGO WeDo clubs after school.

Josh often uses Arduino and Scratch for classroom projects. Many times, he builds the base of projects himself, then students work on adding their own flair and ideas to the basic setup. One such project was an Operation-style game built from found materials, a MaKey MaKey, and using Scratch.

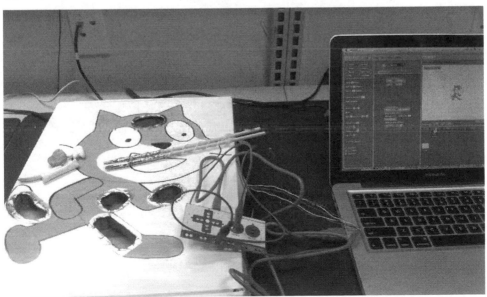

Josh built a very basic prototype to iron out some of the bugs, and test ideas about which materials might be the most useful for students to use. The game consisted of a box with holes that a player would reach inside of using chopsticks.

The goal was to remove the "organs" inside the box while trying not to touch the chopsticks to the sides of any hole. If all of the organs were removed, the operation was successful and the "patient" lived. If a player touched the side of the hole with a chopstick as they attempted to pick up an organ, the circuit was completed, and a signal was sent via the MaKey MaKey. To set this game up, the clay organs were placed under each hole, the chopsticks and the edges of the holes were wrapped with copper tape, and a simple circuit was wired underneath the box. If the chopstick touched the side of a hole, the circuit completed, and the MaKey MaKey sent what looked like a "key press" to the Scratch program. The program waited for a key to be pressed and played a sound signaling the player's failure to win the game and save the patient.

Josh tested this prototype with fifth graders, who helped refine the circuitry and software. With this basic kit, Josh could go into any classroom and students could use the kit to create their own versions, drawing their own characters and wiring their own circuits. Students also enhanced the Scratch program to their liking, changing the sounds and creating dramatic animations that would play

when the chopsticks touched the side of a hole. Some added additional game elements via Scratch, such as virtual characters that got smaller when the player botched the operation, eventually losing their life completely.

Josh says, "Each game is different with the same underlying motherboard design. The Scratch projects work basically the same way, too, utilizing the MaKey MaKey to read a key press, but each project reflects the young makers' personalized design."

In doing this, Josh was able to provide materials and expertise enough for the projects to be successful in short windows of classroom time while still allowing for creativity and personalization.

CREATIVE SPACE DESIGN AND MAKING DO

No matter what tools and materials you use, you will need space for students to create. This is going to be dependent on multiple factors, but here are some considerations.

Once you have decided what kinds of equipment you will begin with, find ways for students to access that equipment that balances safety and security with creativity and a sense of ownership. While the "stuff" in the space is important, you need a space that supports creativity and independence.

Consider whether this space will be in your classroom, like a center. If so, you need to think about how you will manage the space if you are in another part of the room. Can students safely use the space and equipment while you are busy in another part of the room?

If the library is an option, build on the existing advantages. Libraries are cross-curricular, multi-grade, and often have extended hours. All these are advantages for a makerspace. In the past decade, many librarians rebranded themselves as Library Media Specialists; now without changing the acronym, they can be Library Maker Specialists – making meaning, making learning possible, and making things.

If you have the luxury of designing a new space, think outside of the box and optimize for flexibility. Movable furniture maximizes flexibility, but requires space. Plan for more electrical outlets than you think you will need, accessible to anywhere in the room without extension cords. Chalk, whiteboard, or magnetic paint turns walls and tables into brainstorming surfaces. Preserve space to ease traffic flow around busy work centers. This increases safety and opportunities for collaboration.

You may be "making do" within existing school spaces, like shops or science labs. Advantages might include existing water, bench space, and ventilation. There may be things that don't work quite so well, like bolted down furniture or poor lighting. Making do is the heart of being a maker, so just think of your space as one more variable to tinker with!

Space Planning

Design a space that encourages creativity by taking into account both functionality and flexibility. If a space is simply too small, crowded, or uncomfortable, those using it (both children and adults) will be less likely to enjoy working there. The functionality of the space is crucial to making it a better place to work. Good lighting, space to spread out, and organized resources will go a long way towards making your space functional.

Spaces that are flexible in addition to functional will really support creative work. Flexible doesn't just mean that it can be used for multiple purposes, but that it can also be controlled by the people using the space. Can your space support students who want to collaborate just as well as a student who needs to work alone? Can you create comfortable seating that works for brainstorming or reading a good book? Can you create "quiet zones" or a recording studio? When it's safe to do so, can students eat, drink, or work with headphones even if that is not the usual school policy? Giving children choices about how they use this space will increase the creative potential of individual students.

Educators interested in designing productive learning environments need to have *The Language of School Design: Design Patterns for 21st Century Schools* by Prakash Nair and Randall Fielding in their library. Examples of their learning design principles may be found at http://fieldingnair.com.

Safety and Security

Anytime you have electronics, tools, chemicals, or anything else that can cause injury, you must employ proper safety precautions. Valuable and/or dangerous equipment needs to be secured when not in use, for both safety and security. That includes negotiating with cleaning staff to ensure that valuable pieces don't get vacuumed or thrown away. Agreeing upon one day per week when floors will be cleaned allows you and your students to plan for the "big cleanup."

Safety concerns are going to vary widely depending on your materials, equipment, and student projects. Follow school policy, local laws, and manufacturer's instructions regarding ventilation, chemicals, protective eyewear, and other protective gear. Do your homework about the tools and materials you are planning to use and make appropriate rules. Here are a few important points to keep in mind:

- Make sure your first aid kit and fire extinguisher are current and accessible.
- Be cautious, but not overly cautious to the point of never letting children use the tools.
- Think through your project from start to finish. Giving students paper plates and covering the table with a plastic tablecloth might be a good plan for keeping track of parts in a Squishy Circuits project, but if soldering is on the agenda, you've just created a fire hazard!

Be careful that the safety rules don't become curriculum. Rules are important and necessary, but they don't make children safe – careful behavior does. Find examples of safety rules at makerspace and hackerspace sites online. When using someone else's rules, be sure to pare them down to those that directly apply to the tools and materials you have on hand. Too many rules that don't make sense are likely to be ignored.

Makerspace Playbook Contains ideas for makerspace safety and rules. http://makerspace.com/playbook

Project Storage

You will need to decide what to do about projects on their way to completion. Do you have enough space for students to have personal storage? Can you create some shelf space where students can move partial projects and put their names on them?

Organizing materials is highly personal and a matter of style. Some teachers like to maintain pristine kits assigned to specific students or teams of students. Others prefer to group parts by similar size, shape, color, or function in bins or Ziploc bags for use by all students at any time. Cafeteria trays or cardboard boxes may be swell too.

A second option may be required when students create more complex projects that need more of a specific element than comes in a single kit. When every student or team is not building the same contraption, a more liberal sharing of parts may be desirable. In all cases, guard against hoarding and discourage waste.

It can be a challenge to balance the multitude of ways that people use workspaces. It's possible for two reasonable people to look at a mess of wires, tools, and parts completely differently. While one sees exciting inspiration, the other person may see an almost painful outrage. Multiply that by dozens or hundreds of students in the space and you can imagine the challenge of trying to balance everyone's needs. As a teacher, try not to impose your own ideas of order and pick the battles that truly result in improvements for student learning.

An active makerspace may inevitably become a messy makerspace. Cleaning up after yourself and respecting the materials should be an expectation for students at all times. The kindergarten rules of good citizenship apply. However, when constrained by limited time, teachers need to reserve as much time as possible for project work and employ strategies to reduce cleanup time. As long as work may proceed and custodians are not going to vacuum up valuable materials, you might endure some temporary messiness.

Ask for student volunteers to come in during lunch or after school to help collect, sort, and reorganize the materials. You may be surprised by how many kids are willing to help.

Another strategy is to have students reorganize the materials they will need for a specific project at the beginning of that project. This also allows them to become familiar with unfamiliar materials.

Sharing Parts and Tools

If you are using things like LEGO, robotics, or other limited hardware, you will usually have to set some rules about students claiming parts that other students need. Try to make sure you have a wide variety of parts available to start with.

The answer to the question, "How much X do I need?" is that you need enough of X to allow every student to exceed the expectations of your assignment *and* keep their object together long enough for others to admire it. This may require teachers to vary the units of inquiry or stagger the sequence of projects to maximize the use of resources by all kids, classes, and courses.

Students will need to share tools or specific software to work on their projects. One way to manage this is to require some preparation or check-in before a student uses a popular tool. For example, you may require that students get your approval on a CAD drawing before they can use the 3D printer, or that they present a storyboard before they borrow the video camera or use the only high-powered computer capable of video production.

Less Scheduling, More Making

If you are compelled to relegate making, tinkering, and invention to a specific physical space in your school, do everything possible to use that space in a flexible fashion. If you must schedule classes in the makerspace, leave plenty of time for students to drop in to work on projects. You may even encourage an open-door policy where students can work in the space during scheduled classes, as long as they are not disruptive. Run clubs during lunch, recess, and non-school hours to maximize use of your resources. If your 3D printers are robust and safe enough, think about placing 3D printers in public areas, like the library, so students may begin and check on time-consuming processes throughout the day. Let students manage 3D printer queues and teach each other to use your makerspace resources (hardware, software, tools, materials).

SCHOOL IT

Most schools already have existing computers, and along with them, existing rules and policies. As you build your makerspace and resources, you may find conflicts with rules about downloading software, blocked websites, students installing software, and draconian Acceptable Use Policies (AUPs.) This may take time to sort out, but it's worth it. You may need to forge an alliance with the IT department to give your classroom some special leeway. There are certainly reasons that some websites should be blocked. Websites where people have uploaded designs, instructions, and graphics will certainly have the potential for unsavory or inappropriate finds. However, this is not a reason to block *all* students from *all* websites where there is a user forum or shared database.

AUPs are a common offender. When was the last time you actually read it? In many schools, the AUP is the only communication from school to home about the vision of technology use, and yet, it's a negative document, full of complex legalese and threats of punishment. If that's the only message parents get from your school about technology, you are missing an opportunity to set the bar high and share your vision.

SETTING EXPECTATIONS

Here's a great letter home to parents and students, courtesy of Amy Dugré and Kristy Acero at The Willows Community School in Culver City, California. It sets expectations for the "hard fun" that lies ahead.

LIGHT IT UP! ELECTIVE CLASS INFORMATION & EXPECTATIONS

Dear Parents and Students,

We are excited that you joined the Light it Up! Elective. This class is intended to provide students with an opportunity to design, create, and make - anything. We have many wonderful resources, an abundance of materials, enthusiastic teachers, and even a guest engineer. Students in "Light it Up!" will spend the trimester lighting things up with LED lights, tape, & tubing. We will work with conductive thread, conductive paint, conductive and insulating dough, and other materials to connect and power our LEDs in a variety of media.

Throughout this class we will be using real tools to build, connect, and conduct. Tools such as wire, wire cutters, wire-strippers, hot plates, and solder will be used on a regular basis. Yes, we will use actual soldering stations, and they get HOT!

This class will be full of challenges: intellectual, material, and physical. In the spirit of Willows electives, this class will be fun, rewarding and safe, and to that end, it is imperative that all participants remember to treat the work, their classmates, and the space with respect and caution.

We want this experience to be a fun opportunity to expand science, art, engineering, programming, and technology skills for each student. To achieve this goal, we need the cooperation of all participating students. We expect each student to follow these guidelines:

• Give your best effort and be open to create.

• Be courteous and respectful of your classmates and teachers

• Follow ALL safety rules and guidelines.

• Wear safety goggles when working with small parts & solder

• Walk, never run, in the iLab.

• Contribute your thoughts, ideas, and talents

• And most of all…have fun.

Failure to comply with the above expectations may result in disciplinary action or dismissal from the class.

We look forward to the collaborations and creations that will come from this class. We will share our work at this year's Family Arts Night. As always, if you have any questions, please call or email us.

Sincerely,

Amy Dugre and Kristy Acero

INSPIRATION FROM MAKER FAIRES

Make magazine sponsors Maker Faires to "…celebrate arts, crafts, engineering, science projects, and the Do-It-Yourself (DIY) mindset." Since the first Maker Faire in San Mateo in 2006, there have been a number of Maker Faires around the world, many of them run by local DIY enthusiasts. In 2012, the San Mateo Maker Faire had an attendance of over 110,000 people of all ages who saw everything from a robot petting zoo to bands playing on human-powered hand-built electronic instruments, lock-picking workshops, motorized recliner chairs powering around the fairgrounds, and more.

Visit local Maker Faires for ideas, materials, and potential collaborators. Organize a field trip with students or have them exhibit their inventions at the local Maker Faire. Encourage parents to take the whole family – it will help parents see what is possible and will get them excited about your efforts to promote making and tinkering in the classroom.

Licensed Mini-Maker Faire – If you don't have a Maker Faire in your area, why not organize one yourself for your school and local community? *Make* magazine offers guidelines for making your very own official Mini Maker Faire at http://makerfaire.com/mini.

Make your own Maker Day – See our suggestions in Chapter 11.

COMMUNITY SPACES

Schools in need of the space, hardware, or expertise found in a professional makerspace should identify such resources outside of school for use by students during and after the school day. Depending on proximity and transportation issues, you may be able to hold class in a community makerspace. Local makerspaces may also support teacher professional development, fundraising for your school-based makerspace, and mentoring opportunities for students.

In some cases, your school will have the best or only makerspace in an area. If so, you can open your makerspace to the community or perhaps start a maker's club for the community. Interested members of the community can pay dues, help with fundraising. or help invest in hardware you might otherwise be unable to afford. Your makerspace could then be open for community use during non-school hours, much like a swimming pool on campus. Look for opportunities to collaborate with local community colleges, universities, corporations, and clubs.

Young Maker Club Resources – Contains ideas for setting up a local Young Maker Club with projects, getting-started ideas, and mentoring. http://youngmakers.org/resources/

Chapter 10 – Student Leadership

The biggest challenge and the biggest opportunity for the Maker Movement is to transform education. My hope is that the agents of change will be the students themselves. — Dale Dougherty

Creating a classroom makerspace is an opportunity to give students ownership of their own learning as they explore their own passions. Continually ask yourself, "What can my students do instead of me doing it? How can my students be agents of change rather than objects of change?"

This will vary widely at different ages. High school students should be able to take on responsibility for maintaining equipment, planning, research, and many high-level tasks.

However, don't underestimate the capability of younger students. Even students as young as five can learn how to properly take out and put away tools and materials. Slightly older students can share their expertise and teach skills with their peers. As students get older, find ways to challenge them and add more responsibility. When their response to being trusted is to ask to take on even more responsibility, you know you are heading in the right direction.

If you are a tech guru, it may be especially difficult to let go of the reins and not do everything yourself. After all, it is a given that you could do it better and faster. But that's not the goal. The goal is for the students to learn.

This "letting go" is not being a lazy teacher by making students do your job for you. Far from it. A teacher is highly engaged in the art of empowering young people, not getting work done.

SUPPORTING STUDENT LEADERSHIP

Leaders are experts, role models, and mentors no matter what age they are. Some students are natural leaders, while others need assistance to develop those skills.

Expertise: Encourage students to be experts and share their expertise. Make "Three before me" the motto of your classroom, meaning a student should not ask you for help before they ask three of their classmates. If you have a classroom full of students with their hands up chanting, "Teacher, teacher, teacher…" you need to be firm about changing this behavior.

Model this out loud for students. If a student asks you a question, try to find another student and suggest, "Sally, you know how to solder, why don't you teach Jimmy?" Pennsylvania teacher Maryann Molishus says:

> Peer support is especially useful when it comes to technology. Several projects the second graders have worked on have involved using Scratch computer programming. It took me several years to become proficient in using Scratch, and I only became proficient by using it with students and learning with them. Had I waited until I was completely comfortable on my own, I might never have introduced it to my students.

> I can remember first introducing Scratch to second graders. After showing them some basics, they were asked to explore. Minutes later, one student was crying that the computer wasn't doing what he wanted it to do. This was a very bright child for whom most things in school came easily. He was not sure how to handle the frustration and this became a great learning opportunity for him. Others in the class who often struggled became leaders with Scratch and were the ones who would demonstrate new skills and would support those who were having difficulty.

In Maryann's school, her fifth grade students share their Scratch expertise with other classrooms, extending the support for programming school-wide.

Management, logistics, and planning: Hand over as much of these tasks as possible to students. Students can be in charge of cleanup, setup, scheduling, and planning.

Leadership roles: The jobs and roles you give students can be formal or informal. Students can be given badges or ranks that identify them as experts. Escalating privileges, such as being allowed to check out or manage special equipment, could be given along the way. Bringing these students together as a campus leadership club can also benefit you as they take on responsibility, and in turn, it benefits them as they learn leadership, mentoring, and collaboration skills.

Recruiting: Put as much of the recruitment and promotion duties for clubs and events in the hands of students. Josh Burker shares:

Last week I held three promotional meetings for Tech Club during lunch recess. We met in the library since it is a public place where many students already congregate. I found last year that moving Tech Club from an out-of-the-way room to the library got more students to participate. I also asked three girls and a boy who participated last year to help me run the meetings by describing what each of the projects was about, by helping to answer questions, and by taking photos of the meetings.

I made a template that said "I like Tech Club because..." and gave it to students from last year's Tech Club. I asked them to hand write a couple of sentences that answered that question, then I took their photograph. I used the color laser printer to print their photo at the top of the page, then I mounted each of them to construction paper and laminated them before posting them in the 3–5 grade hallway. Many students stopped to read the testimonials from their peers. I figured that the students could do a much better job selling the club than I could.

Teach mentoring explicitly: Students almost always feel that they learn best by doing, but when they become the teacher they tend to lecture. Remind your little lecturers that that's not how people learn best. Teach them how to ask probing questions, be polite, and to not grab the mouse or tools away from the person they are helping.

Community service: There may be opportunities in your community for students to share their new expertise in summer camps, museum programs, or at a local hackerspace. The Make Education Initiative is sponsoring a new form of "Maker Corps" and is currently recruiting young people who will serve as peer mentors and role models in science centers, children's museums, schools, and libraries. These kinds of experiences can give an opportunity for kids to provide service in their communities and share the knowledge gained back at school.

ENGAGED AND EMPOWERED

If you want to build a ship, don't drum up people to collect wood and don't assign them tasks and work, but rather teach them to long for the endless immensity of the sea. — Antoine de Saint Exupéry

You often hear people talk about how technology is so engaging and empowering for kids. But that misses the point. It's not the technology that engages or empowers, it's the outcome of students (or anyone) doing meaningful work. Meaningful to themselves and to the community they are in. Empowering because someone trusted them to do something good and they shouldered the responsibility. Engaging because their passions are made real. These experiences are not something you *do* to kids or *give* to kids.

Teachers can shape a learning environment to favor empowerment over disempowerment. If you never allow a student to make an independent choice, you will certainly not end up with empowered students. But just allowing choice does not guarantee empowerment either.

However, empowered students can be difficult to handle at times. Once students get a taste of what it feels like to be in charge of things, you will have to monitor them to make sure they aren't making life miserable for other students. You may have students who are overly zealous about scheduling and rule-making. You may have students who are passionate advocates for one sort of technology over the other. You may find yourself entangled in endless arguments over versions, updates, operating systems, and other arcane technology details.

Being fair but firm with students is always a good strategy. They may not always agree with you about the tradeoffs in choosing materials or technology, but they will respect you if you are open and share the decision making with them. The time you spend with students discussing options and choices you are making will benefit your classroom in the long run.

Empowered students give one hope for the future of the world. Watching shy awkward young people turn into confident leaders and problem solvers makes you feel like the world is going to be just fine. It's one of the most exciting parts of giving young people the tools to shape their own learning and lives.

Chapter 11 – Make Your Own Maker Day

Tell me and I forget, teach me and I may remember, involve me and I learn.
— Benjamin Franklin

When it comes time to celebrate student making or to build support for such efforts, your school needs a Maker Day! Nothing gets a house cleaned quicker than guests arriving and performance opportunities help students focus on sharing their best work.

A Maker Day is not the same as a science fair. There is often too much "show and tell" or competition at a science fair. A Maker Day is about creativity and collaboration. It celebrates individual ingenuity within the context of the creative culture of shared values. The best way to communicate this message is to have plenty of quick projects that your Maker Day guests can participate in.

You want your Maker Day to send a loud and clear message to your community: "Our students learn by doing. We solve problems with modern tools, materials, and techniques. We value creativity and collaboration. Join us!"

PLANNING

Your Maker Day may be held during a school day, at night, or on a Saturday. You will want one large space as the "midway" and perhaps classrooms for short presentations or more formal demonstrations. Science labs, fab labs, or a stage may also be useful. The Maker Day may be outdoors in nice weather or elsewhere in the community. Why not hold your Maker Day in the local shopping mall?

Just be sure that you have access to needed electricity, water, light, air, and safety equipment wherever you choose to hold your Maker Day!

You may also decide to partner with another school, community organization, museum, or local tech shop in organizing the Maker Day.

Be sure to publicize your Maker Day and design its activities to be fun for the whole family!

Here are some tips for planning and leading a successful Maker Day:

Less Us, More Them

Involve kids in as much of the planning, organizing, and running of the Maker Day as possible. Be sure to include them on committees, have them decorate the venue, design the program, serve as guides, and lead demonstrations. Kids can even write letters to the editor and invite public officials to attend Maker Day. The kids will learn a lot and your event will be more successful.

Make (Nearly) Everything

Students should make as much as possible in preparation for the event. That includes marketing materials, invitations, signage, decoration, goodie bags, the website, the program, and snacks (where permissible).

Set the Tone

Handmade posters and navigational signs should greet guests on Maker Day. Kids should handle ticket and registration activities. They should also serve as guides and operate information kiosks.

One trick we developed at The Constructivist Celebration, Constructing Modern Knowledge institute, and Invent to Learn workshops is to have each attendee design their own name badge. Buy lots of inexpensive solid white stickers and hand one to each person who comes to Maker Day. Then point them to a nearby table loaded with crayons, pencils, paint, glitter pens, feathers, googly eyes, and other craft supplies where they will create their own personal one-of-a-kind name badge to wear throughout Maker Day. You might kick things up a notch by adding LEDs and watch batteries to the junk table.

Be sure to get basic contact information from adult attendees (name, address, phone number, and email address). You will want them to know about your next event and may be able to marshal support for future education initiatives.

Decorate With Examples of Classroom Making

Hang large photographs of students engaged in tinkering projects around Maker Day. Use minimal text to tell the story of those projects. Use this as an opportunity to convince your attendees that making, tinkering, and inventing are educationally sound.

Marketing

A professionally designed poster or flyer may generate interest in your Maker Day, but kids might design these materials as well.

Send press releases announcing the Maker Day to local newspapers, television, and radio stations. This effort serves to advertise the event and have it receive press coverage. Identify parents who may have connections to local media. Reporters often look for interesting hooks to build a story around. Come up with a "never been done before" angle to your day and it will attract more press.

Put flyers or posters in places where they are welcome (store windows, public bulletin boards, the public library), but be sure not to litter or place flyers in postal mailboxes (it's illegal!).

Don't forget to ask kids to create personal Maker Day invitations for their families, friends, and neighbors. This is an opportunity for some persuasive writing and design. Invitations may be handwritten, drawn or colored, or produced on the computer. The more personal the invitation, the larger the turnout will be.

How Many, How Much?

When planning extra-curricular activities, it's often a challenge to guess how many people will actually show up. You want your Maker Day to feel busy and inviting, with plenty of activities for all, yet not have some stations sit empty. Usually, 10–20 activities mixed between drop-in and longer workshops is the right amount.

Let the Kids Enjoy the Day

Strike a balance between kids showing off their inventions or leading hands-on activities with the benefits of them participating in the Maker Day. Be sure to rotate kids on and off stations, feed them, offer activities more than once, and not overschedule young inventors.

ACTIVITIES

Activities that are a little bit messy, surprising, and make you wonder are the best for a Maker Day. Minimize the number of activities that only have one right answer and favor hands-on experiences people may personalize and make their own.

Show Off AND Teach

Kids can set up booths where they share their inventions, but the best part of a Maker Day is the opportunity for attendees to make something or learn by doing. Focus as many stations as possible on action. Kids can lead them in some cases with the assistance of an adult. Allow learners of all ages to experiment, tinker, and most importantly, make things!

Label materials clearly, and where possible provide a handout designed to help a person recreate the experience at home. You may also include those activities on an easy-to-access website that not only advertises your Maker Day, but is a repository of its best project ideas, tips, tricks, shopping lists, videos, and photographs from Maker Day.

Start With a Bang

If you gather everyone at the start of the Maker Day, keep speeches short and to a minimum! A Maker Day is about action! Welcome the audience, acknowledge the local officials in attendance, thank the sponsors, and let the making begin with as little delay as possible. You might even consider thanking people in the program or on signage and skip the ceremony entirely.

If you do gather everyone together, consider having a kid lead everyone in a quick song, chant, or activity designed to get the creative juices flowing. You might even start the day with a quickie project if you can afford it. Why not have everyone make an LED throwie and toss them on the count of three, or make a racket with a handmade noisemaker? Look for opportunities for students to lead these activities.

Make a Schedule

If you wish to manage student presenters and offer maximum experiences for attendees, you need to create a clear schedule. Large versions may be posted around Maker Day, but paper copies should be freely available for attendees. Post the schedule on your Maker Day website prior to the event so people may plan their day in advance.

Have Plenty of Stuff to Do and Plenty of Stuff to Do With

Be sure to have ample supplies for the planned activities. You may also just have a "Maker Playground" area where attendees are free to invent and create with a wide assortment of arts and craft materials, broken toys, LEDs, batteries, hunks of wood, spools, film canisters, hammers, nails, glue guns, glue sticks, colored duct tape, paper/plastic cups, tiles, boxes, paper bags, pipe cleaners, coat hangers, construction paper, streamers, modeling clay, pipe cleaners, little plastic creatures, stickers, paint, etc.

Keep It Moving

While some attendees might spend hours at one station (and that is very cool), brevity is the key to a successful Maker Day. Show people how to do something and then let them do it. This isn't a real estate seminar or boring school class. Let attendees create lots of memories throughout the day by having as many experiences as possible.

Kick It Old School

Be sure to have an area where kids can sand, hammer, and nail wood pieces together resulting in either free-form sculptures or simple projects like toy cars, boats, or tool boxes. Other staples of childhood from bygone eras like cardboard construction, "soapbox derby" races, lanyard making, puppet making, paper airplane flying, and potholder weaving stations create great "make and take" stations.

You might even help participants make pinhole cameras, cigar-box guitars, or hot-air balloons.

Get sticky with your own Diet Coke and Mentos fountains, marshmallow canons, or other kid-safe weapons of mass interaction!

A pegboard marble wall is another great attraction. LEGO, Duplo, or other construction kit building is always a showstopper.

Don't forget to teach soldering under adult supervision and with proper safety precautions in place. Done safely, there is no more exciting experience for a kid.

Let Folks Touch the Future

Tutorials, workshops or demonstrations of Squishy Circuits, robotics, wearable computing, game design, Scratch, or Logo programming will amaze the adults in attendance and demonstrate that your school is on the cutting-edge. Turn the computer lab over to the kids and let them teach what they know. If you have 3D printers or laser cutters, demonstrate those as well.

Identify Experts

Ask parents who work in engineering, computing, construction, mechanics, or carpentry fields to share their expertise in hands-on activities. You may even be able to identify a local hero who can inspire the crowd with their tales of invention.

Make What You Eat and Eat What You Make

Ya gotta have snacks. Everything should be as homemade as permissible. Make your own sundaes, decorate your own cookies or cupcakes, and squish-the-dough-in-a-pan-and-add-your-own-toppings pizzas are yummy and in the spirit of Maker Day. Make ice cream with liquid nitrogen for a dramatic finish!

Perform

Have local or school bands perform throughout the day. This isn't a concert so you want the music to accompany the activity. Work with your music teacher to create small groups of student buskers.

Make a School Improvement

Need a school garden planted or a hallway painted? That seems in the spirit of Maker Day!

Put paint, brushes, plants, tools, etc. in the desired location and invite attendees to *make* your school better. Be sure to have proper safety equipment available and adhere to safe work practices.

Kids can make safety goggles. Note that these are not industry standard safety goggles, but they might be sufficient for safer tasks.

http://makeprojects.com/Project/Soda+Bottle+Goggles/2179/1

Fundraise

A Maker Day is an opportunity to raise some funds for future making. Auctions, raffle tickets, kit sales, T-shirts, buttons, face-painting, temporary crazy hair dying, and refreshments are all potential revenue sources. Be sure to comply with local laws and school traditions.

Cub Reporters

Have kids take photographs, shoot video, and write articles chronicling the Maker Day for the school newspaper, yearbook, local press, or your website.

WRAP IT UP

Announce the Date of Your Next Maker Day

Before people leave, be sure to announce the date for your next Maker Day.

Clean Up!

As the makers of Maker Day, kids should willingly participate in the cleanup activity.

Follow Up

Send thank you notes to volunteers, sponsors, and presenters, including kids.

MAKER DAY PROJECT IDEAS

Marble runs and ramps (small scale)
http://www.ambrosiagirl.com/blog/diy-marble-ramp/

Marble runs and ramps (large scale) http://bit.ly/marbleruns

Scribbling machines or scribble-bots are easy to make and fun to watch. Build robots using scrap materials with pens for legs and a small off-center motor. The vibrating motor causes the robot to dance around and scribble on a large sheet of paper. http://bit.ly/scribblemachines

LED throwies consist of an LED taped to a battery and a magnet. Throwing them creates a crowd-sourced light show.
http://www.instructables.com/id/LED-Throwies/

Cardboard automata (machines made of cardboard)
http://tinkering.exploratorium.edu/cardboard-automata/

Squishy Circuits can be made by mixing up your own dough and creating simple circuits.
http://courseweb.stthomas.edu/apthomas/SquishyCircuits/howTo.htm

Wind Tubes are easy-to-make large upright tubes with a fan at the bottom. Makers can build "stuff that floats" out of recycled materials, put their creations in the tube, and watch them fly up to the sky! http://tinkering.exploratorium.edu/wind-tubes/

Glow Doodle is software that allows you to "paint with light" by capturing a time-lapse picture of a light source moving in a dark room. Build Glow Doodle bottles using color LEDs, a switch and battery, and some simple soldering. Then, use Glow Doodle site or the webcam on a computer to create glowing pictures painted with light.

Glow Doodle site and software: http://scripts.mit.edu/~eric_r/glowdoodle/

Directions for Bottles: http://www.instructables.com/id/Light-Graffiti-Cans-for-Glowdoodle/

Chapter 12 – Making the Case

A ship in port is safe; but that is not what ships are built for. Sail out to sea and do new things.
— Grace Hopper

If you are an educator thinking about incorporating making, tinkering, and engineering in your classroom or school, you may need help. Convincing others, building consensus, and getting the funding are all valid concerns.

People may demand research or "proof" that the maker approach is good for students. Although there is academic research to support these ideas, the most authoritative data may not convince your critics. It is difficult to get people to change longstanding beliefs about education. Everyone is an expert on school, having been a firsthand participant for at least 12 years. The deepest and most closely held beliefs about learning come not from research reports, but personal experience. People cannot choose what they have not seen or experienced. Build consensus in advance by sharing your ideas with the community. Adults who learn by making, even in a brief workshop setting, may be more sympathetic to such approaches being applied in the classroom. Candid discussions with stakeholders about their own learning experiences may generate new supporters.

You should not make the case for making, tinkering, or engineering based on achievement or higher test scores. You may be tempted since some people equate learning with standardized testing. Indeed, there is research at the end of this chapter providing evidence of test score gains and better long-term understanding for children who are exposed to experiential learning, especially in STEM subjects.

However, you may find that if your reasons are based on test scores you will be judged by test scores. Test-prep is cheaper and faster than granting children the time and freedom necessary for creativity and invention. Live by the test and die by the test.

There are growing societal forces at work that can aid you in making the case. Business leaders, politicians, and futurists all agree that creativity and STEM-based making are top priorities for today's young people.

> I want us all to think about new and creative ways to engage young people in science and engineering, whether it's science festivals, robotics competitions, fairs that encourage young people to create and build and invent – to be makers of things, not just consumers of things. President Barack Obama (White House Hangout: The Maker Movement, 2013)

The powerful experiences that occur when you combine children's natural curiosity with amazing technology simply have to be seen to be believed. You may be as successful with Nike's motto of "Just Do It" as you are with trying to make a logical argument using research. This may require you to follow an older adage, "It's easier to ask forgiveness than it is to get permission."

Seeing engaged and excited students using nearly magical tools and technology will ultimately be the convincing factor for many people. Administrators, teachers, and parents will be hard-pressed to deny success when a reluctant student begs to do extra work or a student who "can't focus" creates a project with meticulous attention to detail.

KID POWER

Brian Smith is an ICT Facilitator at Hong Kong International School. His responsibility is to assist teachers in the primary school, primarily grades 3–5, in integrating technology into their curriculum. Brian is a believer in the power of invention and making and his goal is to bridge digital technologies with the physical world through both creating a makerspace for the school and also promoting constructionism in the classroom. Brian is approaching these goals by working on several aspects at once:

- **Use existing space in an informal way.** Brian's workspace is an underused room at the school called the Studio. Brian has opened the Studio before school, during lunch, and at recess for students to build with LEGO and PicoCrickets, take electronic and other devices apart, and free play with electronics and computers. Without announcements or even a scheduled club, students wander through the open door and are invited to build, tinker, and invent. Brian is always on hand to monitor students, and he gives impromptu lessons on robotics, programming, and soldering as needed. This has become popular enough that Brian now has to regulate the traffic to make sure everyone who wants to come in has a chance.
- **Build student capacity to use technology in their own inventions.** By allowing students to experiment and invent, they build skills that can be used in future inventions. This is not a "scope and sequence" of technical skills, but creates confidence in using these materials in a natural way.

- **Providing a platform for sharing.** Knowing that when students participate in personally meaningful projects they naturally want to share, Brian has created an online site for students to share their creations and ideas. This collaborative site can be used as a launching pad for their own websites or blogs around their projects and interests.
- **Give students an opportunity to experience iterative development.** Brian has chosen some projects to create incentives for students to iterate. For example, Glow Doodle is software that allows you to "paint with light" by capturing a time-lapse picture of a light source moving in a dark room. Brian has students build their own Glow Doodle bottles using color LEDs, jumper wires they have to trim and strip, and a switch and battery pack that they build. Then they solder the circuit. When finished, they use the Glow Doodle site or the app on their computer to create glowing pictures painted with light. Students naturally want to continue to build more bottles with different colors so they can make their Glow Doodle pictures better.
- **Build a stock of parts and equipment for projects.** Slowly building up stock of junk parts, used telephone equipment, and other supplies turns the students into detectives looking for recycling opportunities, and casts parents and teachers in the role of willing allies without asking too much time of them.
- **Work with specific students; gain student, teacher, and parent trust.** Besides the open door policy, Brian works with students during class time. Teachers refer these students to him because they are identified with specific interests or learning preferences and occasional behavior problems such as being unable to concentrate or sit still. Brian works one on one or with small numbers on projects of interest to the students.
- **Family nights.** Brian has run evening sessions where family members are invited to the space to see what students are doing and participate in some activities themselves.
- **Summer sessions.** Brian is planning to offer several summer sessions where students can sign up for a 3 weeks of making and inventing workshops.
- **Provide teachers with easy-to-do projects.** Building on a similar offering of weekly math puzzles, Brian creates challenges that students can complete with simple materials found in the Studio and at home. The challenges are similar to the "Weekly Challenge" found on the Instructables website http://www.instructables.com/id/Weekly-Challenges-Archive/
- **Support the curriculum.** Turtle Art provided a way for Brian to work with all fourth grade students and teachers and the school's science and math specialists on a project that combined art, geometry, and programming. These projects were done in classrooms with teachers participating.
- **Acquire 3D printers.** Brian has put in a request for the school to purchase Replicator 2 3D printers. While he waits, he is running projects where

students create digital building renovations to learn 3D design until the printers arrive.

None of these strategies would work in isolation. Brian believes that his best strategy for creating support for the makerspace and learning culture he envisions lies in two key areas: creating notable examples of success and building consensus with all stakeholders, especially students.

By focusing on experiences that the students can have right away, Brian believes that the parents, teachers, and administrators will see the result and be more open to these ideas. Note that the "shopping list" is simply one part of the process Brian sees as a long-term plan to bring more of a maker culture to the school.

Brian told us that his strategy is "Someday/Monday," inspired by Seymour Papert who said, "If you have a vision of Someday you can use this to guide what you do Monday. But if your vision of where it is going is doing the same old stuff a bit (or a lot) better, your efforts will be bypassed by history." (Papert, 1998)

PARENTS AND COMMUNITY

Often parents are torn between their respect for the institution of school and their intuition that something is not working for their child. Be clear while making your case that although your plans may not look exactly like traditional school, you are not abandoning high standards or a quest for learning. The argument for making, tinkering, and engineering should not be as an "alternative" way to learn, but what modern learning really looks like.

Look to your community for allies in making the case. Museums, science centers, colleges, and foundations are all interested in learning and creativity. Many museums, such as the Exploratorium in San Francisco, are taking their expertise in informal learning and engaging interactive displays and opening DIY exhibits and makerspaces. In colleges and universities, you may find allies in all departments from art to engineering. Local makerspaces or tech shops may be able to send speakers to school events or board meetings.

STUDENTS

Convincing your students that school can be different may be more difficult than you think. Kids have been taught through the years to expect teachers to spoon-feed them detailed recipes for success. Removing that safety net may cause some cognitive dissonance, especially for your most successful students. Such students have succeeded at mastering the rules of school and are not going to be happy when their competitive advantage is diminished.

They may also have developed a natural skepticism towards admonitions like, "Mistakes don't matter," when they rightfully suspect a traditional test will be given where mistakes *will* matter. It may take time to establish trust and implement authentic forms of assessment, rather than a pop quiz on 3D printer menu options.

SAY THIS, NOT THAT – ADVOCACY

When you need to advocate for your makerspace, try using some of the following phrases to help structure your argument:

Instead of saying this:
I realize that what I'm proposing is expensive.

Say the following:
- We have made significant investments creating computer labs where too few students have too little access to the resources they need.
- We are spending too much money on segregated art, shop, studio, and computer facilities. A makerspace would unite these resources and produce more opportunities for more students.
- Low-cost insurance and warranties exist for all such equipment.
- A makerspace represents an investment in much needed research and development.

Instead of saying this:
Students need to be prepared for the real world of the future.

Say the following:
- A makerspace offers the potential today for students to engage in the real work of mathematicians, scientists, composers, filmmakers, authors, computer scientists, and engineers, etc.
- We have an obligation to build upon the technological fluency the students bring to us, expand learning opportunities, and amplify human potential.

Instead of saying this:
Technology is so engaging to students.

Say the following:
- Too many of our students "check out" for some or all of their education. We can stem the tide of the growing epidemic of learning disability and students dropping out by increasing the range of experiences available to them.
- A computationally-rich learning environment, complete with physical computing or fabrication, can afford all students unprecedented opportunities to demonstrate their intellectual competence and creativity. This will place fewer students "at-risk" and make them more productive members of the learning community.
- Students will get to apprentice with teachers who also are learning in new ways with new materials.

Instead of saying this:
All students should be technology literate.

Say the following:
- Computers and other maker technologies are integral to the world of our students and it is incumbent upon us to build upon the skills, attitudes, and interests they bring to us.
- Every child in our district should be taught to program computers and understand the critical role computer science is playing across nearly every other discipline. The growing accessibility of fabrication and physical computing greatly expands the range of projects available to learners.
- Computer use must be appropriate, transparent, and ubiquitous across the curriculum, and computer science must be offered to all students when they need more specialized knowledge.

Instead of saying this:
It's just a tool.

Say the following:
- The computer has revolutionized every other aspect of society and the next phase of this revolution is fabrication and physical computing.

Instead of saying this:
All students need to learn to use a 3D printer.

Say the following:
- All students are expected to construct, communicate, and defend original thoughts and inventions to a community of experts and laypeople.

Instead of saying this:
A makerspace offers an alternative way to learn.

Say the following:
- The entire nature of schooling will and must change. If we do not respond to the promise of emerging technology and the challenges posed by social forces, we will not remain viable.
- We complain about student attention spans and yet ring a bell every 37 minutes to interrupt their thinking. Schools that allow students to work on creative inventions have demonstrated routinely that the work students produce without a step-by-step recipe often exceeds our wildest expectations of our students' abilities.
- The empowerment experienced while making, tinkering, and engineering should impact other aspects of teaching, student achievement, and self-efficacy.

SAY THIS, NOT THAT – REBUTTAL

When you are arguing for your makerspace plan:

When someone else says:
Our roofs need repair and there is no toilet paper in the school restrooms.

Answer in the following way:
- It is inexcusable to run out of basic supplies and we will work harder to ensure that it does not occur.
- Roof repair does not come out of the instructional budget and if it did, repairing roofs would do nothing to help us reinvent education for the 21st century or meet the needs of 21st century learners.

When someone else says:
Students will break, lose, or steal these tools.

Answer in the following way:
- Students feel respected when they are trusted with such important devices and have exceeded our expectations all over the world for decades. Neither school laptops nor trombones have proven to suffer abuse, loss, or theft.
- Students are competent and worthy of our trust.

When someone else says:
What about craftsmanship and learning to build real things?

Answer in the following way:
- The maker culture does not privilege the making of one type of artifact over another. However, some projects are more intellectually rich than others.
- Identifying the best strategy, tools, and processes for solving a problem is the goal, regardless of the task or chosen medium.

When someone else says:
What you are proposing is expensive.

Answer in the following way:
- So is our football program. Besides, schools routinely spend more money on the real estate, furniture, and wiring for computer labs that are being used for secretarial work and test taking.
- Instead of building a single purpose television studio or ceramics studio to be used by a handful of students, every student will have a studio that can be customized to create many kinds of products, inventions, and interesting things.
- We have an underutilized "shop" (or other) space that may be converted to a makerspace. However, we advocate making stuff across the curriculum in every classroom as a powerful form of knowledge construction.

- We already own computers and a great deal of tinkering can be accomplished using junk and recycled materials. Limited funds is just an engineering problem to overcome and no excuse for inaction.

When someone else says:
We should teach our teachers about this technology first so they can use it in their lessons.

Answer in the following way…
- We operate on the assumption that teachers love children and are employed to benefit kids. Learning with and alongside students affords teachers an opportunity to see what's possible through the eyes and screens of their students. Experiencing this potential is a powerful motivator.
- Microcomputers have been in schools for 30 years. A generation of children have been robbed of rich learning opportunities while we begged, bribed, cajoled, threatened, and tricked teachers into using the very same technology used everywhere outside of the classroom.
- There is no evidence that teaching a teacher about modern technology outside of the context of their practice will lead to innovative classroom practice.
- Students will lead the way in this learning revolution and there is no need to delay while we teach teachers to use technology and then hope it trickles down to the students.

When someone else says:
Students will look at dirty websites or print inappropriate 3D objects.

Answer in the following way:
- Students will use the computers in purposeful ways in the creation of meaningful projects they care about.
- When the dominant use of the computer is for looking stuff up, it should come as no surprise when kids look up inappropriate stuff. In a makerspace, Web surfing is just about the lamest thing a kid can do.
- You do children no favor by insulating them from some of life's less desirable elements, especially since they already spend so much time using computers. You teach children how to respond to inappropriate images or temptations, just as you teach them not to get in a car with strangers.
- The best filter is a professional educator or caring parent.

When someone else says:
Teachers won't cooperate; they don't use the computers we already have.

Answer in the following way:
- Making things appeals to a primal aspect of being human. Making things with tangible materials has a long tradition in schooling.

- Teachers value hands-on learning. Firsthand experiences with other constructive materials may be an invitation to making things with computational material.
- Making, tinkering, and engineering should be widespread across subjects and grade levels in all classrooms.
- Some teachers may need to rethink their career options.

When someone else says:

This is just a fancy shop class. Our children need to focus on getting into college.

Answer in the following way:

- The 21st century is going to see the integration of these tools into every college major and career choice. This is a matter of agency and personal empowerment. Engineering and art are interrelated; computer programming is mandatory for biologists, musicians, and historians. We can do our children no better service than to introduce them to the powerful ideas that will shape the rest of their lives. Along the way, they will help kids learn everything else.

When someone else says:

We should go slowly and proceed cautiously.

Answer in the following way:

- We owe it to our students to close the digital divide immediately and offer expanded learning opportunities.
- We know that students learn better and invest themselves in learning when it's meaningful and interesting. The time is now to start making this real.
- The opposition to one 3D printer is the same as the opposition to 20. We need to have the courage to lead on behalf of the children we care about.

INSPIRATION

If you need to convince parents, administrators, or funders to support classroom making, lend them a copy of this book or share these inspirational resources:

Learning by Making: American kids should be building rockets and robots, not taking standardized tests by Dale Dougherty (*Slate* magazine online) http://slate.me/132EezD

Make magazine Find an article or video that you think will inspire your community and share it widely. http://makezine.com/

Sylvia's Super Awesome Maker Show is a video series produced by Sylvia, an 11-year-old maker, and her father. The videos are youthful and vibrant examples of playful technology. http://sylviashow.com/

Why I LOVE My 3D Printer (and you will too!) is a video of a passionate talk by 12-year-old Schuyler St. Leger.
http://igniteshow.com/videos/why-i-love-my-3d-printer-and-you-will-too

Joey Hudy Goes to the Whitehouse Joey Hudy is a young maker and entrepreneur who surprised President Obama with a homemade marshmallow cannon in the White House.
http://blog.makezine.com/2012/02/07/joey-hudy-goes-to-washington/

Great Thinkers Endorse Play (quotes)
http://www.thestrong.org/about-play/play-quotes

Cain's Arcade http://cainesarcade.com/

MAKING THE CASE WITH RESEARCH

Research related to making in the classroom can be found to support your case. For some of the newest technology, research is in its embryonic stage. More general research studies going back decades or even further will support the deeper aspects of making the case for a makerspace.

The next few pages provide additional research about invention, tinkering, and engineering in the classroom. This is a very short, very limited selection that we hope is of assistance to the educator trying to make the case or write a grant proposal for making in the classroom. In addition, there are many references in the bibliography and the Resources chapter that point to research used to write this book. Links are provided when possible; for others, ask your librarian for access.

Fabrication and Physical Computing Research

The story of the FabLab@School project provides relevant and recent support for the use of fabrication labs in K–12 schools. (Blikstein, 2013)

Other Fabrication and Physical Computing Resources

- Berry, R. Q., III, Bull, G., Browning, C., Thomas, C. D., Starkweather, K., & Aylor, J. H. (2010). Preliminary considerations regarding use of digital fabrication to incorporate engineering design principles in elementary mathematics education. *Contemporary Issues in Technology and Teacher Education, 10(2),* 167–172.
  http://www.citejournal.org/vol10/iss2/editorial/article1.cfm
- Eisenberg, M., & Buechley, L. (2008). Pervasive fabrication: Making construction ubiquitous. *Education Journal of Software,* 3(4), 62–68.
- Eisenberg, M.(2011) Educational fabrication, in and out of the classroom. *Society for Information Technology & Teacher Education International Conference.* Vol. 2011. No. 1.

- Mellis, David A., and Leah Buechley. (2011) Scaffolding creativity with open source hardware. *Proceedings of the 8th ACM conference on Creativity and cognition.* ACM.
- Resnick, M., Bruckman, A., & Martin, F. (2000). Constructional Design: Creating New Construction Kits for Kids. In A. Druin, Hendler, James (Ed.), *Robots for Kids : Exploring New Technologies for Learning.* San Francisco: Morgan Kaufmann. (Out of print but available used.)
- Two technology associations – SITE and ITEEA – and two mathematics education associations – AMTE and NCTM – recently began a joint exploration of methods for identifying natural connections between mathematics and engineering design in the elementary curriculum. They have recently published some preliminary consideration of methods using digital fabrication to integrate the STEM disciplines in elementary classrooms.

Project-Based, Problem-Based, Inquiry Learning

- "Studies comparing learning outcomes for students taught via project-based learning versus traditional instruction show that when implemented well, PBL increases long-term retention of content, helps students perform as well as or better than traditional learners in high-stakes tests, improves problem-solving and collaboration skills, and improves students' attitudes towards learning."(Vega, 2012) http://www.edutopia.org/pbl-research-learning-outcomes
- "Decades of research illustrate the benefits of inquiry-based and cooperative learning to help students develop the knowledge and skills necessary to be successful in a rapidly changing world." (Darling-Hammond, 2008)
- PBL and inquiry-based strategies have been shown to raise student science and math achievement. (Gordon, Rogers, Comfort, Gavula, & McGee, 2001; Schneider, Krajcik, Marx, & Soloway, 2002)

Two comprehensive online clearinghouses offer resources, videos, articles, and research about project-based learning.

Buck Institute – http://www.bie.org

Edutopia – http://www.edutopia.org

Design, STEM, and the Arts

- *The Art and Craft of Science* in the February 2013 issue of Educational Leadership provides numerous examples and research supporting the integral nature of the arts in developing scientific skills. (Root-Bernstein & Root-Bernstein, 2013) http://bit.ly/artcraftscience

- A study following elementary teachers who were learning how to integrate design and project-based learning into math and science found significant results:

Their students became active learners and problem solvers. Indeed, their critical thinking skills, as evidenced by their ability to pose problems, seek answers, and test solutions, expanded and extended to other curriculum units. Their confidence increased, as they had to take responsibility for their own learning, becoming capable of researching, and finding answers to questions they posed for themselves. The questions became more complex and interrelated. No longer were curriculum areas isolated; mathematics, reading, writing and science are connected through design.

One of the most significant results from units centered on design is the benefit it has for inclusion students or students with special needs. All of the teachers who found that their inclusion students benefited from the experience, in ways they had not from traditional classroom learning activities, realized that the design process enfranchises a variety of learning styles, from the traditional academic instruction to the creative and eclectic. (Koch & Burghardt, 2002) http://scholar.lib.vt.edu/ejournals/JTE/v13n2/pdf/koch.pdf

Other Research

- Institute for the Integration of Technology into Teaching and Learning (2011), University of North Texas, National Science Foundation Innovative Technologies (ITEST) Grant #1030865 Interim Report http://iittl.unt.edu/IITTL/itest/fablab_web/index.html
- Akins, L., & Burghardt, D. (2006). *Work in Progress – Improving K–12 Mathematics Understanding with Engineering Design Projects.* Paper presented at the 2006 Frontiers in Education Conference, San Diego. http://bit.ly/engdesignpaper
- Scientists' early experiences with invention shaped their interest in careers in STEM. (Turkle, 2008) http://bit.ly/passionforobjects

Chapter 13 - Do Unto Ourselves

It is impossible to teach 21st century learners if you have not learned this century. — Gary Stager

Three decades ago, educational computing was built on progressive learning theories, propelled by passion of the civil rights movement and based on a notion that children could invent a better world than had existed for previous generations. Sadly, the powerful ideas have taken a back seat. The powerful ideas of Dewey, Holt, and Papert, not to mention Al Rogers, David Thornburg, Tom Snyder, and Fred D'Ignazio, have been replaced by a focus on filtering policies, meaningless clichés about 21st century skills, and lists of free apps. Too many educational technology conferences seem like a busload of tourists speeding past historical monuments in order to get to the next gift shop.

Tens of thousands of district tech directors, coordinators, and integrators have done such a swell job that after 30 years, teachers are the last adults in the industrialized world to use computers. The question must be asked, "Are the very same employees charged with inspiring teachers to use computers creating dependency and helplessness instead?"

Teachers should not be treated as imbeciles incapable of growth or felons who can't be trusted to show a YouTube video in class.

Educators love the stories of the 11-year-old dot.com millionaire, but would you really want her in your class? Can you build upon the gifts the kids bring to you or will you force them to comply with someone else's curriculum? Would you punish her or classify her with a learning disability for not sitting quietly through a semester of keyboarding?

Failure to embrace the kids' competence, capacity, and creativity leads educators to deprive children of opportunities to achieve their potential. Worst of all, it cheats children out of the rich 21st century childhood they deserve.

CONSTRUCTING MODERN KNOWLEDGE

Six years ago, the Constructing Modern Knowledge (CMK) summer institute was created based on two big ideas: (1) the educational technology community was operating in a vacuum in which it paid too little attention to learning, and (2) the progressive education community gave too little thought to modernity. Progressive education leaders have rarely seen good examples of computer use consistent with the social, emotional, creative, and intellectual development they champion. CMK is our attempt to create a non-coercive constructionist learning experience for educators of all subjects and grade levels.

It is impossible to teach 21st century learners if you have not learned this century. Professional development suffers from being too "meta." Teachers are asked to teach in ways in which they have no personal experience with tools in short supply. CMK addresses this concern by asking participating educators to remove their teacher hat and put on their learner hat for four days of collaboration, tinkering, and project development in a material-rich environment. Being a bit selfish pays dividends for learners when they don't have to worry about how they will teach a particular skill or watch the clock.

The design of professional development, especially efforts involving technology, is too often predicated on a presumption of adult inferiority. We are told that teachers are digital immigrants, that they need more professional development, and that our expectations need to be modest. Therefore, attending a teacher workshop where word processing and Web searching will be taught is viewed as a sophisticated accomplishment. In the world outside of K–12 education, such low-level technology use is assumed for toddlers.

Where there was an expectation 20 or 30 years ago that teachers would become technologically fluent enough to teach their students to program computers, today, the same level of effort is required to get a teacher to use an interactive white board. The continuous lowering of standards for professional conduct is exacerbated by the shift in agency from learner to the system. The computer, once viewed as a revolutionary vehicle for student empowerment, is too often used today as a way to deliver content and monitor achievement. The computer's power as an intellectual laboratory or vehicle for self-expression has been neutralized in the service of doing school a tiny bit better.

Can teachers learn when they feel intellectually powerful? Will they unleash their creativity simply by being treated as adults who care about learning? Is it possible for them to engage in conversation with experts they admire or invent a robot controlled by smiling into an iPad? The answer is a resounding YES. The joyous power of CMK is when teachers exceed their own expectations or report having crossed something off their "bucket list."

Designing a professional learning experience that can change a teacher's perspective on learning, allow engagement in complex project development, and provide first-hand experience with sophisticated materials are but a few goals of Constructing Modern Knowledge.

THE LEARNING ENVIRONMENT

For the past six summers, we have hosted hundreds of teachers at Constructing Modern Knowledge in Manchester, New Hampshire. Transforming a few meeting rooms and the corridors of a hotel into what author Seymour Sarason calls, "a productive context for learning," is an interesting challenge, but serves as inspiration for what is possible in actual schools without sophisticated architectural changes or significant investment. The learning space is the "third teacher" in the parlance of the Reggio Emilia approach. It should inspire, motivate, nurture, and inform practice as much as a parent or teacher. That's why the temporary learning environment of Constructing Modern Knowledge is filled with books, art supplies, laptop computers, robotics materials, LEGO, electronics, toys, recycled objects, marshmallows, bubble-blowing machines, construction kits, 3D printers, cameras, weather balloons, and assorted objects of whimsy. Since the path of a learning adventure is serendipitous, a great variety of provisions are required.

Cynthia Solomon, co-inventor of Logo, teaching programming at CMK

Some materials are used in a deliberate fashion to set a mood or convey a particular message. For example, large Post-It notes are assembled into a make-shift screen in the "theatre" used once a day, but there are no front-of-the-room or whole-class instructional tools in any of the other learning spaces. Finding a solution to your problem with the materials and expertise available is a critical part of the experience.

The CMK environment is designed to support the time-honored traditions of project-based learning, interdisciplinary units of inquiry, classroom centers, and collaboration without explicit instruction in any of these pedagogical practices. Teachers learn by doing in a context one might dream of for students or might never have believed possible.

THE PRACTICE

Piaget reminds us that knowledge is the consequence of experience. Working on personally meaningful projects, within the curriculum or as a hobby, is a powerful way to learn. The personal computer amplifies human potential and supports a greater breadth, depth, and range of projects than would be possible otherwise. The CMK environment affords the luxury of time, abundant materials, and expertise required for such project development.

CMK is unapologetically learner-centered and non-coercive. It honors epistemological pluralism and tacitly reminds educators that it is possible to learn without being taught. Interruptions to the learning process are minimized and learners are free to spend as much time as possible on their projects.

We begin the first day of CMK without much fanfare by engaging in a ritual that is initially daunting for some participants. Butcher paper is hung on walls and we ask for ideas that describe what participants would like to make. We coach the participants away from tool-oriented goals, such as "I want to learn how to use PhotoShop," or teaching-oriented goals, such as "I want to make a lesson about the Civil War." Drawing out project ideas takes time, but usually after 20 minutes the ideas start to flow. After a couple of dozen ideas are recorded on the walls of butcher paper, participants are asked to write their names next to any project that interests them. They are free to tag as many projects as they wish. Folks soon realize that there are more projects than participants and some ideas may be discarded or merged.

After a break, we ask for a volunteer to be the "beacon," not the leader of the project. There are no special responsibilities other than standing somewhere so people who wish to work together know where to meet. Then everybody begins working on a project with no greater plan than a few words you could fit on a Post-It note. Some projects will change personnel or direction dramatically. Others will stick close to the goal on the paper, which hangs prominently as a reminder throughout the institute.

Our expert faculty of gifted educators, inventors, and high-tech pioneers then spend four days supporting the project-based learning of participants. There are no lectures or workshops on specific tech skills. However, the faculty is happy to lead mini-tutorials alongside learners when initiated by the participants.

Learner initiative is critical. One year, when the small tank of provided helium failed to fill the five-foot weather balloon that a group of teachers needed, they had to rely on their ingenuity. A trip to a party store was required, but it would be impossible to use a regular car to transport the balloon back to CMK once it had been inflated. So they charmed the hotel shuttle bus driver into taking them to buy helium. Once at the party store, they received a stern lecture on the worldwide shortage of helium before the gas they needed was sold to them. This serendipitous event led to all sorts of new questions and learning opportunities. Where does helium come from? Why is there a shortage?

What will happen tomorrow when we go back to the party store for more helium because we accidentally popped the weather balloon?

As in the preschools of Reggio Emilia, CMK has appointments, but not strict schedules. Flexibility is prized and participants are treated as grown-ups. However, once a day everyone comes together for a conversation with a guest speaker. These speakers are carefully chosen to bridge the gap between progressive education and the frontiers of science, technology, engineering, and mathematics, with the arts and social justice thrown into the mix. Guest speakers have included astronomer Derrick Pitts, filmmaker Casey Neistat, historian James Loewen, project expert Lilian Katz, educator and MacArthur Genius Deborah Meier, author Alfie Kohn, science educator Bob Tinker, author Jonathan Kozol, Reggio Emilia Approach authority Lella Gandini, *Make* magazine editor Mark Frauenfelder, artist Peter Reynolds, and 11-year-old Web phenomenon, Super Awesome Sylvia. Guest speakers are encouraged to spend time sitting with participants and discussing their projects. The value of this experience for participants is priceless. Not only do they have an audience for their work-in-progress, but also the person showing an interest in them may be a personal hero.

Even CMK's seemingly casual approach to meals is by design. With the exception of one institute dinner, participants are free to make new friends and go out for lunch in a nearby restaurant. Some people bring food back or have it delivered in order to keep working on their projects. The benefits of setting your own pace and being trusted with autonomy are greater than the result of micromanaging. You are responsible for your time and learning. That learning continues even during top-secret late night missions seeking ice cream or margarita sampling.

Nothing is more thrilling than learning that a group of participants had breakfast with Lilian Katz or made plans to collaborate with one of our guest speakers after the institute. It isn't uncommon for FedEx to arrive with supplies ordered by a participant. Five recent CMK alums from different schools formed a panel discussion at the World Maker Faire in New York City to share their perspectives on classroom tinkering and learning by making. A community has been created that is the basis for collaboration across great distances long after the event.

In addition to our guest speakers, expert faculty, project-based learning, and materials-rich classroom, no "lifelong kindergarten" is complete without a field trip. Each year, CMK transports participants to Boston for a night on the town beginning with a reception hosted by a professor at the legendary MIT Media Lab. Each year, a different professor concerned with the intersection of learning, technology, and creativity talks about their work and CMK participants get a sneak peek at the Media Lab. After the brief reception, some participants tour Boston or go to a Red Sox game. Others participate in an optional "fireside chat" at MIT with Marvin Minsky, one of the fathers of artificial intelligence and one of the world's greatest scientists. Minsky is a generous and brilliant provocateur who delights in discussing any topic of interest with the assembled educators.

The morning after last year's trip to the Media Lab, CMK participants began work on projects incorporating the ideas and approximations of the technology being developed at MIT. Light-up paper origami made with a watch battery, LEDs, conductive tape, and paint emerged, and attempts were made to draw a piano with a graphite pencil that could then be played. Knowing that such possibilities are just around the corner is one thing. Engaging in the process of inventing your own versions of such technology represents a new level of empowerment for K–12 educators. Total success may remain elusive, but CMK participants join a community of engineers, composers, scientists, mathematicians, filmmakers, and more through their learning adventures.

THE PROJECTS

A few examples represent the multiple dozens of clever projects created by educators at Constructing Modern Knowledge.

Kate Tabor is a middle school English teacher and Shakespeare scholar. She spent her first CMK writing a computer program in MicroWorlds to generate random Elizabethan insults. The following year, she returned with photographs of Islamic tile patterns she observed in Spain. Using Turtle Art, she explored the geometry of those patterns and wrote programs to create new but similar patterns on the computer.

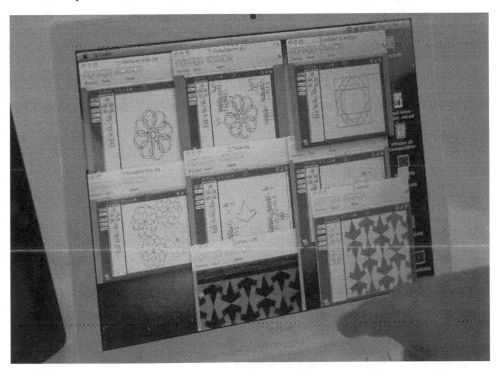

Islamic tile patterns in Turtle Art

Rick Weinberg announced during the brainstorming ritual that begins CMK that he wanted to be able to charge his iPhone while riding his bicycle to work. Eleven people said they were interested in collaborating, but Rick was soon working alone. By the end of day one, he had a small LEGO vehicle that could generate enough electricity to turn on a tiny LEGO light. The second morning, a local participant brought Rick an actual bicycle to use. By the end of CMK, Rick was riding the bicycle through the hotel lobby and charging an iPhone! The entire contraption was made of LEGO and string.

When Rick presented his work, he told a poignant tale of how his engineer father would try to calm his fears when he was a scared young boy aboard a roller coaster or airplane. His dad would say, "Don't worry. It's over-engineered." Rick confessed that he never really understood what that meant until 30+ years later when he built his iPhone charger. Learning that lesson was very important to him and connected his own understanding to a deeply personal childhood memory. Rick also explained that he now viewed the world differently. When asked by an admiring CMK participant if he was an engineer, Rick replied, "No. I'm a social studies teacher."

Two years ago, very few people had heard about wearable computers, but teachers at CMK not only learned about them, they began working with Lilypad Arduino materials. Young teachers were able to make a hat with a switch that allowed the wearer to switch between their "teacher hat" and "learner hat" by switching an LED pattern from T to L. They sewed LEDs into their school T-shirts and programmed a dancing pattern to illuminate their logo. What was science fiction a few years ago is now a fifth grade Father's Day present.

Similar materials have allowed CMK participants to invent cup holders that alert a consumer when the can gets warm, or electric piano keyboards made of bananas. Now, with the rapidly expanding toolkit of easy-to-use, affordable materials we've talked about throughout this book, teachers can expand their bag of tricks to support student projects.

Not all projects need to be high tech. The goal is to stretch personal boundaries and venture out of comfort zones. One summer, teachers co-wrote and performed a silly play with students at a community center in Rwanda, using Skype and simple tools. A school principal, an architect, and a teacher choreographed a dance for a video attempting to explain the Higgs Boson discovery that was recently in the news. When they arrived at MIT, they were able to discuss the science with Professor Minsky. Dance, technology, filmmaking, and conversation with a great scientist make a powerful brew for understanding complex phenomena. These experiences provide teachers with a deeper understanding of their own learning processes so they can be more aware of their students' individual learning processes.

Perhaps the finest example of serendipitous learning and exceeding expectations comes from the experience of three teachers who attended CMK together. They began working on a computer programming project and quickly became frustrated. Knowing that the expectation was to be doing something, they looked around for something to do. On the table filled with toys and miscellaneous gadgets was a kit to build a replica of an Edison cylinder phonograph. They thought, "How hard could this possibly be?"

They soon found out when they opened the package and realized that the building instructions were in Japanese. A combination of guilt and responsibility propelled them forward since they had broken the seal. Off they went to figure out the instructions, learning the Japanese necessary to build a phonograph that records sound by scratching a plastic drinking cup and then plays the sound by reading the same scratches. When the phonograph was eventually completed, it seemed to work properly. However, the recording volume was imperceptible. With a sense of urgency the team grabbed a microphone, downloaded and installed the audio editing software Audacity, recorded the phonograph playback, figured out how to amplify the recording digitally, and then waited to hear if their invention worked. Boy, did it!

When the voice of one of the teachers was reproduced by the plastic cup phonograph, a history teacher on the team exclaimed, "Holy sh#t, I sound just like Eleanor Roosevelt!" Then she got somber for a moment and confessed, "I'm a good history teacher and pride myself on using primary sources with my students. I play newsreels of Hitler and Stalin and Roosevelt so students can hear their voices. It never occurred to me before that maybe Eleanor Roosevelt didn't sound like Eleanor Roosevelt! Perhaps that's how she sounded because of the recording technology of that era? I wonder if linguistic patterns changed in the culture because the populace thought that is how important people talk?"

All of these questions led to explorations into linguistics, culture, and the impact of technology on society. The promises Edison made for how the phonograph would revolutionize education were compared to Steve Jobs' similar claims for the iPad. Along the way, a wooden automata puppet of Edison was built so he could make his bold claims in the video they spontaneously shot and edited.

Jonathan Kozol listens to the plastic cup phonograph

So, teachers with beginner technology skills were able to build a working phonograph, teach themselves to record and edit audio on a computer, engage in historical and linguistic inquiry, build a puppet, and shoot and edit a film in less than four days – all because they didn't wish to continue working on the first project they started.

When a kindergarten teacher gleefully shares her first molecular simulation with a scientist, or a music teacher and art teacher collaborate on an animated music video, but switch roles "for fun," or an English teacher uses computer science and mathematics to investigate Islamic art, this is not your standard computer workshop for teachers. Skills are not learned in isolation, but deeply embedded in the pursuit of personal project goals. The boundaries between subject areas and disciplines evaporate and educators realize that they are not alone in wanting more for their students than test-prep.

Most of all, the CMK experience demonstrates that teachers are competent. Like all learners, an educator is not a vessel to be filled, but a lamp to be lit.

Chapter 14 – Resources to Explore

Sometimes the questions are complicated and the answers are simple. — Dr. Seuss

This chapter contains numerous resources including books, websites, articles, videos, and toys. Some are repeated from the previous chapters. We have included articles that are primarily research or evaluation in the chapter on Making the Case and many books are listed in the Bibliography.

As with all links in this book, we apologize in advance if they have changed by the time you read this book. We list these resources (and more!) at the companion website http://InventToLearn.com and will update those links.

PROJECT COLLECTIONS, TUTORIALS, AND INSPIRATION

- **Howtoons** – Comic strip stories to inspire building, designing, engineering and inventing. http://www.howtoons.com/
- **How Stuff Works** – Diagrams and explanations of how machines and everyday objects work. http://www.howstuffworks.com
- **Instructables** – A DIY online community http://www.instructables.com/
- **Make Magazine Projects** – Projects in electronics, craft, science, art, robots, and many more categories in all ranges of challenge.
  http://blog.makezine.com/projects/
- **FabLab@School** – Main site for projects, video tutorials, blog posts, and more about the global network of FabLabs in K–12 schools http://fablabatschool.org/
- **Toy-A-Day Blog** – Fun toys to inspire and delight.
  http://toy-a-day.blogspot.com/
- **Geek Dad Blog** – Besides writing books, Geek Dad blogs at Wired.com about doing projects with kids. http://www.wired.com/geekdad/

- **Sylvia's Super Awesome Maker Show** – 11-year-old Super-awesome Sylvia and her father produce a whimsical video show showing how to build fun electronic projects. http://sylviashow.com
- **Invention Projects** – A list of activities to make your own lightbulb, gramophone, and other famous inventions from the Spark!Lab at the National Museum of American History in Washington, DC http://sparklab.si.edu/spark-experiments.html
- **The Caberet Mechanical Theatre** – Projects, blogs, and kits for building whimsical moving mechanical sculpture. http://www.cabaret.co.uk/

Supplier Site Projects

Many manufacturers, publishers, and stores, and have project libraries, tutorials, and resources for educators. These are just a small sample.
- **Makerbot 3D Printing Education** – Tutorials and STEM fabrication projects. http://curriculum.makerbot.com/
- **Sparkfun Tutorials** – Beginner, intermediate, and advanced tutorials for Arduino, electronics, wearable computing, and more. http://learn.sparkfun.com/curriculum
- **Adafruit Learning System** – Projects, guides, and tutorials on Arduino, microprocessors, components, tools, and more. http://learn.adafruit.com/
- **Adafruit for Educators** – Special blog for educators focusing on making in the classroom around the world. http://www.adafruit.com/blog/category/educators/

Good Starter Projects

- **Digitally Interfaced Book: Paper, Graphite, Makey Makey, Scratch, and Imagination** – Instructions for completing an interactive book project http://digitalis.nwp.org/resource/4885
- **Marble runs and ramps** – Small scale versions http://ambrosiagirl.com/blog/diy-marble-ramp/
- **Marble runs and ramps** – Large scale versions http://bit.ly/marbleruns
- **Scribbling machines or scribble-bots** – Easy to build robots using scrap materials with pens for legs and a small off-center motor. The vibrating motor causes the robot to dance around and scribble on a large sheet of paper http://bit.ly/scribblemachines
- **LED Throwies** – An LED taped to a battery and a magnet creates a crowd-sourced light show http://www.instructables.com/id/LED-Throwies/
- **Wind Tubes** – Easy to make large upright tubes with a fan at the bottom. Makers can build "stuff that floats" out of recycled materials, put their creations in the tube and watch them fly up to the sky! http://tinkering.exploratorium.edu/wind-tubes/
- **Glow Doodle Software** – Software to create pictures with glowing light http://scripts.mit.edu/~eric_r/glowdoodle/
- **Glow Doodle Bottles** – Make bottles for glowing light pictures http://www.instructables.com/id/Light-Graffiti-Cans-for-Glowdoodle/

Books

These books (and more) can be found at: http://InventToLearn.com/books

- *Unbored: The Essential Field Guide to Serious Fun* – A zillion high- and low-tech project ideas with suggestions for amusing yourself.
- *The New Way Things Work* – Every classroom needs at least one copy of David Macauley's beautifully illustrated book of how things work.
- *Geek Dad: Awesomely Geeky Projects and Activities for Dads and Kids to Share* – The first book in this terrific series
- *The Geek Dad's Guide to Weekend Fun: Cool Hacks, Cutting-Edge Games, and More Awesome Projects for the Whole Family* – The second volume in the Geek Dad series
- *The Geek Dad Book for Aspiring Mad Scientists: The Coolest Experiments and Projects for Science Fairs and Family Fun* – The third Geek Dad book
- *Geek Mom: Projects, Tips, and Adventures for Moms and Their 21st-Century Families* – More fun projects for families to build together
- *50 Dangerous Things (You Should Let Your Children Do)* – By Gever Tulley and Julie Spiegler
- *The Big Book of Hacks: 264 Amazing DIY Tech Projects* – Really cool and beautifully photographed tech projects ideas for kids and adults alike.
- *Photojojo!: Insanely Great Photo Projects and DIY Ideas* – This book is filled with insanely creative ways to turn your photographs into amazing products and crazy ways to capture photographs you won't believe. Fun for the whole family!
- *Fifty Dangerous Things (You Should Let Your Children Do and Why)* – Gever Tulley's self-explanatory classic on messing-about in the real world wth real stuff, just like real kids.
- *62 Projects to Make with a Dead Computer: (And Other Discarded Electronics)* – Computer hacking takes on a whole new meaning when you're going at it with a screwdriver and hammer.
- *The Best of Instructables Volume I* – Do-It-Yourself Projects from the World's Biggest Show & Tell
- *Recycle This Book: 100 Top Children's Book Authors Tell You How to Go Green* – Essays from renowned children's book authors provide an informative and inspiring call to kids of all ages to understand what's happening to the environment, and take action in saving our world.
- *Steven Caney's Invention Book* – Steve Caney's books are mostly out of print, but available used online. All his books are full of whimsical projects that are good to have in a makerspace for inspiration.

Parenting Advice

- **Free-range Kids** – Common sense advice about parenting http://www.freerangekids.com/
- *Beware Dangerism!* – By Gever Tulley (Kindle Single) http://amzn.to/ZhB47i

Online Clubs for Kids

- **DIY.org** – Maker "Scouts" – online tutorials, upload pictures of creations with a phone app and collect badges http://diy.org
- **Built By Kids Club** – Project ideas, tool tutorials, and weekly projects for club members http://builtbykids.com/

MAKERSPACES AND HACKERSPACES

- **Makerspace Directory** – Worldwide list of makerspaces. http://makerspace.com/makerspace-directory
- **Hackerspaces.org** – A list of hackerspaces worldwide, events, challenges, resources, and more http://hackerspaces.org/
- **Hackerspace Meetup groups** – http://hackerspaces.meetup.com/
- **Makerspace Meetup groups** – http://makerspaces.meetup.com/
- **TechShop** – Shared workshop spaces in seven communities, more planned to open soon. http://www.techshop.ws/

In Museums and Libraries

- **Tinkering Studio** – Experiments, projects, blogs, and events from the Exploratorium Museum in San Francisco http://tinkering.exploratorium.edu/
- **Learning Technology Center** – Exploring design and informal science learning at the Science Museum of Minnesota http://www.smm.org/ltc
- **New York Hall of Science** – NYSCI features the largest collection of hands-on science exhibits in New York City and runs hands on maker events. http://www.nysci.org/
- **A Librarian's Guide to Makerspaces: 16 Resources** – Resources and sites about makerspaces in public and school libraries. http://oedb.org/blogs/ilibrarian/2013/a-librarians-guide-to-makerspaces/

Fab Labs

- **K–12 Digital Fabrication Labs Discussion Group** – A google group of K–12 educators who share ideas, projects, and resources. http://bit.ly/k12fablabgroup
- **FabLab@School Blog** – A group blog with contributions from over 400 global fablabs in schools worldwide. http://fablabatschool.org/profiles/blog/list
- **Fab Central** – Organizing website for worldwide fab labs maintained by the MIT Center for Bits and Atoms http://fab.cba.mit.edu

MAKE MAGAZINE

Make magazine has spawned a number of websites, organizations, events and more.

- **Make Magazine** – A print and online magazine for inventors and tinkerers of all ages http://makezine.com/

- **Craft** – Crafting projects. The magzine is no longer in print, but the website has good resources http://www.craftzine.com
- **Makers Faire** – See and share inventions around the world http://makerfaire.com/
- **Mini-Makers Faires** – Small, independently-run Makers Faires http://makerfaire.com/mini
- **Young Makers** – Connecting youth makers with adult mentors http://www.youngmakers.org/
- **Maker Education Initiative** – Promotes a Young Maker Corps and Maker Clubs http://makered.org/
- **Makerspace Playbook** – Ideas for schools starting a makerspace or planning a local Mini-MakerFaire http://makerspace.com/playbook
- **Maker Corps** – A volunteer organization to support makerspaces in schools http://makered.org/makercorps/

VIDEOS

- **Making in Education** – Gary Stager's interview with Steve Hargadon at the 2012 San Mateo Maker Faire http://youtu.be/RVJfba1TAhg
- **FabLab@School: One Fabrication Lab per School** – A TEDx talk by Paulo Blikstein http://youtu.be/ylhfpDAniqM
- **Leah Buechley's TED Talk, "How to Sketch with Electronics"** – Inspiring and beautiful video. http://bit.ly/sketchwith
- **Mike Eisenberg's plenary address** based on his paper, "*Constructionism: New Technologies, New Purposes.*" at the Constructionism 2012 Conference in Athens, Greece. Anyone interested in learning, emerging technology, creativity, the arts, science, or craft would be wise to watch this terrific presentation. http://vimeo.com/49891132
- **Tinkering School** – A four minute TED Talk by Gever Tully showcasing learning by tinkering http://bit.ly/tinkeringschool
- **Tinkering as a mode of knowledge production in a Digital Age** – John Seeley Brown http://vimeo.com/2183356

Videos by Kids

- **Why I LOVE My 3D Printer (and you will too!)** – A passionate talk by 10 year old Schuyler St. Leger http://igniteshow.com/videos/why-i-love-my-3d-printer-and-you-will-too
- **Joey Hudy Goes to the Whitehouse** – Joey Hudy is a young maker and entrepreneur who surprised President Obama with a homemade marshmallow cannon in the White House http://blog.makezine.com/2012/02/07/joey-hudy-goes-to-washington/

ORGANIZATIONS

- **DIYAbility** – "Where McGyver meets Assistive Technology" Projects, workshops and resources on making and hacking for children with disabilities. http://www.diyability.org/
- **Citizen Scientists League** – A group of scientists and science hobbyists dedicated to promoting the tools and skills of science. http://citizenscientistsleague.com
- **Code.org** – Code.org is a non-profit foundation dedicated to growing computer programming education. http://www.code.org/

CONSTRUCTIONISM RESOURCES

Here are some web-based papers and articles you might read if you are interested in learning more about Seymour Papert's theory of constructionism.

- **The Eight Big Ideas of the Constructionist Learning Lab** The father of constructionism explains what it looks like in this guide for laypeople http://stager.org/articles/8bigideas.pdf
- **Constructionism vs. Instructionism** by Seymour Papert http://papert.org/articles/const_inst/const_inst1.html
- **Constructivism(s): Shared roots, crossed paths, multiple legacies** – a brilliant overview of constructivism and constructionism by Edith Ackermann http://linkedith.kaywa.com/files/PaperConstr.2010.EA.Final.pdf
- **Computer as Material: Messing About With Time** by George Franz and Seymour Papert http://papert.org/articles/ComputerAsMaterial.html
- **A Critique of Technocentrism in Thinking About the School of the Future** by Seymour Papert http://papert.org/articles/ACritiqueofTechnocentrism.html
- **Epistemological Pluralism and the Revaluation of the Concrete** – an incredibly powerful paper by Sherry Turkle and Seymour Papert http://papert.org/articles/EpistemologicalPluralism.html
- **Computer as Mudpie** by Seymour Papert http://bit.ly/fUik9v
- **What's the Big Idea? Toward a pedagogy of idea power** by Seymour Papert http://web.archive.org/web/20060501165026/ also as a PDF from the IBM Systems Journal http://www.research.ibm.com/journal/sj/393/part2/papert.pdf
- **Situating Constructionism** – The first chapter from the book *Constructionism*, edited by Idit Harel and Seymour Papert http://papert.org/articles/SituatingConstructionism.html
- **Climbing to Understanding: Lessons from an Experimental Learning Environment for Adjudicated Youth** By David Cavallo, Seymour Papert, and Gary Stager http://stager.org/articles/ICLS%20stager%20papert%20cavallo%20paper.pdf
- **Papert.org** – Online collection of articles, speeches, and book chapters by Seymour Papert http://www.papert.org/
- **DailyPapert** – a collection of quotes from Seymour Papert curated by Gary Stager. http://dailypapert.com

Constructionism Books

- *Constructionism in Practice: Designing, Thinking, and Learning in A Digital World* by Yasmin B. Kafai and Mitchel Resnick

Books by Seymour Papert

Seymour Papert's seminal books were written over a span of several decades and explore different aspects of constructionism. In short, the three books all explore constructionism but from different points of view, respectively, that of the learner, the teacher, and the parent. Links to these books (and more) can be found at: http://www.InventToLearn.com/books

- *Mindstorms: Children, Computers, And Powerful Ideas* – Constructionism explained as the way people naturally learn. In it, Papert explores how learning to program computers and gain mastery over them can influence how children learn everything else.
- *The Children's Machine: Rethinking School In The Age Of The Computer* – Looking back on the first decade of computers in schools and where we need to go now.
- *The Connected Family: Bridging the Digital Generation Gap* – How parents can understand computers as thinking and learning partners rather than a menace.

REGGIO EMILIA APPROACH

- *The Hundred Languages of Children* – The definitive book on the Reggio Emilia Approach by Carolyn Edwards, Lella Gandini, and George Forman, Editors
- **Reggio Children** – The international resource for educators interested in the Reggio Emilia approach http://zerosei.comune.re.it/inter/reggiochildren.htm
- **Learning Materials Workshop** – Books, videos, and toys inspired by the Reggio Emilia Approach. This company also sells gorgeous books from Italy (in English) http://learningmaterialswork.com/
- *Beautiful Stuff: Learning with Found Materials* – By Cathy Wiseman Topal and Lella Gandini

ADVOCACY, REPORTS, AND ARTICLES

- **Running On Empty** – Report on the failure to teach computer science from the Association for Computing Machinery (ACM) http://www.acm.org/runningon-empty/
- **Innovation, Education, and the Maker Movement** – Final report from the New York Hall of Science 2010 Making Workshop http://www.nysci.org/media/file/MakerFaireReportFinal122310.pdf
- **Design-Make-Play: Growing the Next Generation of Science Innovators** – Final report from the New York Hall of Science 2012 Making Workshop http://www.nysci.org/media/file/DMP-Report-2012.pdf

- **Engaging Students in the STEM Classroom Through Making** – By Ann Marie Thomas http://www.edutopia.org/blog/stem-engagement-maker-movement-annmarie-thomas
- **Extreme Marshmallow Cannons! How the government and private sector can turn American kids on to science through "Making"** – By Thomas Kalil http://slate.me/YYnZjV
- **Learning by Making: American kids should be building rockets and robots, not taking standardized tests** – By Dale Dougherty (Slate magazine online) http://slate.me/132EezD

RESEARCH GROUPS

- **High-Low Tech group at MIT** – Engages diverse audiences in designing and building their own technologies and develops tools that democratize engineering. http://hlt.media.mit.edu/
- **MIT Media Lab Lifelong Kindergarten Group** – Mitchel Rensick's constructionist research group at MIT http://llk.media.mit.edu/
- **MIT Center for Bits and Atoms** – Neil Gershenfeld's fabrication research lab at MIT http://cba.mit.edu/
- **FabLab@School** – A Stanford Education School project supporting school-based FabLabs http://tltl.stanford.edu/projects/fablabschool
- **Craft Tech Lab** – Mike Eisenberg heads this research group at Colorado University, Boulder interweaving computation and craft materials. Website offers research, resources, and community outreach events. http://l3d.cs.colorado.edu/~ctg/Craft_Tech.html

INVENTORS AND INVENTING

- **Edison Muckers** – All about Edison and inventing http://www.edisonmuckers.org/
- **Invent Now** – A non-profit that supports invention through contests, camps and hosts the National Inventors Hall of Fame, including an online database of inventors. http://www.invent.org/
- **Inventions, Inventors, and Invention Stories** – Articles, video, classroom resources, and an audio database of famous inventors and invention from the Smithsonian's Lemelson Center for the Study of Invention and Innovation. http://invention.smithsonian.org/

PLAY RESOURCES

- **American Journal of Play** – Peer reviewed but accessible for a wide audience, the journal covers the history, science, and culture of play to increase awareness and understanding of the role of play in learning and human development and the ways in which play illuminates cultural history http://www.journalofplay.org/

- **The Strong** – An educational institution in Rochester, NY devoted to the study and exploration of play. The National Museum of play features exhibits, collections, and research, plus the National Toy Hall of Fame and the International Center for the History of Electronic Games. http://www.thestrong.org
- *Play: How it Shapes the Brain, Opens the Imagination, and Invigorates the Soul* – By Stuart Brown

PLACES TO PURCHASE PARTS AND SUPPLIES

- **Sparkfun Electronics** – Specializes in hobbyist electronic components, tools, and kits. The website features a project blog, buying guides, and tutorials from soldering to using a breadboard. Ask for educator discounts. http://www.sparkfun.com
- **Adafruit** – "Unique and Fun DIY Electronics and Kits." Check the Young Engineers section for selections that are whimsical and fun. Ask for educator discounts. http://www.adafruit.com
- **Maker Shed** – Vetted by Make Magazine. Specializes in kits for learners of all ages http://www.makershed.com/
- **Electronics Goldmine** – Extensive supply of cheap electronic parts. Look for deals and bulk purchases, for example, a container of 200 LEDs costs $5.00. http://www.goldmine-elec.com/
- **Jameco Electronics**. Another popular source of electronics parts and kits. http://www.jameco.com

3D PRINTING AND FABRICATION

- **The Edutech Wiki** – 3D printer guide for educators http://edutechwiki.unige.ch/en/3D_printing
- **Instructables Introduction to 3D printing** – Simple introduction to 3D printing with many photographs http://www.instructables.com/id/3D-Printing-1/
- **Make Magazine (Winter 2013) – 3D Printer Buyer's Guide** – Extensive product comparisons and recommendations for printers of various types and price ranges. http://amzn.to/17ccaGR
- **Makerbot** – Printers, materials, tools, blogs, and community forums about 3D fabrication. http://makerbot.com/
- **Thingiverse** – Thingiverse is a place to search for or share digital designs with the world for laser cutters, CNC machines, 3D printers, and even automated paper cutters. The site is hosted by 3D printer manufacturer MakerBot. http://www.thingiverse.com/
- **Fab Central** – MIT Center for Bits and Atoms (CBA) clearinghouse for global projects, tools, events, etc. using 3D fabrication. http://fab.cba.mit.edu/
- **3D Printing News** – News articles about global 3D fabrication in industry, medicine, art, and more. http://on3dprinting.com

Software for 3D Design

- **SketchUp** – A free, easy to use 3D modeling program. There is an online warehouse of models to download or contribute to. http://www.sketchup.com
- **Autodesk's 123D** – Free 3D modeling program, available both browser-based and as a downloadable app. Options include creating paper sliced or folded creations. http://www.123dapp.com/
- **Shapesmith** – Free, open source, browser-based 3D modeler. http://www.shapesmith.net
- **3DTin** – Free use 3D modeling program, charges for storage. Browser-based (WebGL enabled browser required). http://www.3dtin.com
- **Printcraft** – Print your Minecraft creations on a 3D printer http://www.printcraft.org
- **ReplicatorG** – Open source CAM program http://replicat.org
- **Blender** – Blender is a widely used 3D creation tool, free to use for any purpose and supported by a worldwide developer and user community. Blender has a high learning curve but may interest students who are fans of 3D animation or video games. http://www.blender.org/

3D Printing Services

- **Shapeways** – Upload a design and it will be printed and delivered to you. Also offers a community and marketplace to sell your own designs. http://shapeways.com
- **Ponoko** – Create your own design or modify someone else's with an easy to use "Personal Factory." Your object will be delivered to you in plastic, wood, metal, ceramics, acrylic, or other materials. http://ponoko.com
- **Sculpteo** – Print your 3D object in a variety of materials. Browse designer collections or open a 3D object store. Offers plugins for SketchUp and Blender. http://sculpteo.com

Cutters

- **Laser cutters** – Although we do not directly address laser cutters in this book, they can be a part of a school makerspace. Adafruit has a terrific tutorial and buyers guide for those thinking about laser cutters http://learn.adafruit.com/all-about-laser-cutters/overview
- **Programmable vinyl cutters** – Roland, US Cutter, and other companies make vinyl cutters. Look for large format printer companies in your area. http://www.rolanddga.com/ or http://www.uscutter.com/
- **Cutter software** – You will need a vector graphics program such as Adobe Illustrator, or the free open source Inkscape (also many cutters come with their own software) http://inkscape.org/

COPYRIGHT AND INTELLECTUAL PROPERTY

- **Creative Commons** – Free, easy-to-use copyright licenses provide a simple, standardized way to give the public permission to share and use your creative work — on conditions of your choice. http://creativecommons.org/
- **"It Will Be Awesome if They Don't Screw it Up: 3D Printing, Intellectual Property, and the Fight Over the Next Great Disruptive Technology"** by Michael Weinberg. http://www.publicknowledge.org/it-will-be-awesome-if-they-dont-screw-it-up

ELECTRONICS

- **Instructables How to Solder** http://instructables.com/id/How-to-solder/
- **Sylvia's Maker Show How To Solder** – Fun handout on how to solder with great tips and safety instructions http://sylviashow.com/printables/how-solder
- **Circuit Playground (app)** – This $2.99 app gives quick access to useful electronics information such as resistor & capacitor codes; calculate power, resistance, current, and voltage; convert between decimal, hexadecimal, binary or ASCII characters http://adafruit.com/circuitplayground
- **Adafruit Electronics Coloring Book** – Cute introduction to electronics http://adafruit.com/coloringbook/
- **Adafruit's Circuit Playground** – A is for Ampere (Episode 1) http://www.adafruit.com/blog/2013/04/02/circuit-playground-a-is-for-ampere-episode-1/
- *Make: Electronics* – Charles Platt's thorough text explaining the world of electronics – a great resource for your library.

PHYSICAL COMPUTING

Arduino

- **Arduino website** – Open source electronics prototyping platform and robotics controller for interactive projects. http://www.arduino.cc/
- **Make Magazine Arduino** – Videos, project ideas, how-tos, kits, parts, and blog posts about what people are doing around the world with the Arduino. http://blog.makezine.com/arduino/
- **Modkit** – An iconic programming environment for controlling Arduino, Lilypad, and a number of other popular microcontrollers http://modk.it
- *Programming Arduino: Getting Started with Sketches* – By Simon Monk. Clear, easy-to-follow downloadable examples show you how to program Arduino in C. This is a must have book for learning to use the Arduino.
- *Getting Started with Arduino* – A handy little guide to getting started on Arduino by Massimo Banzi

Arduino Project Collections

- **Sylvia's Super Awesome Maker Show Simple Arduino Projects** – Super Awesome Sylvia presents video tutorials for two simple Arduino projects. http://sylviashow.com/episodes/s1/e3/full/arduino
- **Instructables Arduino Projects** – Offers a number of Arduino projects at varying levels of complexity. http://www.instructables.com/id/Arduino-Projects/
- **Make Magazine Arduino** – Videos, project ideas, how-tos, kits, parts, and blog posts about what people are doing around the world with the Arduino. http://blog.makezine.com/arduino/
- **HacknMod Arduino Projects** – HacknMod specializes in projects that "mod" (modify) one kind of thing into another. For example, projects that mod an Xbox Kinect into a virtual piano or motion sensing interface. http://hacknmod.com/topics/arduino/

Raspberry Pi

- **Raspberry Pi Foundation** – Main website for all things Raspberry Pi http://www.raspberrypi.org/
- **Make Magazine Raspberry Pi** – Many projects, ideas, and resources for using the Raspberry Pi http://blog.makezine.com/category/electronics/raspberry-pi/
- **Raspberry Pi Quick Start Guide** – Even if you are an "I don't read instructions" kind of person, you should at least look at this 3 page illustrated quick start guide for the Raspberry Pi. http://www.raspberrypi.org/quick-start-guide
- **Raspberry Pi Education Manual** – Written by a team of UK teachers from Computing at School (CAS) available at the Pi Store or as a PDF. http://www.raspberrypi.org/archives/2965

Wearable Computing and E-Textiles

- **Lilypad Arduino** – A special Arduino board for projects using textiles and wearable electronics. http://bit.ly/XB0MDq or http://www.arduino.cc/en/Main/ArduinoBoardLilyPad
- **LilyPond** – Lilypad and other e-textile projects and workshop ideas from the inventors of the Lilypad. http://lilypond.media.mit.edu
- *Arduino Wearables* – by Tony Olsson. This book is a project-based introduction to wearable computing, prototyping, and smart materials using the Arduino platform. Each of the ten chapters takes you all the way from idea to finished project, gradually increasing in complexity and challenge.
- **Getting hands-on with soft circuits** – An e-textile workshop facilitators guide by Emily Lovell (e-book) http://web.media.mit.edu/~emme/guide.pdf
- **Soft Circuit Saturdays** – Tutorials and project ideas very suitable for kids from Angela, a maker in New England. http://softcircuitsaturdays.com/

LEGO Engineering

- **Fred Martin's Art of LEGO** – Fred Martin, the engineer behind the RCX brick, wrote a terrific paper explaining LEGO engineering principles. http://www.stager.org/lego/fredmartin.pdf
- **The Art of LEGO Posters** – One-page color photos illustrating commonly used LEGO mechanisms. Well-suited for classroom posters. http://www.stager.org/lego/artoflego2.pdf
- **Motion models** – These invaluable step-by-step pictorials demonstrate how LEGO machines may be used to generate motion in a range of ways required in robotics projects. http://www.picocricket.com/motion.html
- **LEGO WeDo** – An early-childhood robotics construction kit that may be controlled via Scratch. http://bit.ly/ZhtXMk
- **LEGO Education** – Main LEGO website for education products and resources. http://legoeducation.us
- **LEGO Mindstorms NXT** – Robotics construction kits for middle school/high school students http://mindstorms.lego.com/en-us/default.aspx
- **Enchanting** – Alternative programming language for LEGO NXT http://enchanting.robotclub.ab.ca/
- **FIRST LEGO League** – Worldwide robotics competitions for youth ages 9–16 http://www.firstlegoleague.org/
- *The Unofficial LEGO Technic Builders Guide* – A new full-color guide to building machines out of LEGO Technic! Mechanical principles are explained clearly.
- *The LEGO Technic Idea Book Fantastic Contraptions* – Yoshihito Isogawa's three magnificent wordless books of LEGO Technic project ideas are like the holy books of LEGO construction. There are enough ideas contained within to keep you building for years!
- *The LEGO Technic Idea Book Wheeled Wonders* – More amazing LEGO Technic ideas.
- *The LEGO Technic Idea Book Simple Machines* – Even more LEGO Technic projects. You need all three!
- *Lego Crazy Action Contraptions* – Great, simple LEGO machine projects with mechanical concepts that may generalized into larger personal projects.

Robotics

- **GoGo Board** – Open source hardware platform for programmable projects using sensors and robotics. Works with MicroWorlds and Scratch. http://www.gogoboard.org/
- *Make: LEGO and Arduino Projects: Projects for Extending MINDSTORMS NXT with Open source Electronics* by John Baichtal, Matthew Beckler, and Adam Wolf
- **Great robotics challenges** – Gary Stager's 13 favorite problem-solving prompts for inventing with robotics. http://www.stager.org/lego/challenges.pdf
- **New Pathways into Robotics** – This paper discusses strategies for educators to broaden participation in robotics activities. http://bit.ly/176guY9

- **Probot** – A car-shaped floor turtle, complete with a pen for drawing geometric "trails" on paper http://www.terrapinlogo.com/pro-bot.php
- **Big Trak** – Our late friend, Steve Ocko, invented this programmable floor turtle (robot) for Milton Bradley in 1979. There has never been a more powerful easy-to-use robot available for kids since. The good news is that some lunatic bought the rights to the Big Trak and is manufacturing new ones 30+ years later. Kids from 5+ will play and learn with Big Trak for ages.
- **iRobot Create Programmable Robot** – The Roomba company has created a programmable floor robot http://store.irobot.com/product/index.jsp?productId=2586252&cp=2591511
- **Robotics Competitions** – List compiled by NASA of many robotics competitions http://robotics.nasa.gov/events/competitions.php

PROGRAMMING

Logo, Scratch, and Variations

- **MicroWorlds and MicroWorlds EX** – Modern multimedia versions of the Logo programming language, with robotics control with an optional robotics version from Logo Computer Systems International (LCSI) http://microworlds.com/
- **Scratch** – Free programming language for simple storytelling and games. Graphic interface. Materials and videos for educators and classrooms. Scratch works with http://scratch.mit.edu/
- **WeDo programming and Scratch** – Scratch also may be used to program LEGO's early childhood robotics set called WeDo. Plug the WeDo into your computer, boot Scratch and new blocks appear for robotics control. info.scratch.mit.edu/WeDo
- **ScratchED website** – For educators who teach with Scratch http://scratched.media.mit.edu/
- **S4A (Scratch for Arduino)** – A block-based version of Scratch intended for programming and controlling an Arduino microcontroller http://seaside.citilab.eu/scratch/arduino
- **Snap!** – Scratch with first-class objects added to make more complex programming projects possible http://bjc.berkeley.edu/
- **Turtle Art** – A simple yet elegant variation of Logo with an iconic interface intended to create beautiful images http://turtleart.org
- *Super Scratch Programming Adventure!: Learn to Program By Making Cool Games* – A full-color project book for learning Scratch programming. It even includes a chapter on using the external Picoboard.

Other Programming Languages and Environments

- **Processing** – A powerful graphic programming language. Be sure to explore both the "learning" and "reference" tabs http://processing.org
- **Learning Processing** – Excellent guide to learning Processing by Daniel Shiffman http://www.learningprocessing.com/
- **Python** – (Mac, Windows & Linux) Download, share code, and learn about the Python programming language http://www.python.org/
- **Introduction to Python** – Free e-book by Mark Clarkson (PDF) http://bit.ly/intropythonpdf
- **Squeak** – Squeak is the vehicle for a wide range of projects including multimedia applications, educational platforms, and commercial Web application development. Scratch itself was created in Squeak. http://www.squeak.org/
- **Etoys** – Created in Squeak, the Etoys software provides microworlds for kids to explore powerful mathematical and scientific concepts http://www.squeakland.org/
- **AgentSheets** – AgentSheets is part of the Scalable Game Design project to teach young people around the world about computer science and science. AgentCubes is a recently released 3D version http://www.agentsheets.com/
- **LiveCode** – A "Hypercard on steroids" cross platform development engine. http://www.runrev.com/
- **MIT App Inventor** – Create apps and games for Android devices with this software. Code samples, tutorials, and extensive educator resources are on the MIT website. http://appinventor.mit.edu/

KITS

- **MaKey MaKey** – An "invention kit for everyone," MaKey MaKey should be a part of any tinkering classroom. MaKey MaKey creates a simple alligator-clip-based interface between the computer and everyday objects. It plugs into the USB port of any computer, even a Raspberry Pi, and turns household objects into a keyboard or joystick. http://www.makeymakey.com/
- **Drawdio** – Allows you to turn a pencil into a simple music synthesizer. You can play music while you write! Build your own or buy a kit. http://web.media.mit.edu/~silver/drawdio/
- **Minty Boost** – A small kit that lets you create a battery-powered cellphone charger that fits inside a tiny gum tin. The kit doesnÕt come with the tins, so you might wish to purchase those too. http://www.ladyada.net/make/mintyboost/
- **TV B Gone** – A tiny contraption that turns off (or back on) any television in your vicinity. This has serious mischief potential and can make your colleagues want to kill you, but kids love it and learn a bit about electronics too (before being chased from the mall.) http://www.ladyada.net/make/tvbgone/

CREATIVE MATERIALS OLD AND NEW

- **Sugru** – Miraculous shapeable air-cured rubber, because "the future needs fixing!" http://sugru.com/
- **Tapagami** – Tapigami is an art form using masking tape created by Danny Scheible. http://tapigami.com/
- **Bare (conductive) Paint** – Paint pens and interactive card kits. This is a UK-based company; some of their materials are available at ThinkGeek and Amazon. http://bareconductive.com

Squishy Circuits

- **Squishy Circuits** – The home of all things related to Squishy Circuits http://courseweb.stthomas.edu/apthomas/SquishyCircuits/
- **Squishy Circuits Store** – Kits of LEDs and other parts that work well with squishy circuits http://squishycircuitsstore.com
- **Sylvia's Super-Awesome Maker Show about Squishy Circuits** – Super-Awesome Sylvia explains Squishy Circuits to kids of all ages. http://sylviashow.com/episodes/s2/e7/mini/squishycircuits

Cardboard

- **Rolobox** – Wheel sets for cardboard boxes. Great for use with Makedo and other materials. http://www.rolobox.com/
- **Makedo** – Wicked cool reusable connectors, hinges and child-safe saws for building cardboard constructions. http://mymakedo.com/
- **The Story of Caine's Arcade** – Caine Munro and his cardboard arcade have inspired millions of people around the world to be more playful and creative. http://cainesarcade.com
- **Cardboard automata** – Machines made of cardboard http://tinkering.exploratorium.edu/cardboard-automata/

Software

- **Tech4Learning** – Kid-friendly art, animation, publishing and creativity software for schools. http://tech4learning.com
- **HyperStudio** – Multimedia authoring, video editing, interactive Web and iBooks publishing, and Arduino programming http://hyperstudio.com
- **Animationish** – Peter Reynolds' easy-to-use animation program, complete with video tutorials. http://bit.ly/ZhBwTg
- **Pics4Learning.com** – Database of free, copyright friendly photographs submitted by educators and students around the world. http://www.pics4learning.com
- **Audacity** – Free audio editor and recorder software. This is a must have! http://audacity.sourceforge.net/

Filmmaking and Photography

- **Go Pro Cameras** – Go Pro Camera – Go Pro has a line of small, sturdy cameras built to strap onto helmets of extreme sports enthusiasts. This also makes them perfect for school projects where you want to put a camera on a robot or a weather balloon. The HERO3 is the latest and most affordable option – accessories are available separately or in more expensive bundles. http://gopro.com
- **Casey Neistat** – Filmmaker Casey Neistat creates incredibly creative short videos using everyday cameras and simple, easy to reproduce production effects. http://caseyneistat.com
- Collection of early films on DVD – This collection of early films, including productions by Melies and Edison, should inspire young filmmakers http://bit.ly/115rOlF
- *101 Things I Learned in Film School* – A terrific easy-to-read book full of helpful tips and tricks for creating compelling videos or films.
- *Making Real-Life Videos* – A fine guide for teenage filmmakers
- *How to Photograph Your Life: Capturing Everyday Moments with Your Camera and Your Heart* – This book shows how to capture great photographs by comparing great examples next to terrible ones of the same scene.
- *Screenplay: The Foundations of Screenwriting* – Syd Field's bible of screenwriting is a perfect text for high school students.
- *Pinhole Cameras: A DIY Guide* – By Chris Keeney. A practical guide to making and using pinhole cameras.

PROFESSIONAL DEVELOPMENT, CURRICULUM, AND STANDARDS

- **Constructing Modern Knowledge** – Summer institute for educators hosted by Gary Stager. http://constructingmodernknowledge.com/
- **Engineering is Elementary** – K–6 engineering curriculum, educator resources, and kits from the Boston Museum of Science. http://www.eie.org/
- **Project Lead the Way** – Project-based STEM curriculum for middle and high schools, resources, and professional development http://www.pltw.org/
- **Engineering byDesign** – The International Technology and Engineering Educators Association engineering curriculum for Grades K–12 http://www.iteea.org/EbD/ebd.htm
- **Buck Institute** – Project-based learning resources for educators http://www.bie.org
- **Edutopia** – Online articles on project-based learning from the George Lucas Educational Foundation http://www.edutopia.org
- **Next Generation Science Standards** – In spring 2013, the National Research Council, the National Science Teachers Association, the American Association for the Advancement of Science, and Achieve released the Next Generation Science Standards to modernize science teaching and learning in US schools. http://www.nextgenscience.org/

OTHER BOOKS AND RESOURCES

- *Makers: The New Industrial Revolution* – This new book about the maker revolution is by the former editor of Wired Magazine, Chris Anderson.
- *Young Investigators: The Project Approach in the Early Years* – By Judy Harris Helm and Lillian G. Katz
- *Design Make Play: Growing the Next Generation of STEM Innovators* – A book edited by Margaret Honey and David Kanter of essays, case studies, and research explore innovative programs using creative materials and technology to inspire young people about STEM subjects.
- *Engaging Children's Minds: The Project Approach* – By Lillian Katz and Sylvia Chard
- *I Won't Learn From You and Other Thoughts on Creative Maladjustment* – By Herbert Kohl
- *Making Learning Whole* – By David Perkins
- *The Book of Learning and Forgetting* – By Frank Smith
- *The Second Self: Computers and the Human Spirit* – By Sherry Turkle

SCHOOL DESIGN

- *The Language of School Design: Design Patterns for 21st Century Schools* – The premiere lavishly illustrated guide to school architecture and designing learning spaces by Prakash Nair and Randall Fielding
- *Make Space: How to Set the Stage for Creative Collaboration* – By Scott Doorley and Scott Witthoft from the Stanford Design School. This book is is full of good ideas for all spaces and budgets for changing surroundings to enhance the ways in which teams and individuals communicate, work, play – and innovate.

AUTHOR WEBSITES AND BLOGS

- **Invent To Learn website** – The companion website for this book contains purchasing information, news from the world of making, tinkering, and engineering, all resources (plus new ones!) http://InventToLearn.com
- **Sylvia Martinez at the Generation YES blog** – Sylvia writes about how empowering students can improve school and change lives http://blog.genyes.org
- **Gary Stager's website** – A collection of articles, resources, and videos http://www.Stager.org
- **Gary Stager's blog** – Gary writes thoughtful, provocative essays on many topics http://stager.tv/blog
- **Generation YES** – Sylvia is President of Generation YES, a global non-profit dedicated to empowering students with technology to improve education for all. http://genyes.org

Bibliography

Ackermann, Edith. (2007). Experiences of Artifacts: People's Appropriations / Objects' 'Affordances'. In E. v. Glasersfeld (Ed.), *Key Works on Radical Constructivism* (pp. 249–259). Rotterdam, NL: Sense Publishers.

Ackermann, Edith. (2010). Play: What's to be learned from kids? Retrieved March 29, 2013, from http://blogs.walkerart.org/ecp/2010/02/05/play-whats-to-be-learned-from-kids-part-1/

Akins, L., & Burghardt, D. (2006). *Improving K–12 mathematics understanding with engineering design projects.* Paper presented at the 2006 Frontiers in Education Conference, San Diego.

Banzi, Massimo. (2008). *Getting Started with Arduino*: Make Books.

Belland, Brian R. (2012). Habitus, Scaffolding, and Problem-Based Learning: Why Teachers' Experiences as Students Matter. *The Role of Criticism in Understanding Problem Solving*, 87–100.

Berry, R. Q., III, Bull, G., Browning, C., Thomas, C. D., Starkweather, K., & Aylor, J. H. (2010). Preliminary considerations regarding use of digital fabrication to incorporate engineering design principles in elementary mathematics education. *Contemporary Issues in Technology and Teacher Education, 10(2),* 167–172.

Blikstein, Paulo. (2013). Digital Fabrication and 'Making' in Education: The Democratization of Invention. In J. W.–H. C. B. (Eds.) (Ed.), *FabLabs: Of Machines, Makers and Inventors*: Bielefeld: Transcript Publishers.

Bonawitz, Elizabeth, Shafto, Patrick, Gweonc, Hyowon, Goodmand, Noah D., Spelkee, Elizabeth, & Schulz, Laura. (2011). The double-edged sword of pedagogy: Instruction limits spontaneous exploration and discovery. *Cognition, 120*(3), 322–330.

Brand, Stewart. (1988). *The Media Lab: Inventing the Future at M.I.T.* NY: Penguin.

Bronson, Po, & Merryman, Ashley. (2010, July 10, 2010). The Creativity Crisis. *Newsweek.*

Brosterman, Norman. (1997). *Inventing Kindergarten*. New York: Harry N. Abrams

Brown, Stuart, & Vaughan, Christopher. (2010). *Play: How it Shapes the Brain, Opens the Imagination, and Invigorates the Soul*. New York: Penguin Group.

Campbell, Thomas, Williams, Christopher, Ivanova, Olga, & Garrett, Banning. (2011). Could 3D Printing Change the World? Technologies, Potential, and Implications of Additive Manufacturing *Strategic Foresight, Report*.

Cheryan, Sapna, Plaut, Victoria C, Davies, Paul G, & Steele, Claude M. (2009). Ambient Belonging: How Stereotypical Cues Impact Gender Participation in Computer Science. *Journal of Personality and Social Psychology, 97*(6), 1045.

CNN. (2013). $1.99 iPhone app saved Oscars film. from http://money.cnn.com/video/technology/2013/02/19/t-iphone-app-oscar-film.cnnmoney/

Code.org.). What's wrong with this picture?   Retrieved March 31, 2013, from http://www.code.org/stats

Csikszentmihalyi, Mihaly. (1991). *Flow: The Psychology of Optimal Experience* (Reprint ed.). NY: Harper Perennial.

Csikszentmihalyi, Mihaly. (1996). Creativity: Flow and the Psychology of Discovery and Invention. New York: Harper Collins Publishers.

Darling-Hammond, Linda, Barron, Brigid. (2008). Teaching for Meaningful Learning: A Review of Research on Inquiry-Based and Cooperative Learning *Powerful Learning : What We Know About Teaching for Understanding* Jossey-Bass

Dewey, John. (1938). *Experience and education*. New York,: Touchstone.

Dougherty, Dale. (2013). The Maker Mindset. from http://llk.media.mit.edu/courses/readings/maker-mindset.pdf

Duckworth, Eleanor. (2005). A Reality to Which Each Belongs. In B. S. Engel & A. C. Martin (Eds.), *Holding Values: What We Mean by Progressive Education*. Portsmouth, NH: Heinemann.

Edwards, Carolyn, Gandini, Lella, & Forman, George (Eds.). (2012). *The Hundred Languages of Children: The Reggio Emilia Experience in Transformation* (3rd ed.). Santa Barbara, CA: Praeger.

Eisenberg, Michael. (2011) Educational fabrication, in and out of the classroom. *Society for Information Technology & Teacher Education International Conference*. Vol. 2011. No. 1.

Eisenberg, Michael, & Buechley, Leah. (2008). Pervasive Fabrication: Making Construction Ubiquitous in Education. *Journal of Software, 3*(4), 62–68.

Farivar, Cyrus. (2013). "Download this gun": 3D-printed semi-automatic fires over 600 rounds. *ars technica*. Retrieved from arstechnica.com website: http://arstechnica.com/tech-policy/2013/03/download-this-gun-3d-printed-semi-automatic-fires-over-600-rounds/

Foremski, Tom. (2012). Chris Anderson: Why I left Wired – 3D Printing Will Be Bigger Than The Web. *ZDNet*. Retrieved from http://bit.ly/leftwired

Frauenfelder, Mark. (2011). *Made by Hand: My Adventures in the World of Do-It-Yourself*: Portfolio.

Gardner, Howard. (1983). *Frames of Mind: The Theory of Multiple Intelligences*. New York: Basic Books.

Gershenfeld, Neil. (2007). *Fab: The Coming Revolution on Your Desktop–from Personal Computers to Personal Fabrication*: Basic Books (AZ).

Gordon, PR, Rogers, AM, Comfort, M, Gavula, N, & McGee, BP. (2001). A Taste of Problem-based Learning Increases Achievement of Urban Minority Middle-School Students. *Educational Horizons, 79*(4), 171–175.

Harel, Idit. (1991). *Children Designers: Interdisciplinary Constructions for Learning and Knowing Mathematics in a Computer-Rich School*. Norwood, N.J.: Ablex Pub. Corp.

Hawkins, David. (1965). Messing about in science. *Science and Children, 2*(5), 5–9.

Hill, Sally. (n.d.). A. C. Gilbert Illustrated: From Magic to Merchant. Retrieved April 4, 2013, from http://bit.ly/gilbertac

Institute for the Integration of Technology into Teaching and Learning (2011), University of North Texas, National Science Foundation Innovative Technologies (ITEST) Grant #1030865 Interim Report http://iittl.unt.edu/IITTL/itest/fablab_web/index.html

Kalchik, Stephanie, & Oertle, Kathleen M. (2010). The Theory And Application Of Contextualized Teaching And Learning In Relation To Programs Of Study And Career Pathways.

Katz, Lilian, & Chard, Sylvia C. (2000). *Engaging Children's Minds: The Project Approach*: Praeger Pub Text.

Kay, Alan. (2007). Educomm Keynote Presentation. Anaheim, CA.

Koch, Janice, & Burghardt, M. David. (2002). Design Technology in the Elementary School—A Study of Teacher Action Research *Journal of Technology Education, 13*(2).

Kohn, Alfie. (2010). News Archive. from http://www.alfiekohn.org/miscellaneous/newsarchive.htm

Kyle, W. C., Bonnstetter, R. J., Gadsden, T. Jr., & Shymansky, J. A. (1988). What Research Says About Hands-On Science. Science and Children, 25(7), 39–40.

Latour, Bruno. (1987). *Science in Action: How to Follow Scientists and Engineers Through Society*. Cambridge, MA: Harvard University Press.

Levy, Steven. (2010). *Hackers: Heroes of the Computer Revolution* (1st ed.). Sebastopol, CA: O'Reilly Media.

Mellis, David A., and Leah Buechley. (2011) Scaffolding creativity with open source hardware. *Proceedings of the 8th ACM conference on Creativity and cognition.* ACM.

Minsky, Marvin. (1988) The Society of Mind. Touchstone.

Monk, Simon. (2012). *Programming Arduino : Getting Started with Sketches.* New York: McGraw-Hill.

National Research Council. (2012). *A Framework for K–12 Science Education: Practices, Crosscutting Concepts, and Core Ideas*: Committee on Conceptual Framework for the New K–12 Science Education Standards.

National Science Board. (2012). *Science and Engineering Indicators 2012.* Arlington, VA: National Science Foundation (NSB 12–01).

Negroponte, Nicholas. (1995). *Being Digital.* New York, NY: Alfred P. Knopf

Next Generation Science Standards. (2013): National Research Council, National Science Teachers Association, American Association for the Advancement of Science, Achieve.

Norton, Michael, Mochon, Daniel, & Ariely, Dan. (2011). The 'IKEA Effect': When Labor Leads to Love. *Harvard Business School Marketing Unit Working Paper*(11–091).

Papert, Seymour. (1972a). Teaching Children Thinking. *Programmed Learning and Educational Technology, 9*(5), 245–255.

Papert, Seymour. (1972b). Teaching Children To Be Mathematicians Versus Teaching About Mathematics. *International Journal of Mathematical Education in Science and Technology, 3*(3), 249–262.

Papert, Seymour. (1980). *Mindstorms: Children, Computers, And Powerful Ideas.* New York: Basic Books.

Papert, Seymour. (1986). Constructionism: A New Opportunity for Elementary Science Education. Massachusetts Institute of Technology, Media Laboratory, Epistemology and Learning Group: National Science Foundation. Division of Research on Learning in Formal and Informal Settings.

Papert, Seymour. (1993). *The Children's Machine: Rethinking School in the Age of the Computer.* NY: Basic Books.

Papert, Seymour. (1996, October 27). Computers in the classroom: Agents of change, *The Washington Post Education Review.*

Papert, Seymour. (1998). Technology in Schools: To support the system or render it obsolete. *Milken Exchange on Education Technology.* Retrieved June 1, 2010, from
http://www.mff.org/edtech/article.taf?_function=detail&Content_uid1=106

Papert, Seymour. (2000). What's the Big Idea? Toward a Pedagogical Theory of Idea Power. *IBM Systems Journal, 39*(3&4), 720–729.

Papert, Seymour. (2005). You Can't Think About Thinking Without Thinking About Thinking About Something. *Contemporary Issues in Technology and Teacher Education, 5*(3), 366–367.

Papert, Seymour. (2006, Dec. 4). *Keynote: From the Math Wars to the New New Math.* Paper presented at the Seventeenth ICMI Study: Technology Revisited, Hanoi, Viet Nam.

Papert, Seymour, & Franz, George. (1987). Computer as Material: Messing About with Time. *Teachers College Record, 89*(3).

Papert, Seymour, & Solomon, Cynthia. (1971). Twenty Things to do with a computer *Artificial Intelligence Memo # 248.* Cambridge, MA: Massachusetts Institute of Technology.

Patri, Angelo. (1917). *A Schoolmaster of the Great City*: Macmillan.

Piaget, Jean. (1976). *To Understand is to Invent: The Future of Education* (G.-A. Roberts, Trans.): Penguin Books.

Polya, George. (1945). How to Solve It: A New Aspect of Mathematical Method Princeton, NJ: Princeton University Press.

Resnick, Mitchel. (2007). *All I Really Need to Know (About Creative Thinking) I Learned (By Studying How Children Learn) in Kindergarten.* Paper presented at the Proceedings of the 6th ACM SIGCHI conference on Creativity & cognition.

Resnick, M., Bruckman, A., & Martin, F. (2000). Constructional Design: Creating New Construction Kits for Kids. In A. Druin, Hendler, James (Ed.), *Robots for Kids : Exploring New Technologies for Learning.* San Francisco: Morgan Kaufmann.

Rheingold, Howard. (2011). Mitch Resnick: The Role of Making, Tinkering, Remixing in Next-Generation Learning. 2012, from http://bit.ly/DMLresnick

Rinaldi, Carlina. (2006). *In Dialogue with Reggio Emilia: Listening, Researching and Learning* London ; New York: Routledge.

Robinson, James. (2011, August 26, 2011). Eric Schmidt, chairman of Google, condemns British education system, *The Guardian.* Retrieved from http://bit.ly/schmidtsays

Root-Bernstein, Robert, & Root-Bernstein, Michele. (2013 February 2013). The Art and Craft of Science. *Educational Leadership, 70,* 16–21.

Schneider, Rebecca M, Krajcik, Joseph, Marx, Ronald W, & Soloway, Elliot. (2002). Performance of students in project-based science classrooms on a national measure of science achievement. *Journal of Research in Science Teaching, 39*(5), 410–422.

Schunn, Christian D. (2009). How Kids Learn Engineering: The Cognitive Science Perspective. *The Bridge, 39*(3), 32–37.

Scientific American Frontiers: You Can Make it On Your Own. (2003). *Scientific American Frontiers*: Connecticut Public Television and Radio.

Shearer, Branton. (2009). *MI at 25: Assessing the Impact and Future of Multiple Intelligences for Teaching and Learning*. New York: Teachers College Press.

Silverman, Brian, & Kay, Alan (Producer). (2013). Session 4 – Powerful Ideas. *Learning Creative Learning MOOC*. [video] Retrieved from http://youtu.be/yNlyDr8dem8

Stager, Gary S. (2006). *An Investigation of Constructionism in the Maine Youth Center*. (Ph.D.), The University of Melbourne, Melbourne.

Stanley, Norm. (2002). *Amateur Science, 1900–1950: A Historical Overview (With Emphasis on Amateur Chemistry)*. Paper presented at the First Annual Citizen Science Conference. http://philosophyofscienceportal.blogspot.com/2008/04/home-chemistlong-gone.html

Taylor, R. (1980). The Computer in the School: Tutor, Tool, Tutee.

Tinker, Robert. (1992). Thinking About Science. *CEEB*, 57.

Turkle, Sherry. (1984). *The Second Self: Computers and the Human Spirit*. New York: Simon and Schuster.

Turkle, Sherry. (2008). A Passion for Objects. *Chronicle of Higher Education, 54*(38), B11.

Turkle, Sherry, & Papert, Seymour. (1991). Epistemological Pluralism and the Revaluation of the Concrete. In I. Harel & S. Papert (Eds.), *Constructionism* (pp. 161–191). Norwood, NJ: Ablex Publishing Corporation.

Upton, Eben, & Halfacree, Gareth. (2012). *Raspberry Pi User Guide*. West Sussex, UK: Wiley.

Vega, Vanessa. (2012). Project-Based Learning Research Review. from http://www.edutopia.org/pbl-research-learning-outcomes

Vygotsky, Lev S. (1978). *Mind in Society: The Development of Higher Psychological Processes* (14th ed.). Cambridge, MA: Harvard University Press.

Watson, Bruce. (2002). *The Man Who Changed How Boys and Toys Were Made*. New York, N.Y: Viking.

White House Hangout: The Maker Movement. (2013, March 27, 2013). Retrieved from http://www.whitehouse.gov/blog/2013/03/27/white-house-hangout-maker-movement

Index

BRING *INVENT TO LEARN* TO YOUR SCHOOL, DISTRICT, UNIVERSITY, OR CONFERENCE!

The authors of *Invent To Learn: Making, Tinkering, and Engineering in the Classroom* have extensive experience as keynote speakers, workshop leaders, and consultants around the world.

Gary Stager and Sylvia Martinez are available to speak at your conference, lead workshops, or collaborate in the creation of your makerspace.

For detailed information on how *Invent To Learn* services may be tailored to the needs of your school, district, or conference, go to www.inventtolearn.com or send email to education@inventtolearn.com.

Continue the learning adventure online!

Go to InventToLearn.com for the latest news, tools and resources about making, tinkering, and engineering. Every link in this book is just a click away!

Made in the USA
San Bernardino, CA
18 April 2017